BICYCLING
MEXICO

ACKNOWLEDGEMENTS

We would like to thank the following companies for their generous donations of help and equipment:

Cascade Designs Inc.

Graber Products Inc.

Elizabeth Strode of McCutchen, Doyle, Brown & Enerson

Raleigh Cycle Company of America

Rhode Gear USA

Sierra Designs

Stanyon Cyclery, San Francisco

Our thanks also to the following people for assistance along the way:

Patrick Christiano

Bob and Ellie Deckwar

Susan Erlich and John Ziakoff

Amy Goldfarb

Tom Hauser

Vicente Kramsky

Diana Osuna and Tom Stallings

Ramon Perez Gil Salcido

Bella Riley

Ursula Viola and Klaus Stromer

Heartfelt thanks to the people of Mexico who looked with kindness upon the company of strangers.

Lastly, we thank our publisher Michael Hunter, who, if he had doubts this book would be completed, kept them to himself.

BICYCLING MEXICO

Ericka Weisbroth

Eric Ellman

HUNTER
PUBLISHING INC

Hunter Publishing, Inc.
300 Raritan Center Parkway
Edison NJ 08818
(201) 225 1900
FAX (201) 417 0482

ISBN 1-55650-252-4

Printed in Singapore through Palace Press

Maps by Joyce Huber, PhotoGraphics

Photo Credits

Authors: 32, 38, 45, 59, 62, 80, 93, 102, 114, 120, 130, 152, 154, 164, 219, 230, 233, 256, 266, 281, 287, 294, 318, 320, 323. Klaus + Uschi: 85, 111, 145, 178, 188, 210, 332. L. Verplanken: 283. Secretaria de Turismo de Mexico: 174, 240, 251, 270, 335.

CONTENTS

INTRODUCTION: WHY MEXICO?

Mexico, the most popular destination for travellers from the United States, is *made* for bicycle touring. The country is exotic, inexpensive and, no insignificant factor, it's right next door. Phoenix is less than a day's drive to the thriving bordertown markets of Nogales, and El Paso is but a short bus ride from Ciudad Juarez, a major gateway to the south. San Diego is within an afternoon's pedalling distance of the Baja peninsula, a land of remote beaches, imposing mountains and forests of desert cactus. The dense jungles and Maya ruins of the Yucatan are a 60-minute flight from downtown Miami. Mexico's vast interior offers a tableau of both man-made and natural wonders, of culture and history, regional cuisine, climate and geography, sport and relaxation. Its western shoreline, all 7,141 kilometers of it, boasts magnificent beaches and extraordinary seafood. Great adventure potential so nearby has made it inevitable that bicycle tourists put Mexico on their agenda.

The advent of sturdy mountain bikes and the cushioned ride of fat-tires have helped tame Mexico's most rugged roads, making even remote villages accessible. Bicycle tourists are privy to the sorts of experiences which do not filter through a tinted glass windshield. Overtaking a burro-drawn cart and exchanging "Buenos dias!" with the happily surprised driver, waving at a *campesino* laboring in his cornfield, or pulling into a small town to discover that its residents have come out to greet you, create durable and pleasant memories.

Since private cars remain a luxury, riding a bicycle in Mexico is not considered mere recreation. Grown men ride bikes and were doing it long before young, urban, cholesterol-fearing professionals saddled up for the office. Range-toughened *vaqueros* pedal from the ranch to their grazing herds on old single-speeders. Bicycle riding is a respected mode of transportation, and the ramifications for the touring cyclist are several. Despite your scientifically-engineered, aerodynamically-streamlined, tight-fitting clothes you'll be regarded as a novelty rather than an oddball. It means you will find bicycle repair shops in towns of any consequential size. But, most important, it means that the traffic you do encounter is not unused to bicycles on the road's narrow or non-existent shoulder and they will treat you with a modicum of regard.

The paucity of private vehicles in so large a country has spawned a slew of independent bus companies. This rolling armada includes silver-sided luxury liners indistinguishable from their northern Greyhound cousins, and vintage Kenworth's old enough to have carried Glenn Miller on his first national tour. The extensive routes of these entrepreneurial caissons include the most unlikely villages and forgotten towns. If the service they provide is austere, it is at least frequent. It's a great comfort to know that no matter how inconvenient a moment your axle chooses to crack, there's a 40-year-old school bus soon to come lumbering around the bend. It's hard to get so far afield that a bus can't bring you home again. With storage bays below, welded luggage racks overhead and the price of a ticket a pittance, they are Everyman's sagwagon.

If public transportation is the safety net of Mexican bike travel, the climate makes it easier still. Loaded panniers will have never seemed so light. The warm year-round weather (there are exceptions) obviates the need for heavy clothing. Leave all but a sweater at home. Likewise your fenders. The rainy season occurs throughout the country between May and October but it seldom rains for hours at a time. A review of our Climate, Rainfall, and Altitude Chart will help determine the seasonal specifics of your trip.

Camping is rarely a necessity on the tours outlined in BICYCLING MEXICO and, with a little planning, even most of these occasions can be circumvented. You may sometimes want to splurge on a hotel, but decent shelters in the $4-to-$7 range abound. This book is not intended as an accommodations guide. Both *Frommer's* and *Let's Go: Mexico* are good references for the budget-minded traveller. Our Road Notes will alert you to uncommon bargains and lodging in villages overlooked by most guidebooks and will help you pace your daily riding schedule. There's little sense in pushing to the next village before nightfall, only to discover there's nowhere to sate your hunger or rest road-weary bones.

Nothing distinguishes a culture as much as its language and its cuisine. While you cannot hope to command Spanish by the end of a two- or three-week vacation, for a thoroughly rewarding gustatory adventure, master the menu. Restaurant prices throughout the nation are a remarkable bargain. Eat out. Leave the cooking gear at home with the tent, the fenders, and the kitchen sink.

The idea for a bicycle guide to Mexico arose out of our discovery that none existed when we needed one. The Mexican highway system is, of course, not nearly as diverse or developed as in the United States. But we were not prepared for the overall lack of road information. Riding conditions generally, and as they specifically pertain to the cyclist, were simply not available.

Much of Mexico's traffic confines itself to high-speed expressways where cycling is unpleasant, dangerous, and sometimes illegal. But a wonderful network of old two-lane interstates forms an extensive framework for travelling the country by bicycle. All of the suggested routes in BICYCLING MEXICO have been researched by bike unless otherwise indicated. For portions of road which proved too fearsome or otherwise unenjoyable, we recommend a combination of bike and bus travel.

This book is written with two groups of travellers in mind. People new to cycle touring who want to maximize the efficiency of their vacation with a scouted route itinerary will find this a valuable planning manual, a security blanket of sorts. Experienced cycle tourists, those intrepid souls who are about to venture south of the border for the first time or again, will find BICYCLING MEXICO an informative catalyst. Read our tours to learn what to anticipate, then yield to curiosity. Stir the cauldron of your imagination, get a map and go explore. We embark on a journey with the expectation that it will broaden our perception and enrich our lives. Touring Mexico by bicycle is a terrific way to attempt this worthy goal.

Happy cycling!

PLANNING YOUR TRIP

Mexico! The name conjures images of ancient ruins, hot chilies, and mariachi music, a land of glistening sands, splashy resorts and endless, sun-bleached, cactus-covered deserts. True enough, but hardly more than ad-man's rhetoric. Whether arriving by plane or train, car, bus or bicycle, it takes only a few minutes to realize you really are in a *foreign* country. Modern Mexico is a complex blend of European and indigenous cultures, given expression by the variety of regional dress, crafts, and cuisine, architecture and ceremony.

Travelling by bicycle can't help but expose you to the most intimate details of community life, an excellent reason for attempting this kind of travel. But no matter what mode you choose, a little planning will facilitate a successful journey, and some advance reading will deepen your understanding of what you encounter.

Because of Mexico's continuing devaluation of the peso, prices quoted in this book cannot possibly be accurate. During our research, the peso's value fell from 2,000p to 2,300p per dollar. As of this writing the exchange rate hovers around 2,600p to the dollar. The prices we quote are based on 2,300p per dollar and should be used as a guideline, only.

YOU BIKED *HOW MANY* KILOMETERS?!

With the exceptions noted in the text, either or both of us have bicycled every inch of road discussed.

When Ricky agreed to collaborate with Eric to research and write this book, she was one month short of her 43rd—not a typo!—birthday and hadn't been on a bicycle in at least 20 years. A self-described slug, her idea of exercise was meeting a friend for lunch.

We started riding together in the Yucatan, one of Mexico's flatter regions and a good place to begin building muscle. If you haven't biked in a while, consider starting there. Certainly there is no shortage of things to see and do while getting in shape for the tougher stuff.

Throughout Mexico we met nationals from many countries who were touring by bike. It is our guess that 35% of these cyclists were women. One, a 55-year-old grandmother we met in Bahia Concepcion in Baja, had cycled from the U.S. border and was soon continuing south.

Can anyone do it? There's no getting around it, most of Mexico is mountainous and riding is a challenge. A successful, satisfying trip requires the flexibility to travel more slowly than you thought you might. But keep in mind that Mexico has an expansive bus system, not unaccustomed to carrying all manner of freight. If you want to cover hundreds of miles in a matter of hours, or if you are simply too tired to continue on for the day, combine bus travel with biking. That being the case, we believe Mexico is accessible to anyone crazy enough to try it.

WHEN TO GO

The best time of year to visit Mexico depends on personal schedule as well as destination. Great weather can be found in some part of the country during any given period. If it's too cold in the highlands of Chiapas, it's probably just right in the otherwise steamy Yucatan peninsula. Unbearably hot along the southern shoreline? Cool out in the mountains around Oaxaca or Cuernavaca. Miserably wet in Tasco? It's crackling dry in La Paz. Our Temperature and Rainfall Chart at the end of this chapter will facilitate making a choice.

Mexico is a great country for celebrations, but holidays and fiestas can also affect travel plans. Banks may be closed, hotels booked, busses full. In Appendix 2 we have listed national holidays and many local fiestas, but in reality they are only a few of the hundreds which occur throughout the year. Every town has a patron saint which is honored by a celebration. Such unanticipated festivals frequently proved to be a delightful vacation highlight.

GASOLINE?

Some people may choose to combine a car and bicycle tour of Mexico. Be advised that unleaded gasoline, called *Extra,* is hard to find in many parts of the country (Baja is the exception). Leaded gas, *Nova,* is almost always available.

SOLO, DUO, OR GROUP TOURING?

Simply put, there are benefits and shortcomings to all of these choices. If you travel alone, there's no one else to blame for foolish decisions, but at least there's no haggling in making the decision. Go where you want, when you want. Undoubtedly, too, there is greater cultural immersion; you're not only more approachable by strangers, your own need for communion becomes a driving force in meeting people. But it can get pretty lonely, especially if your knowledge of Spanish is limited.

The advantages of travelling with a companion seem pretty obvious. You don't get *as* lonely. If on a tight budget, sharing expenses can affect how long a trip will last. In addition, someone else shares responsibilities such as getting bus or ferry tickets, scouting out hotels, or safeguarding the gear. All of this is true for groups, too, but there are more opinions to consider. And, not to be underestimated, there are group dynamics. Consider all the angles before deciding to travel as a group.

For women especially, there is the added component of safety in numbers. Camping alone can make for some very uneasy nights. Women should be leery of accepting an invitation to spend the night in a man's house. Traveling with a friend, be it another woman or a man, will help eliminate questions about one's virtue. But it will only help. Face it ladies: You're in the land of the double standard. Men do as they please and it's okay. Women do as men please, which means "nice" girls stay home. Women who travel are considered fair game (in an outrageously unfair game!).

GETTING READY TO GO

Let's start with bicycles. Even in a land where bicycles are common, so few places rent them as to be insignificant. Bikes of Mexican manufacture are inferior to the many excellent brands available in the industrial countries, and they're not inexpensive. Plan to bring your own bike along.

You are not allowed to sell your bicycle in Mexico and your tourist card may indicate possession of one. Bringing a bicycle into Mexico can be problematic, too, if the bike just looks too shiny and new. We know a guy who bought a bike for his own use just before bussing to El Paso from the East Coast. He transported the bike, boxed, to the border and planned to assemble it on the

Mexican side, but was not permitted to bring a new bike in. So he assembled it on U.S. soil, muddied it up a bit, and rode into Mexico without further ado. Sometimes a small "tip," say $5, helps settle matters. If that doesn't work wait for the *aduana* (border guard) shift to change.

The predominance of bicycles means that repair shops can be found in nearly every town. The people who run them are experienced in patching together the most obdurate and obscure bicycle parts, sometimes in a quite unorthodox but functional manner. Large cities usually have well-stocked bicycle shops. Still, it behooves you to carry a decent tool and spare parts kit.

We don't intend to get stuck in the mountain-versus-touring-bike skirmish but—alas!—do have a few observations. Prior to researching this book, Eric had been to Mexico twice on a touring bike. We did all of our riding for BICYCLING MEXICO on mountain bikes. We met people who swore by each, as well as all manner of in-betweeners. In Yucatan we crossed paths with a man from India who was travelling the world on a single-speed bike. In Cuernavaca we met a young Irish woman who'd bought a three-speeder in San Diego, biked Baja, transversed the mainland from Pto. Vallarta, and was heading for South America. She was alone, we hasten to say, but not without some serious hassles. One fellow was travelling on a recumbent. Many of rural Mexico's roads are dirt, gravel, or poorly paved. Road bikes are suitable for most of the rides in this book, but mountain bikes, while slower on pavement, are more versatile.

Bicycles must be boxed for shipment by air. Cartons are available at most bicycle stores for free or for a nominal charge. In Mexico, however, when preparing to fly home, expect to do some looking to find an adequate bike box. It shouldn't be a problem, but may take longer than you anticipated. If you happen to be returning from Mexico City, cartons can be found at the "Benotto" bicycle factory, located on Calz. de Tlalpan #744.

When travelling within Mexico by bus, train or ferry, bikes can be transported without being boxed.

WHAT TO BRING

As little as possible! The rule is, lay out everything considered *essential* for a trip, divide the pile equally, return half to your closets and drawers, and pack the rest into your panniers. At the end of this chapter we list suggestions for clothing, personal items, and a bicycle tool kit.

But there are a few other considerations to keep in mind.

The Properly Equipped Cyclist

Wearing headgear is absolutely basic to riding in Mexico. At the very least, a cotton bandana will help protect against sunstroke, and it can be dampened for the cooling effect of evaporation. Optimally, though, you'll cycle wearing a helmet. There will be times when a helmet is mandatory, situations where, of course, you would never cycle and there you are doing it—riding in the rain, or alone on a steep, curvaceous, gravelly downhill, or at night.

Equally important are good sunglasses; a sunblock of at least SP15; lipbalm with sunblock; and gloves. Because of the scarcity of traffic it's easy to be lulled into thinking you're the only one on the road. A rearview mirror will alert you to oncoming traffic. Don't forget a bicycle pump. Or water bottles. Carry at least two of the liter size.

An odometer is important, too, and should be set for kilometers rather than miles.

Last, bring a padlock and cable rather than a cumbersome U-lock. Generally speaking—large cities and resorts are the exceptions—theft is not a big problem in Mexico. In nearly all situations where it is necessary to lock a bike, a cable will suffice, and in more threatening circumstances the bike shouldn't be left unattended anyway. Yet, occasionally, such situations arise. Besides locking the bike, consider enlisting the aid of someone in the vicinity, the fruit stall lady, the news stand man, the museum entrance guard. With rare exception, they will happily keep an eye on your bicycle.

The Properly Loaded Bike

There are nearly as many opinions about what is proper as there are cyclists. Here's ours. Place heavier gear lower inside your panniers, but keep the things you use most often near the top. The bags on the left and right side should weigh about the same, but carry the heavier bags on the front rack. Trial and error will reveal at what point safe handling of the bike is encumbered. A seat wedge pack will hold most tools, and a removable handlebar bag is good for carrying a camera, a few oranges, and the kinds of valuables that shouldn't be left on your bike during a lunch stop or while exploring an archaeological site. Remember, *you* get to carry it all. Large panniers tend to fill up. Think small.

Riding Decorum

For both men and women, riding in Mexico requires a higher degree of modesty than many cyclists are accustomed to. With the possible exception of the Yucatan, bareback riding is considered improper. Skintight riding shorts are okay while straddling a bike, but expect to be stared at if strolling around town or sightseeing in them. It's easy enough to keep an extra pair of shorts handy, to pull over your riding shorts when deemed necessary.

While cycling, women will probably experience occasional harassment, no matter what they are wearing. Try riding in loose, lightweight cotton pants that can be rolled very high both for comfort and a great tan, but can be rolled down on arrival in town. Or keep a skirt accessible. Likewise, if wearing a tanktop or any other style that can be construed as immodest, it's best to cover up with a "town" blouse. Resist the temptation to cycle wearing a halter.

Other Essentials

We assume people are going to sleep indoors most nights, and will eat in restaurants whenever possible. Take only minimal gear for those rare outdoor nights, and so that you have your own bedding should a family offer shelter. Restrict this equipment to a drop cloth, an inflatable Therm-A-Rest pad, sleeping bag and washable liner.

Of course the length of time you plan to travel will also affect the need for a variety of gear. A tent comes to mind, but during months of research we never used a tent on the mainland, except once along the Costa Grande to combat mosquitoes. In Baja we carried tents because we expected to camp a lot and even then used them rarely.

Rain gear and bicycle fenders are unnecessary except when necessary. Leave them at home.

MAPS

Mexico's Department of Tourism goes to considerable lengths to make state and local maps available to foreigners. A visit to the tourist office is always one of our first stops when arriving in a new city. The government's Green Angels ply Mexico's highways in search of troubled motorists. But they will gladly offer assistance to cyclists. They carry maps and many agents speak English. Look for their distinctive green trucks and don't be shy about waving one down. Some even carry drinking water.

Pemex, the nationalized petroleum company, puts out a good, inexpensive road atlas. It is available (sometimes) at gas stations, cultural centers and bookstores.

The best overall map of Mexico we found is put out by AAA, the American Automobile Association.

A cautionary note: Many maps contain inaccuracies. Whenever there is a significant variance between our Road Notes and, say, the Pemex map, we believe our records are correct. Please bear in mind that even our Road Notes should be used as close approximations only. Odometers vary slightly from brand to brand and bike to bike. In addition, as soon as you backtrack two-tenths of a kilometer to buy that soda after all, your distance is no longer in sync with ours. Therefore, except in a few instances where exactness is critical to the directions, we have rounded the kilometers in our Road Notes to the nearest whole number.

DOCUMENTS AND MONEY

Entry Requirements

U.S. citizens do not need passports or visas to travel in Mexico but they do need tourist cards. These can be obtained in Mexican consulates, at border crossings, and on air flights into the country. You will need to show proof of citizenship, however, and a passport is the most readily accepted form of identification. It will also facilitate cashing traveller's checks or using a credit card for purchases or a cash advance.

A tourist card is good for up to six months and cannot be renewed without leaving the country.

Other foreign nationals should check with the Mexican Consulate for entry requirements.

International Certificate of Vaccination

Depending on where you are entering into Mexico from, you may be required to produce a current record of vaccination. Yearly updates on the status of worldwide disease and inoculation requirements are available through the International Association for Medical Assistance to Travellers (IAMAT). Members receive a World Immunization Chart and, most valuable, a booklet with the names of reputable doctors around the globe who charge specified rates for their services. IAMAT's address is: 417 Center Street, Lewiston, NY 14092-3633. Membership is free but the organization exists on donations. Send $20 if you can.

Another good source of information is the Centers for Disease Control. CDC publishes *Health Information for International Travel, 1990,* a compendium of vaccination and travel health information. To order a copy send $4.95 to the Superintendent of Documents, U.S. Government Printing Office, Washington, DC 20402. Ask for the pamphlet by name.

Pre-Departure Preventive Measures

The following information should be taken as a guideline only, pursuant to seeking qualified medical recommendations.

Certain diseases are endemic in Mexico and precautions against them should be taken before leaving home. A tetanus-diphtheria booster and a poliomyelitis booster are considered routine immunizations recommended to all travellers regardless of age or global destination.

Infectious hepatitis (Type A) is prevalent wherever conditions are unhygenic and travellers may want to get a gamma globulin shot. It should be administered two to four weeks after other vaccines, so plan ahead, and it is effective for only six months.

Far more critical, in our opinion, is the risk of malaria, which occurs in many parts of Mexico. (IAMAT publishes a World Malaria Risk Chart). Before leaving home, fill a prescription for chloroquine pills. Get the kind that can be taken weekly. To be effective chloroquine must be taken for two weeks prior to, during, and six weeks after potential exposure to malaria.

Rabies is also widespread and travellers should exercise caution in befriending stray dogs and other animals. Famous advice. While camping in Baja, Eric spent the night cozied up with an abandoned kitten.

Health measures while in Mexico are discussed in Chapter Two.

Money

It's a good idea to carry some U.S. dollars, 100 or so. Smaller bills are useful when you run low on pesos and the banks are closed for the next three days because of a fabulous holiday weekend of parades, dance, and general hilarity, and the only place around that will deign to change money charges an unconscionably high fee. Bring some singles and a couple of fives—nothing larger than a twenty. The bills should be clean and untattered.

Most of your money, however, should be in the form of traveller's checks and, truth be known, American Express really are the least troublesome to cash.

Keep your traveller's check record separate from the checks. The same holds true for other documents, i.e., passport, tourist card or visa, credit cards and airline tickets. Airlines sometimes replace lost or stolen tickets if you are able to provide the ticket number.

Visa and Mastercard are the most widely accepted credit cards, but expect to be able to use them for purchases only in the most touristy hangouts. Their *real* benefit to the traveller is the cash advance, a godsend when you've just been ripped off, or are ready to fly home and can't find the airline ticket. Be sure cards won't expire during the period of travel.

Hiding Places

Nothing's foolproof, but here are some ideas: Wear a passport purse inside your shirt; sew pockets inside underpants or pants; stash some cash inside the bicycle seat tube; and distribute valuables throughout your bags. Suggestions?

Emergency Money or, For That Matter, Emergencies

Cabling money is such a hassle for both the sender and sendee, it's really worth trying to avoid. Having said that, the most expedient way to send money is through a large international bank that has a correspondent bank in Mexico. *Bancomer* and *Banamex* are two likely choices. The sender must know *your* passport number as well as the name and address of the recipient bank. In Guadalajara or Mexico City the money may arrive within a day. Elsewhere, even in state capitals, it can take weeks.

Money can be sent through American Express, but only the AmEx offices in Mexico City and Acapulco can receive money.

Exchanging money internationally by way of Western Union is complicated, expensive, and less than reliable (not Western Union's fault).

When really in a pinch—if you are seriously ill or lose your documents and money—it may be time for a trip to the nearest consular office. U.S. consulates maintain lists of English speaking doctors and dentists. Money can be sent through the State Department's Citizens Emergency Center to the U.S. Embassy in Mexico City or a specified consulate. See Appendix 3 for locations.

Traveller's Insurance

Everyone agrees it's a wise idea to carry travel insurance, and many companies offer both health and theft coverage. The best place to start looking for one is in the telephone yellow pages. Students who join CIEE (the Center for International Educational Exchange) receive an International Student ID card which provides partial accident and illness coverage. CIEE offices are located in large cities, and information is available on most campuses.

PURCHASES

You can bring up to $400 in purchases, including one liter of alcoholic beverage, home from Mexico without having to pay duty. If you have anywhere near that total it is a good idea to save receipts as proof of value.

It is illegal to bring many types of products into the United States. These include agricultural products, live animals (those permitted in will be quarantined), and items made from endangered wildlife. A few examples: *all* sea turtle products (including skin cream), snakeskins and most reptile skins and leathers, wild birds, feathers and skins. The list is long, and you will not be compensated for goods confiscated by customs or wildlife officials. The U.S. Customs Service puts out a booklet called *Know Before You Go,* available through local offices or by writing U.S. Customs, P.O. Box 7047, Washington, D.C. 20044.

On the Mexican side of the law, it is illegal to export any products made from wildlife, endangered or not. Unfortunately, this law is flagrantly violated because enforcement is inadequate.

MAIL

It takes at least a week for mail sent from the United States to reach Mexico. Once there, it will be held, usually for two weeks, before being returned as undeliverable. On the other hand it takes *about* ten days for mail from Mexico to reach its U.S. destination. It's easy to send weekly postcards to the folks back home, but if you hope to ever receive mail, give some thought to scheduling.

Letters addressed to you should have your last name capitalized and underlined. The address for general delivery is: *a/c Lista de Correos,* name of city, state, and country. On the lower left the sender might add *Favor de retener hasta legado,* please hold for delivery.

When mailing packages home don't seal the box until postal authorities have inspected the contents. This requirement varies from one state to the next (or maybe one post office to the next). As a result of leaving cartons open for a looksee, no one has ever bothered to actually go through our packages, but we do know people who sealed theirs and had to reopen them. Much easier to just bring wrapping paper, tape and string to the post office.

DRUGS

The Hassle of Your Life: A Handbook for Families of Americans Jailed Abroad, and *Coming Home: A Handbook for Americans Imprisoned in Mexico* are both published by the International

Legal Defense Counsel. Sobering material, best read before it is needed. These and other booklets concerning international incarceration can be ordered for $5.00 each from the ILDC, 111 South Fifteenth Street, Philadelphia, PA.

Need we say more? Well, yes. Marijuana and psychedelics, drugs, bountiful drugs, are illegal in Mexico. As a tourist, you're already a marked man or woman. Be more than merely careful. NEVER carry drugs. Even a roach can cost you dearly. Remember that the person you buy from may make money at the other end by turning you in.

SUGGESTIONS FOR PACKING

When deciding what clothing to take, consider how long you hope to travel as well as local climate. On some of these rides altitude changes encompass sweltering plains and chilly mountain plateaus. Even in summer many places are quite cold. Choose clothing which layers easily to optimize versatility. While all clothing should be broken in before leaving, shoes *really* should be.

Clothing:

pants

riding or sweat pants

2 pairs shorts, or roll-up pants for women

skirt, cotton knit won't wrinkle

bathing suit

heavy sweater

long-sleeved shirt

3 t-shirts or light blouses

underpants, bras

1 pair of shoes, a walking/riding combo

shower thongs, a health precaution

bath towel

4 pairs of socks

Personal Items:

insect repellent

chloroquine, a malaria preventive

sunblock, at least SP15

lipbalm with sunblock

comb or brush

tooth paste and brush

prescription medicines

First Aid kit:

  bandaids

  antibacterial such as Betadine ointment

  tweezer

  thermometer

  Pepto-Bismol lozenges to relieve diarrhea

  antihistamine to combat allergies

  aspirin or Tylenol

  snake bite kit, to ensure you don't need it

  (which is why we don't recommend taking condoms . . . besides, they're readily available in Mexico; the kind lubed with Oxynol-9 cost about $.75 each)

for women, the birth control of choice

eyeglasses, contact lenses and solution, and the prescription should they need replacement

tampons and pads, available in many places but carry some spares

shampoo

soap

razors

Miscellaneous Items:

small flashlight and extra battery

pocket knife

bungee cords
laundry soap
extra Ziploc plastic bags
a few feet of strong lightweight rope
toilet paper, available in markets but not in johns
water purification tablets
camera, extra battery, and extra film

Tool and Spare Parts Kit:

tire patch kit and extra patches
Phillips and flathead screwdrivers
small wrenches
adjustable wrench
pliers/wire cutter combo
Allen wrenches
tire irons
tire guage
spoke wrench
free wheel tool
chain tool
extra spokes
plastic fasteners
lubricant
spare tire
2 spare inner tubes

UNITED STATES EMBASSY

Mexico City, D.F.
phone: 211 00 42

UNITED STATES CONSULATES

Ciudad Juarez, Chih. 3 40 48
Guadalajara, Jal. 25 29 98
Hermosillo, Son. 3 89 22
Matamoros, Tamps. 2 52 50
Mazatlan, Sin. 1 29 05
Merida, Yuc. 5 54 09
Monterrey, N.L. 46 06 50
Nuevo Laredo, Tamps. 4 05 12
Tijuana, B.C. 86 10 01

UNITED STATES CONSULAR AGENTS (call Embassy if no phone number is listed)

Acapulco, Gro.
Cancun, Q.R. 4 16 38
Durango, Dgo. 1 11 07
Mulege, B.C.S. —call consulate in Guadalajara
Oaxaca, Oax. 6 06 54
Pto. Vallarta, Jal. —call consulate in Guadalajara
San Luis Potosi, S.L.P.
Tampico, Tamps.
Veracruz, Ver.

ANNUAL AVERAGE TEMPERATURES AND RAINFALL

CITIES	ALTITUDE	JAN T	JAN R	FEB T	FEB R	MAR T	MAR R	APR T	APR R	MAY T	MAY R	JUN T	JUN R	JUL T	JUL R	AUG T	AUG R	SEP T	SEP R	OCT T	OCT R	NOV T	NOV R	DEC T	DEC R
Acapulco, Gro.	23	78	0.4	78	0.0	79	0.0	80	0.0	83	12.	83	17.	83	8.6	83	9.8	82	14.	82	6.7	81	1.2	79	0.4
Aguascalientes, Ags.	6258	55	0.5	58	0.2	63	0.1	68	0.1	72	0.7	70	4.8	69	5.8	67	4.1	67	3.6	66	1.3	64	0.7	56	0.6
Apatzingan, Mich.	2237	78	.16	80	.28	84	.06	86	.04	90	.56	88	3.5	84	7.4	82	6.8	83	6.6	83	1.8	81	.32	78	.63
Campeche, Camp.	26	72	0.7	74	0.4	77	0.5	79	.02	81	1.7	81	6.1	80	7.0	81	6.7	81	5.7	80	3.4	76	1.2	74	1.2
Chetumal, Q. Roo	13	73	3.0	75	.86	77	1.1	80	1.2	81	5.5	82	7.0	82	5.1	82	4.2	81	5.5	79	8.4	75	3.4	75	3.7
Chihuahua, Chih.	4690	49	0.1	52	0.2	59	0.3	65	0.3	74	0.4	79	1.0	77	3.1	75	3.7	72	3.7	65	1.4	56	0.3	49	0.8
Chilpancingo, Gro.	3800	66	0.1	67	0.2	70	0.1	72	0.2	73	2.8	70	6.0	70	7.8	69	6.6	69	6.2	70	3.4	69	0.9	67	0.8
Cd. Obregon, Son.	131	65	.27	68	.20	72	0.6	77	.16	81	0.0	90	0.7	93	.27	93	1.8	91	1.7	85	.57	75	1.7	67	.51
Cd. Victoria, Tamps.	1053	60	1.4	64	1.0	70	0.8	76	1.5	79	5.0	81	4.8	81	4.1	82	2.7	79	7.9	74	4.3	67	1.7	60	0.6
Colima, Col.	1657	72	0.5	72	0.3	74	0.0	77	0.0	79	0.3	79	5.7	78	7.7	78	7.2	77	7.7	78	3.1	76	0.9	73	1.3
Cordoba, Ver.	3049	61	1.8	63	1.5	67	1.5	62	2.2	73	4.3	72	13.	70	15.	70	16.	70	18.	68	9.1	65	3.7	63	2.1
Creel, Chih.	7724	41	1.9	41	.31	42	.59	50	.55	55	1.1	63	5.3	63	5.3	61	5.5	59	1.1	54	2.6	44	1.3	39	1.8
Cuernavaca, Mor.	5000	65	0.1	67	0.2	70	0.3	72	0.3	74	2.1	70	7.8	68	8.6	68	8.7	68	9.7	68	3.1	67	0.3	66	0.1
Culiacan, Sin.	216	67	0.4	69	0.4	71	0.2	74	0.0	79	0.1	83	1.2	83	5.8	82	6.8	82	4.6	80	1.6	73	0.4	67	2.1
Durango, Dgo.	6209	53	0.5	56	0.4	60	0.0	65	0.1	69	0.5	62	2.4	69	4.9	69	3.6	67	4.0	64	1.2	58	0.6	54	0.7
Fortin, Ver.	3326	61	1.9	64	1.5	67	1.6	70	2.1	72	5.0	71	14.	71	15.	70	16.	70	18.	69	8.5	64	3.5	62	2.4
Guadalajara, Jal.	5220	58	0.7	61	0.2	65	0.1	70	0.0	72	0.7	71	7.6	69	10.	68	7.9	67	7.0	65	2.1	61	0.8	59	0.8
Guanajuato, Gto.	6835	57	0.5	60	0.3	64	0.2	68	02	71	1.1	68	5.4	67	6.6	66	5.5	67	6.0	63	2.0	60	0.7	59	0.6
Guaymas, Son.		64	0.3	66	0.2	69	0.2	73	0.1	73	0.1	84	0.0	87	1.8	87	3.0	86	2.1	81	0.4	72	0.4	65	1.1
Hermosillo, Son.	638	60	0.1	63	0.6	68	0.2	73	0.1	79	0.1	88	0.1	90	2.8	88	3.3	87	2.5	79	1.6	70	0.2	60	1.0
Ixtapan la Sal, Mex.	6349	84	0.6	67	0.5	70	0.3	72	1.2	75	2.3	73	6.4	68	7.3	68	11.	69	9.5	67	0.6	66	0.6	66	0.3
Jalapa, Ver.	4540	58	2.1	60	2.1	63	2.1	63	2.3	68	4.7	67	12.	66	8.5	66	8.0	65	11.	64	5.1	60	2.8	52	1.9
La Paz, B.C.	59	64	.13	68	.45	71	.03	74	0.0	79	0.0	81	0.0	88	.25	88	1.6	85	2.0	80	.37	72	.54	60	1.3
Leon, Gto.	6180	58	0.5	61	0.2	66	0.2	70	0.1	73	0.9	71	4.3	68	6.6	68	5.5	68	5.2	66	1.5	61	0.7	60	0.5
Manzanillo, Col.		75	0.9	74	0.5	74	0.0	76	0.0	79	0.1	81	4.0	83	5.4	83	7.4	81	15.	81	5.0	79	0.7	77	2.1
Mazatlan, Sin.	3	67	0.5	67	0.4	67	0.1	70	0.0	75	0.0	79	1.1	81	6.6	81	9.6	81	10.	79	2.4	74	0.5	69	1.7

Station (altitude, ft)	T	R	T	R	T	R	T	R	T	R	T	R	T	R	T	R	T	R	T	R	T	R	T	R
Merida, Yuc. 30	73	1.2	74	0.6	78	0.8	81	1.0	82	3.2	81	5.9	81	5.5	81	6.0	79	4.0	75	1.2	74	1.2	74	1.2
Mexico, D.F. 7240	54	0.2	56	0.3	61	0.4	63	0.5	65	0.2	63	4.2	61	4.9	61	4.1	59	4.6	58	1.3	54	0.6	54	0.3
Monterrey, N.L. 1749	59	0.8	62	0.9	68	0.6	74	1.1	78	1.7	81	3.3	81	2.9	81	2.5	72	8.1	63	4.3	57	1.0	57	0.9
Morelia, Mich. 6234	57	0.5	60	0.3	64	0.3	67	0.3	69	1.7	67	5.2	65	6.8	64	6.4	63	6.2	60	2.3	58	0.8	58	0.2
Oaxaca, Oax. 5068	63	0.1	66	0.1	70	0.4	72	1.0	73	2.4	71	4.9	70	3.7	69	4.1	67	6.7	65	1.6	64	0.3	64	0.4
Orizaba, Ver. 4079	59	1.8	61	1.6	64	1.0	68	1.9	70	5.3	68	14.	67	15.	67	13.	66	17.	61	7.3	66	3.9	66	2.1
Pachuca, Hgo. 7999	53	0.2	55	0.5	58	0.6	61	0.7	61	1.3	60	2.8	59	2.3	59	2.1	56	3.1	54	1.9	55	0.8	55	0.2
Patzcuaro, Mich. ...7180	57	0.8	56	0.5	61	0.3	64	0.2	68	1.5	68	7.9	63	0.8	63	9.5	61	8.5	58	3.1	55	1.0	55	0.9
Progreso, Yuc. 46	73	1.3	74	.67	76	.59	80	.70	79	2.1	80	2.9	80	1.8	80	1.8	79	2.1	76	2.7	74	.80	74	1.0
Puebla, Pue. 7200	54	0.2	60	0.2	62	0.5	65	0.5	66	2.9	64	6.2	63	5.4	63	5.8	61	7.4	58	2.2	56	0.8	56	0.3
Queretaro, Oro. 6160	57	0.4	60	0.1	64	0.2	68	1.4	70	1.1	69	3.7	67	4.1	67	3.4	63	4.8	61	1.3	59	0.4	59	0.5
Sn. Cristobal L.C., Chis. 7087	54	0.3	55	0.0	57	0.4	60	0.3	60	5.1	60	10.	60	5.6	60	6.3	59	9.9	55	6.0	55	0.9	55	0.6
San Jose Purua, Mich. ..6335	57	0.7	60	0.6	63	0.3	67	0.4	70	0.2	71	6.3	69	7.1	69	6.6	65	7.0	64	2.5	60	0.8	60	2.5
San Luis Potosi, S.L.P. .6157	55	0.5	59	0.2	63	0.4	69	0.2	70	1.2	70	2.8	67	2.3	65	1.7	63	3.4	59	0.7	57	0.4	57	0.6
Tampico, Tamps. ...39	65	2.1	68	0.9	71	0.5	77	0.4	80	2.0	82	7.9	82	5.8	82	5.9	78	13.0	72	7.0	67	2.2	67	1.7
Tapachula, Chis. ..551	77	.28	78	.24	80	1.2	81	2.9	80	12.0	78	19.	78	12.	78	13.	77	18.	77	16.0	77	3.4	77	.45
Taxco, Gro. 5500	66	0.0	69	0.2	72	0.4	75	0.9	76	3.0	72	10.0	70	12.	69	14.0	69	13.0	68	3.5	67	0.2	67	0.1
Tehuacan, Pue. ...5509	60	0.1	62	0.1	65	0.6	68	0.6	70	2.6	69	3.7	68	2.8	68	2.2	65	4.7	61	1.3	61	0.2	61	0.3
Tehuantepec, Oax. ...328	58	1.5	66	0.3	69	1.4	72	1.4	74	3.6	72	6.5	71	4.9	69	3.2	68	8.5	67	3.6	66	1.5	66	0.6
Tepic, Nay. 3000	63	1.2	63	0.8	65	0.0	70	0.0	71	0.1	74	6.8	74	14.0	74	12.0	73	8.1	78	1.9	64	0.3	64	2.1
Tlaxcala, Tlax. ...7500	55	0.2	57	0.1	61	0.3	63	0.7	64	2.9	63	5.0	61	5.3	61	5.9	60	5.4	58	1.9	57	0.3	57	0.2
Toluca, Mex. 8712	49	0.4	52	0.4	55	0.0	57	1.1	59	2.0	58	5.3	56	3.6	56	5.7	54	6.0	52	1.9	50	0.8	50	0.3
Torreon, Coah. ...3720	54	0.5	60	0.2	65	0.0	70	0.2	81	0.5	83	1.5	81	2.1	80	0.9	74	1.4	62	0.9	56	0.5	56	0.5
Tuxpan, Ver. ...	67	1.6	70	1.0	72	1.5	78	1.5	81	3.4	83	8.0	82	6.9	81	6.7	78	12.0	72	8.9	78	2.1	78	1.5
Tuxtla Gutierrez, Chis ..1759	71	0.0	73	0.2	77	0.4	80	.22	81	3.0	79	9.2	78	7.0	77	6.1	76	8.0	73	3.2	70	.16	70	.25
Uruapan, Mich. 5500	61	0.6	62	0.8	68	0.3	70	0.2	72	1.3	71	11.0	69	14.0	69	13.0	68	16.0	64	7.1	61	1.5	61	1.2
Valladolid, Yuc. ...72	70	2.5	73	1.0	77	1.0	80	3.0	81	4.7	80	6.0	80	5.5	79	6.3	77	7.0	73	5.7	72	1.9	72	2.2
Villahermosa, Tab. ...33	72	5.5	75	3.9	77	1.8	80	3.0	83	3.5	83	8.0	82	8.0	82	7.6	80	10.0	76	11.0	73	5.6	73	7.1
Zacatecas, Zac. 8187	49	0.4	51	0.2	54	0.1	59	0.1	62	0.9	61	2.1	57	3.5	57	2.3	56	3.0	52	0.9	50	0.6	50	0.5

T = Temperature in °F • R = Rainfall in inches • Altitudes are in feet

WHEN YOU GET THERE

Getting oriented in foreign surroundings is always a challenge and doing it with a bicycle hardly simplifies the task. A little forethought will help your cycling vacation off to a fast, smooth start.

Whether your first steps in Mexico are through the streets of Tijuana or down the aisle of a DC-10, the cultural transition is dizzying. Arrival is an excellent occasion to splurge on a hotel. Cull a few names from an accommodations guide before leaving for Mexico. Knowing where to stay that first night will help decrease your anxiety and there will be plenty of opportunity to bargain hunt later. Settle in, get accustomed to the food, dust off the old high school Spanish. Get used to being in Mexico. Then, get used to being in Mexico on a bicycle.

Those initial goals seem modest enough, but marshaling all that gear can involve a number of choices. When flying into Mexico City, or any of the larger cities, it's best to transfer your bike, still boxed for shipping, by taxi to a hotel. But, if arriving at a regional airport where the terminal is tiny and only a few miles from town, align handlebars and attach pedals on the spot and bike off.

If you are returning home from the same point as arrival, a bicycle transit bag can be checked at the airport or bus station baggage depot until the end of your trip. Ask the attendant to put a note on the package saying approximately when you'll pick it up. Storage fees are reasonable.

THE PLAZA

The *zocalo,* or plaza, is the heart of all Mexican towns. Weekends and in early evening, the *zocalo* serves as the point of social interaction for generations of families. Peals of childish laughter carry on a warm summerish breeze, grandmas cluster and indulgently gossip, couples stroll or chat with neighbors, and eligible girls and boys promenade, eyeing each other shyly. Most plazas are bordered by cafes and restaurants and provide excellent vantage for people watching.

LODGING

In our parlance "great" lodging is safe, reasonably comfortable, and inexpensive. If you haven't yet found lodging for the night, the main *zocalo* is the place to begin looking. Older, budget-priced hotels are found near the plaza, usually the oldest district in town.

The modest roadhouses scattered throughout rural Mexico are not fancy. A favorable disposition to tropical fauna is helpful. Visits to the toilet may involve a short walk to the outhouse, and the beds . . . well, Eric frequently sleeps on the floor. Armed with a self-inflating Therm-A-Rest pad, any hotel can be a haven. Besides the enticement of a shower at the end of each riding day, the freedom that comes with locking your gear away for the evening adds incomparably to peace of mind. Go to the plaza, see a movie, have a few drinks and don't worry that the campsite will be robbed while you're away.

TOURIST OFFICES

Most cities of consequential size have a government tourist office and it is our practice to seek it out soon after arrival in any town where we intend to stay more than a night. Helpful staffs are ready with stacks of free maps, brochures and recommendations on places to go, and some offices coordinate tours of the city and surrounding environs.

FOOD

Belongings safely tucked and maps in hand, it's time to eat. Newcomers to Mexico won't be long in discovering that Mexican food is more than burritos. The national diet of rice, beans, and corn combine with regional cuisines to make Mexican cooking deliciously varied.

Comida, the day's big meal served between 1:00 and 4:00 p.m., is a good opportunity to indulge in regional cooking. *A la carte* dining is increasingly the mode in Mexico but a set dinner, called *comida corrida*, is still provided by many restaurants. *Comida corrida* is the traditional working man's meal, found in hole-in-the-wall establishments called *fondas* as well as fancier restaurants. The day's choices, posted in the doorway or attached to the menu, are usually two or three entrees served with rice, beans, soup, dessert and beverage. Prices range from US$1 to US$5. Restaurants which specialize in *mariscos,* seafood, rarely offer *prix fixe* meals.

American-style foods, though slow to penetrate the market, are making headway. Pepsi and Coke are found everywhere. *Exquisitos,* hot dogs grilled with a bacon wrapping, are a popular north-of-the-border import. And there is, of course, that most famous American food, the *hamburguesa.*

Late Night Dining

Too late for *comida?* Your best bet for nighttime eating is the plaza. At dusk vendors with carts appear in the *zocalo* and set up stands which prepare *tacos, hamburguesas* and *exquisitos, tamales* and steaming bins of *elotes*—corn on the cob, slathered with mayonnaise, cheese and chile powder. Most stay open until the wee hours. Other places to look for vendors are outside movie theatres, bars, at the market and in bus stations.

Eating On the Road

Large towns will have several eating places to choose from, and even small ones will have tiny restaurants, called *fondas* or *comedors,* which serve simple meals. Road-side stores sell soft drinks (generally warm) and junk food. Keep an eye on the map and our Road Notes as you travel so as not to be left hungry.

Botana

Botana is complimentary food served with drinks during the *comida* hour at decrepit little *cantinas* and upscale watering holes which prefer to be identified as "bars." Foods range from simple appetizers to fiery soups, generous servings of fried fish and local delicacies. Taxi drivers are a wonderful source to discover the best *botana* bar in town, a search that happens to be one of our favored pastimes.

Cantinas and Bars

The word *cantina* generally indicates a classic dive, while a bar has loftier pretensions. The cantina is an altar of inebriation, long on atmosphere and short on facilities. In some cases, the men's bathroom may be little more than a wall designated for urinating upon. There are no facilities for women. In fact, women, as well as uniformed police and soldiers, are prohibited from entering most *cantinas,* but allowances for tourists are commonly made. It is inappropriate for a woman or small group of women to go into a *cantina* without a male escort, and even then his asking for permission to enter is an essential courtesy.

Bars are generally more sophisticated than *cantinas,* and, especially in cities, it is acceptable for women to enter unescorted. The term "ladies bar" certainly indicates that women are welcome, but it may also mean prostitutes work the place. It shouldn't take long to figure out which type of ladies bar you've entered.

Drinking Water

Three culprits are responsible for most cases of *turista:* e. coli, *shigella flexneri* and *salmonella typhi.* They can usually be avoided by drinking bottled beverages. But, if you use ice cubes, you may be interested in these statistics: 78% of the *shigella,* 82% of the *salmonella* and 97% of the e. *coli* are killed after a day in the freezer. Using Coke as a mixer eliminates another 50% of the survivors. This sounds good until you get a serious bout of diarrhea, nausea, and stomach cramps.

Despite considerable gains in municipal efforts and growing public awareness of health issues, untreated water is still not safe to drink. Dehydration from diarrhea is the major cause of juvenile mortality in Mexico. Bottled drinking water has become the norm among urban Mexicans, and you will often see little refreshment stalls using commercially sold water. Five gallon decanters of *agua purificada* are standard in many hotels, or sometimes a specific wall spigot provides filtered water. Fill your water bottles at every opportunity. If the locals don't drink tap water, you certainly shouldn't. In our experience, obtaining sufficient clean water has seldom been a problem. Requests to fill our bottles have never been refused, although in some rural areas where *agua purificada* deliveries are less frequent, we've been asked to take only what we thought we'd really need.

Tiendas or stores throughout the countryside sell *aqua mineral,* bottled carbonated water, and in a pinch buy a couple of them to fill your water bottles.

Water Treatment

When some form of purified water simply cannot be found, there are three options for treating the available water: pumps, pills, and boiling.

Several good water filter pumps are sold which remove virtually all impurities except the hepatitis virus—a big consideration in Mexico. In addition, all water filters require frequent cleaning.

Boiling is a good method of purification but necessitates hauling a stove, fuel, and a pot. It takes 10 minutes plus one minute for each 1,000 feet above sea level at a rolling boil to kill the most resistant microbes, a process which is time consuming and uses lots of fuel. White gas is not readily sold and you can forget about propane cartridges.

Because of the infrequent need to sterilize water, we think chemicals—light, cheap and reliable—are a good choice. Iodine is very effective but excessive use can destroy the body's natural flora along with the target pathogens. Halazone is unstable and ineffective against giardia. We recommend "Potable Aqua," a brand name germicide widely available in camping and sporting goods stores.

STAYING HEALTHY

Staying healthy calls for common sense. Get enough rest and eat well. Compromise, if you must, on hotels rather than food. Food that has been carelessly prepared or dishes that have been inadequately washed are fertile breeding grounds for bacteria. This doesn't mean avoiding street food or the marketplace, but it does require exercising judgment. Take note of the vendor's level of hygiene, avoid excessively greasy foods and those which have been cooked in cloudy oil.

Regaining Health

Sometimes you become ill anyway. If—perhaps it is more realistic to say when—it happens, here are a few suggestions to follow:

1. Avoid dehydration. Drink lots of fluids and avoid such diuretics as coffee and alcohol.
2. Get plenty of rest. Cut back on cycling, especially during the heat of the day.
3. Some people swear by the curative powers of fresh papaya mixed with yogurt.
4. Try the potion that unites grandmas around the world, *sopa de pollo.*
5. Fast. Drink bottled mineral water only. Starve the little buggers out.
6. Take antibiotics only as a last resort. Though effective in the short run, they knock out the body's natural defenses, leaving you highly susceptible to re-infection.

Plan ahead. A list of recommended doctors who charge set fees can be obtained from IAMAT (see Chapter One for the address). In the event of something more serious, emergency treatment can be gotten at one of the government's IMSS hospitals. Whenever you receive medical care abroad it is advisable to check in with your personal physician upon returning home.

The AIDS crisis in Mexico is a growing health concern. Condoms lubricated with Oxynol-9 are the most effective means of preventing transmission. They are widely available in pharmacies and cost about $.75 each. Best think twice about the brand that sells three for a dollar, *Buena Suerte* ("Good Luck")!

Heat and Sun Exposure

Cyclists should be particularly alert for symptoms of overexertion.

Prolonged exposure to hot temperatures and direct sunlight can lead to heat exhaustion and heat stroke. Both result from the body's inability to maintain an adequately cool internal temperature. Heightened physical activity, high relative humidity and hot weather are all contributing factors. If not acted upon promptly, heat exhaustion can escalate to heat stroke, a life-threatening situation. The initial symptoms of heat exhaustion are not always obvious but may include dizziness, nausea, headache and a rapid, weak pulse. The sufferer does not necessarily perspire, yet her or his skin may be cool to the touch. If either heat exhaustion or stroke is suspected, it is essential to lower the body's internal temperature. This can be accomplished by shading the person, wetting him with water and fanning to enhance evaporation. Aspirin should *not* be administered.

To prevent overheating, drink lots of fluids, don't ride in the heat of the day, and wear head protection. Helmets should be light colored and incorporate air-flow design, or wear a wet bandana to keep your brain from boiling.

Altitude Sickness

Pulmonary edema is the accumulation of fluid in the lungs, a condition which strikes even physically fit individuals who are not acclimatized to altitudes above 8,000 feet. Symptoms begin one to three days after achieving high altitude and are first apparent in fatigue and shortness of breath, followed by disorientation, drowsiness and bloody sputum. Early on, pulmonary edema can be treated by evacuation to a lower altitude, but the afflicted person is in increasingly grave peril until oxygen can be administered.

Anyone climbing Mexico's volcanoes should be aware of the risks of high altitude recreation. Atop Orizaba, 18,700 feet, oxygen levels are reduced by 50% relative to sea level. The potential for altitude sickness is great. The Paso de Cortes (Tour #10) crests near 14,000 feet, high enough to merit caution.

RIDING CONDITIONS

Mexican roads hide few surprises. They are sometimes ragged, usually narrow, and always without shoulders. Sounds pretty dangerous, huh? Let's not kid ourselves, bicycle touring anywhere involves risk. Turning your back on strangers who overtake you in high-speed vehicles is truly an act of faith.

We believe cyclists arriving in Mexico will be pleasantly surprised to find riding conditions better than expected. In our experience the drivers of commercial vehicles, the bulk of traffic outside urban areas, are skilled and courteous. Highways are of a quality considered secondary backroads in the developed nations but the scarcity of traffic compensates for deficiencies. For the

most part the macadam is whole, the amount of glass manageable, and thorns a problem only offroad. Bicyclists from around
the world routinely cross Mexico on standard touring bikes with
28c tires and get no more flats than usual. We prefer mountain
bikes because there are so many unpaved roads to explore, not
because the pavement requires them.

ROAD SIGNS

International road signs are used throughout Mexico. Most
meanings are clear, but one symbol may leave you puzzled. Speed
bumps, called *topes,* appear as a horizontal chain of ovals, or as
two symmetrical black hills against a yellow backdrop. Typically,
one or two rows of *topes* are placed on all roads either entering or
leaving town. They are made of concrete or domed metal. Be careful not to hit them dead on. They'll rattle your innards and the
surfaces can be slippery.

BUSSES

Private cars remain a luxury in Mexico, making busses the major source of mass transportation. To the cyclist they are both a
blessing and a bane. The "squeeze play," when two busses from
opposite directions pass as they simultaneously overtake you, is
bicycling Mexico's single worst hazard. Be alert. Continuously
scan the road for emergency pull-offs and always be prepared to
get off the road in a split second.

In truth, the service which the nation's many bus fleets perform
and their safety record is exemplary. Their efficiency, low cost
and sheer abundance add a new dimension to bicycle touring.
Far-flung regions can be visited in one short vacation and long,
uninteresting sections of ground can be skipped over quickly.

Bus 'n Bike Travel

You can board a bus almost anywhere along its route, but the
hassle and tension of stuffing a bicycle into the storage bay in
only a few seconds, while the driver's assistant impatiently urges
you to hurry, can be reduced by catching the bus at its point of
origin.

Bus stations in Mexico, called the *camionera central* or *estacion
de autobuses,* are exciting places, reminiscent of airports in the

Highway Signs

ALTO
STOP

NO REBASE
NO PASSING

ANCHO LIBRE
HORIZONTAL CLEARANCE

PESO MAXIMO
MAXIMUM WEIGHT (METRIC TONS)

NO
NO PEDESTRIANS

LIMITE
PARKING LIMIT

UNA HORA
ONE-HOUR PARKING

NO
NO LEFT TURN

NO
NO U TURN

NO
NO PARKING

CONSERVE SU DERECHA
USE RIGHT LANE

INSPECCION
INSPECTION

NO
NO TRUCKS

PEATONES A SU IZQUIERDA
PEDESTRIANS KEEP LEFT

100 km/h
MAXIMA
SPEED LIMIT (IN K.P.H.)

CONTINUA
CONTINUOUS TURN

NO
NO BICYCLES

CIRCULACION
KEEP RIGHT

NO
DO NOT ENTER

SLIPPERY ROAD LOOSE GRAVEL

STEEP HILL

CEDA EL PASO
YIELD RIGHT-OF-WAY

LANDSLIDE AREA

BUMPS

NARROW BRIDGE

DIP

TWO-WAY TRAFFIC

TRAFFIC CIRCLE

SIGNAL

R.R. CROSSING

CATTLE

SCHOOL CROSSING

MEN WORKING

4.20 m
VERTICAL CLEARANCE

TRAILER CAMP

AIRPORT

HOSPITAL

MECHANIC

FERRY

500 m
RESTAURANT

RESTROOMS

1 km
TELEPHONE

1 km
GAS STATION

Most Vehicles Give Cyclists Wide Berth

industrial countries. The major carriers provide top-notch service
and the drivers are accorded the status of professionals. Everything about them, from their impeccable uniforms to the impe-
rial manner with which they treat the baggage handlers and
ticket takers, makes it clear that these guys are big-time. Our
esteem for their abilities is high.

It is a good idea to affect a respectful attitude toward the driver
when travelling by bus. Even when there's room for a bicycle and
panniers in the baggage bay, the driver always has the final say.
How much to charge is usually left to his discretion, so some
bikes ride free, others don't. We generally consent to any charge
up to half the passenger fare, at which point we dig in. No one
yet has called our bluff.

Many bus lines sell reserved seats. Try to get seat numbers three or four, front row right. In addition to the best view and extra leg room, you'll be the first off to unload bike and gear.

Hitching Rides with Busses

Should mechanical failure beset you, a bus can be flagged down. Most busses do make impromptu roadside stops so if one doesn't respond to frantic arm waving, it's either full or there is no room for a bicycle. Sit tight. Another is not far behind, so be prepared for the moment when a bus does pull over. Have panniers, pump, water bottles and cycle computer—all removable items—stripped from the bike for quick, efficient loading. Some second-class busses, those most likely to stop, carry baggage on the overhead rack. If stowing a bike overhead, lash it down with a bungee cord or rope.

TRAINS

Trains are another way to cover territory you'd rather not bike, and are sometimes the only means of transportation to regions otherwise inaccessible. Trains in Mexico are slower than busses and, unless travelling pullman class, cheaper as well. Not all trains include a freight car, so make inquiries in advance. To get a bicycle to Creel, for instance, the jumping-off place for Barranca del Cobre, it is necessary to ship a bike the day before you ship yourself.

Freight charges are based on weight ,usually a few dollars for a bike. A ticket is attached to the bike and the owner gets a receipt. If possible, oversee the bike's loading and attach a cable lock. It will provide a little peace of mind for the time your bicycle is out of sight.

A FINAL WORD

Always leave a margin of time for the unanticipated. Often, the things which make a trip memorable are those which are impossible to plan. Remember that itineraries were made to be modified. If for any reason you fall hopelessly out of sync with the schedule you so carefully crafted, tear it up. You'll feel so much better.

INTRODUCTION TO
THE YUCATAN

There is no better place to begin bicycle touring in Mexico than the Yucatan. Its level terrain and gently rolling hills provide an excellent training ground for the less experienced cyclist and permit the experienced biker to rack up extraordinary mileage. The roads consistently are the best in Mexico and in most places traffic is light.

Add to this the fact that Yucatan's best weather is during the United States' and Europe's worst, November through February. The temperature hovers in the 80's, the skies are sunny and clear (yes, there are occasional storms called *nortes*), and there is a delightfully warm, steady breeze. Airfares from both the U.S. and Europe are low, and staying in Mexico is inexpensive. For women there is the extra attraction of its being almost hassle-free. We recommend that women travel in groups of two or more if you plan to camp. On longer solo ventures plan to stay in hotels. There is no other area in all of Mexico that is as safe for women travellers.

The Yucatan peninsula hangs on the eastern tip of Mexico like a geologic afterthought. From it, Central America stretches its shaky arm, clasping onto the whole of South America. It is comprised of three states, Yucatan, Campeche, and Quintana Roo. The Spanish conquistadors first invaded the peninsula around 1527, but it was not until 1542 that the Yucatan was secured and Merida founded on the remains of the Mayan city of Ti-Ho. The Spaniards brought with them disease, slavery and war. The decline of the native population was rapid; some estimate the *indigenas* were reduced from 25 million to one million within 100 years. What remained of Maya civilization collapsed utterly. Magnificent cities disappeared beneath soil and vegetation as surely as the foundations of their culture were systematically destroyed.

Maya cities sprawled far beyond the boundaries of the restored buildings that you see at most sites. Whole municipalities lie buried. In Mayapan alone, 3,000 suspicious humps in an other-

wise flat terrain indicate the presence of a once-thriving city.
One is tempted to think, "Oh, another pyramid." But these cities
are architecturally diverse and track the progress of Maya civilization over a period of many centuries. The Puuc Hill and Caribbean tours include the most famous Maya ruins in the Yucatan,
Uxmal and Chichen Itza, as well as the lesser known, equally
marvelous Sayil and Labna.

Besides great riding to great ruins, the peninsula is replete with
caves and limestone sinkholes, called *cenotes*. A massive carbonate shelf, relic of prehistoric high sea levels, it is too porous to
support a river system. They are all underground and have
carved an extensive subterranean network. Where the erosive
process has broken through the earth's surface, *cenotes* have
formed. When filled with water, they make for good swimming.
The Maya frequently call any cave with a body of water in it a
cenote. We were taken to one, which we've described in Tour #2,
and were awed to see the deepest, clearest pool of water imagina-
ble. It stretched far beyond our willingness to explore. Several
caves, or portions of enormous caves, have been made accessible
to tourists. They are lighted and groups are led by a guide. We
think the cave of Loltun, also in Tour #2, is not to be missed.

THE COAST

The north and east coasts of the Yucatan, the Gulf and the Caribbean, offer very different kinds of pleasures. The Gulf Coast
makes for a hardier tour. The wind blows stiffer, the hotels, if
there are hotels, are simpler. The tour takes you past henequen
fields, jungle, beach and swamp, and an array of avian life that is
simply magnificent. The Caribbean, of course, needs little intro-
duction, but in addition to the gorgeous and heavily touristed
areas around Cancun, we have included information south as far
as untramelled Punta Allen.

WHERE HENEQUEN WAS KING

The far reaching effect of the henequen industry in the Yucatan
is readily apparent. You ride past mile after mile of tended and
abandoned henequen fields. A large, spikey succulent with fibrous leaves, the plant is used to make sisal rope. Between the
mid-1800's and 1940, henequen was king in the Yucatan. Large
haciendas owned by single families controlled vast tracts of land
and the lives of hundreds of peasants. Towns evolved solely to

serve the needs of the *hacienda*. At the end of World War II, the industry collapsed. Today, towns once dependent on a plantation system which provided them a harsh but certain existence, are scratch poor. You will find plenty of sisal products for sale, such as hammocks, bags and hats, but they will never compensate for the loss of the sailing and rope markets.

Certain Yucatecan peculiarities are worth noting. On first arrival it appears you've entered barber heaven. It's all those *guayabera* shirts the men are wearing. Except for having either short or long sleeves and bland variations in color, they are identical. You will see some spectacular variations in *huipiles*, however— the traditional garb for Maya women. Although the market is flooded with machine-sewn polyester *huipiles*, the dresses worn by most native women are decorated with beautifully hand-stitched flowers of fine embroidery thread. *Huipiles* and *rebozos*, the shawl no traditional woman is seen without, display distinctions peculiar to each village. As you travel throughout Mexico you will continue to see marked differences in these traditional clothes.

Hammocks come to mind when you think of the Yucatan. There are two major hammock weaving centers which these tours pass through, Tixkokob and Chumayel. Visit the home of a hammock maker. They won't undercut the prices of their Merida distributors but you'll get a good quality hammock and a grand look behind the scenes. Hammocks available on the street tend to be of lighter weight and looser weave, but at least they're cheap, around 12,000p ($5.25). Depending on size, quality and material, most hammocks cost between 22,000p and 140,000p.

In Maya Scrabble sets, "X" is only a one-point letter. It's widely used and causes English speakers no end of problems. This flys in the face of the local population's insistence that Maya and English are actually two similar languages. Perhaps, if you speak neither. In any case, try pronouncing "X" like "ish", which means X-Can sounds like "Ish-Can." Tixkokob is pronounced "Tish-co-cobe."

INCREDIBLE EDIBLES

Yucatecan cuisine is generally mildly spiced but accompanied by a dish of *salsa piquante*. The green chilies are really hot, the orange ones (called *habaneros*) which look deceptively like grated

carrot would make the devil himself beg for mercy. Forewarned is forearmed.

Some other not-to-be-missed Yucatecan foods are *panuchos,* which are *tostadas* with beans precooked inside. They're piled high with lettuce, chicken and tomatoes. Sweet onions pickled in a peppery vinaigrette are the crowning touch. The Maya word for orange is *china,* pronounced "chee-nuh." Peeled, split, and topped with salt and chili, the unusual combination is a potent thirst quencher. *Pibil*-style means wrapped in banana leaves and stewed in its own juice. It's a particularly meritorious way for a chicken to be recycled. *Poc-chuc* transforms pork the way *pibil* does chicken, rendering it tender and tasty. *Papadzules,* a big hit with vegetarians, are enchilladas stuffed with hard boiled egg and covered with a thick pumpkin seed sauce. *Sopa de lima,* lime soup, shows what Latin genius has done for an old Jewish favorite. Fried tortillas and a bobbing lime unleash the latent greatness of a humble bowl of chicken soup. When it's really done right the tortillas are stuffed with meat (Mexican kreplach!). It might be the greatest soup in the world if it weren't for *sopa de ajos,* garlic soup, which is strictly for the purist.

There are three regional Yucatecan beers, Montejo, Carta Clara, and Leon—two lights and a dark. Highly recommended. The cheapest store-bought beers are sold in *depositos,* beverage centers which display sale banners. Drinking on the premises, while technically illegal, is usually permitted. Ask, and consume discreetly.

Drinking *Xtabentun,* an anise and honey liquor, is a great way to spend an evening with a bunch of new friends or old strangers.

MERIDA

Merida, capital of Yucatan, is a city of lovely, overt affection. In the balmy weather of its winter days Meridians promenade in the square, couples young and old holding hands or arms wrapped around each other. The plaza clock tower chimes four times an hour. Dawn and dusk are marked by a flag ceremony, accompanied by the music of a military band. People here, like

Vegetable Market, Merida

those we met elsewhere in the Yucatan, are friendly, generous, and instinctively trusting. Merida is a convenient staging ground for two-wheeled forays throughout the peninsula. You may want to make it home base during your visit to the Yucatan.

THE GULF: YUCATAN'S "OTHER" COAST

ROUTE: Merida—Sisal—Progeso—Dzilam de Bravo—Merida.
DISTANCE: 280 k.
RIDING TIME: 4 or 5 days.
DIFFICULTY: As easy as it will ever get.
TERRAIN: Virtually flat. Well paved except for a 27k stretch of dirt-sand-mud road.
BEST TIME: October through March.
ATTRACTIONS: Topographic changes include jungle, swamp and seashore. Typical, kempt villages and a marvelous variety of birds.

The Yucatan's Gulf Coast tour initiated our working together as bicyclists cum travel writers. We began here for three main reasons: The flat terrain was an essential training ground for Ricky who, almost 43, had never cycle-toured; it's a wonderfully relaxing place to sightsee; and, the weather is hot and humid for much of the year. We did this tour in early February.

In addition to the terrain being virtually level, with the exception of one 27k stretch, the roads are exceptionally good—probably the best in Mexico—and lightly trafficked. From Sisal to Dzilam de Bravo the view encompasses vast, windswept, nearly deserted beaches, the ocean wild and rolling, and huge *cienegas,* wetlands inhabited by a stunning variety of aquatic birds. In fact, the route is a bird watcher's paradise and is of more than passing interest to the average observer. And there are some memorable meals to be had along the way.

Leaving Merida

Getting out of Merida takes some doing. The inner city streets are all one-way and on Sundays and holidays (which seem to be frequent and take the uninitiated by surprise) the central ones are closed to vehicular traffic. That term includes bicycles, we

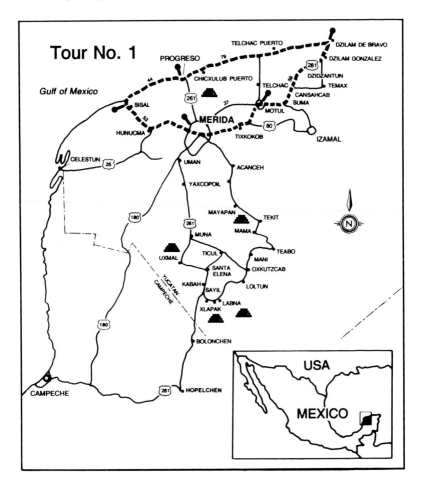

quickly learned. The streets are well-marked but a street/road map is essential. They're available for free at the local tourist office on Calles 60 and 57 in Merida.

From Merida head west on Calle 61 to its terminus at the Centenario Zoo. On the far side of the zoo turn right and follow Avenida de las Itzaes one block north to Calle 59A. Turn left. It's almost free sailing now and traffic diminishes perceptibly. By k 7, neatly stacked limestone fences appear, marking the start of the henequen fields. The road stretches ahead, flat, well-paved, and almost empty. The scent of jungle flowers fills the air. Exotic birds fly through the bush.

Typical Yucatecan Towns

The first town you will reach, Caucel, does not appear on most maps. It is impossible to determine why it doesn't or why, for that matter, certain others do. Caucel and Ucu, the next town you will ride into, are typical of most Yucatecan towns. The outskirts are marked by extensive roadside garbage dumps—a quite shocking blight after rolling through the glorious, untainted countryside. Flocks of black feathered buzzards pick through the rotting, half-incinerated debris.

But the ugliness is confined to the village perimeter. Speed bumps (called *topes*) appear, wide corrugated concrete affairs that rattle your innards every time you pass over one. Carefully tended yards line the street, each separated by a low stone fence. Beautiful thatched-roof structures, elliptical in shape and the traditional Maya home, called *na*, dominate each neatly defined plot. Chickens, turkeys and geese strut about, scratching out a living under the shade of orange and papaya trees. Children play, dogs lie about, women tend to household chores. Each town is foreign in a similar way, until they all start to seem reassuringly familiar.

The center of virtually every town you will enter (the upcoming Sisal is an exception) is the main plaza or *zocalo*. With remarkable consistency the plaza is overshadowed by the presence of a huge, ancient church, a testament to rapacious Spanish conquest. There are thought-provoking socio-political inconsistencies to be found here. The Maya cling proudly to a culture which is uniquely theirs, yet have totally embraced the Catholicism of their conquerors.

As you near most town plazas, *bodegas* and kiosks appear where you will be able to sate your thirst and perhaps deflect your appetite. Many of the towns in the Yucatan do not have even one restaurant. Neither sufficient tourism nor fluidity of local cash exists to support them. What you can expect is a steady supply of bottled sodas and junk food. But a restaurant almost invariably appears sometime during the course of the day.

One of the delights of the Yucatan is its fruit. Generally even the most meagerly appointed town will have a citrus-seller. The ritualized preparation of an orange, called *china* in Maya, involves turning the fruit on a handcranked brass lathe. The peel falls to the ground in a long, ribbon-like strand, the bitter rind pared from the sweet fruit. Sliced in half and sprinkled with chile and salt, the combination is an invigorating and delicious thirst quencher.

We biked the 39k to Hunucma before stopping for lunch. The town was bustling with activity as we pulled in, just in time, it turned out, for us to enjoy the local festival for the Virgin of Tetiz. Rather than try to penetrate the chaos with loaded touring bikes we chose to eat at the **Restaurant D'Iran** because of its easy access. After a good meal at a great price (3,000p each, about $1.40), which included beer and *chimole,* a breast of chicken in a piquant, oily sauce, the restaurant owner urged us to leave our bicycles in the safety of his large kitchen, so we could enjoy the fair unencumbered. We happily did so.

A rickety bullfighting stadium, erected yearly for this celebration, commanded the landscape. Behind it a ferris wheel and merry-go-round spun celebrants of all ages. Food stands and fruit stalls sold tantalizing refreshments, vendors hawked cotton candy and popcorn. There were even a few games of chance. We were surrounded by Mayans, the women adorned in gorgeous, stark white *huipiles,* their necklines and hems embroidered in richly saturated colors. Remarkably, despite legions of gooey-fingered children, their dresses remained impeccably clean.

The bullfight was supposed to begin in a few hours. In the stadium cowboys practiced with their lariats, cowgirls put their equine mounts through paces. After wandering around, snapping pictures and talking with strangers, we declined invitations to stay for the 4 p.m. bullfight. We mounted our own trusty steeds and left for Sisal, the first day's goal.

While the terrain between Hunucma and Sisal remains flat, the face of the surrounding countryside begins to change noticeably. Untended acres of henequen give in to the jungle. A dozen kinds of brilliant flowers catch your eye. Unobserved against a protective

backdrop until they move, birds fly off in a stunning display of color. Fields of salt marsh appear, densely covered with mangroves. This strip of road is a condensed lesson in shifting ecosystems.

The Gulf Coast

Sisal is a desolate fishing village. For two months of the year Sisal, as well as the other small towns along this route, come alive with a deluge of Mexican tourists attempting to escape the intense summer heat of inland Yucatan. The rest of the year the hotels and restaurants lie fallow and the towns go about fishing as usual. Much of Sisal's appeal comes from its lack of interest in the tourist dollar.

A paved road, which becomes narrow and funky only upon reaching Sisal, leads directly to the Gulf. A hectic wind blows choppy little waves against the shore, snapping at the row of beached fishing dinghies just beyond reach. On our visit the only open food establishment was a snack bar. There were no hotels. Anticipating this, we'd brought along sleeping bags. Now, after seeing the sand piled up against buildings and feeling the strength of the wind, that option became less than appealing. We decided to ask around about possible rooms for rent.

Eric tried his Spanish on three men who were standing in a doorway. No, they didn't know of any hotels. Yes, camping was permitted on the beach. . . . "Well," said Francisco, "perhaps." He had a second house which was being renovated and maybe we would want to spend the night there, but he would not even know what to charge.

Eric suggested that a price of 4,000 or 5,000 pesos might be fair. "Okay," said Francisco. "If you like it I will charge 4,000p."

We ended up staying the night. For another 4,000p we were invited into their home and Francisco's wife made us a fish dinner which has made subsequent meals pale by comparison. Francisco and his brothers, all fishermen, plan to open a seafood restaurant by the time you read this. It will be called **El Paso del Pescador** and, if our dinner was any indication, this restaurant will be worth your checking out.

Maps indicate an "improved" road extending east from Sisal. Francisco insisted it did not exist. The truth lay in between.

There is a road of sorts, built during the henequen plantation era, which has long since fallen into decay. Judging by the trail of shell casings we found, it is now used mostly by duck hunters. Apparently it was once paved; here and there bits of concrete still cling together. But for the most part the road is dirt, sand and mud, 27k of it. The dirt is negotiable; the sand and mud are not. In addition, at various points two parallel roads have been sliced through the jungle. When the sand on one becomes too tiresome, it's necessary to shift across to the other. A word of caution: At certain times the road becomes a maze of the detours and cross-cuts. It is not difficult to maintain your general direction, but it is easy to lose track of your companions if you don't stay in sight.

Be sure also to fill your water bottles before leaving Sisal. There are no facilities along this stretch. We bought oranges, bread and cheese. We treated our water with purification tablets and pur-chased a large container of juice. The treated water was so wretched, we were sorry we hadn't bought more juice.

This slow route often requires walking, but the road between Si-sal and Dzilam de Bravo offers compelling visual rewards. There are times when the strip of land you traverse becomes so narrow, that while looking due east you can see the azure Gulf waters on the left and an extensive salt marsh on the right. Large aquatic birds sail overhead—pelicans, seagulls and ducks; snow white egrets and dark heron stalk prey in the swamp. Across the shal-low water an occasional tree spreads its naked limbs. Nearby a startled iguana clumsily skitters into the bush. On the horizon a stand of palm trees looms, while long driveways lead to aban-doned buildings in varying states of decay.

It is a strange and oddly appealing landscape. After three hours the plodding ahead through the midday heat begins to seem end-less. After four hours Chuburna appears heaven-sent. We drank beers and ate *ceviche,* then pushed on for Chelem.

We spent the night at the **Hotel Villa Nueva,** one of the few open establishments in a 17k row of summer homes and guest houses. Most are open only in July and August, during the annual influx of Mexican tourists. The silent, lonely buildings lend an eerie ghost-town ambiance to the surroundings. As the sole guests of the Villa Nueva's new owners, we were mercilessly assailed by their slightly askew efforts to be attentive. The discovery of a colony of ants in Ricky's bed necessitated a change to new quarters, but only after the innocent young desk clerk who had assigned us the room had been thoroughly upbraided by the hotel manager. This same guy awoke her at 7 a.m. to enquire whether he could begin cleaning the room. His energies would have been more appropriately directed at fixing his boiler. Despite repeated assurances of hot water, our showers were short, brisk affairs. The cost of this idyll was 16,500p (about $7).

Progreso

Had we known better, we'd have pushed the last 9k to Progreso, where more polished facilities and better prices are available. In addition to a wider choice of both lodging and restaurants, you will be advantageously positioned for the next day's ride.

Progreso's busy streets and thriving market offer pleasant diversion. And the Gulf Coast's most popular beach for swimming and sunbathing forms the city's northern boundary. On the western edge of town an impressive two-kilometer-long pier, open to automobile and pedestrian traffic, juts out into the water. The extraordinary length of the pier, built during the henequen heyday to facilitate the exportation of sisal around the world, was necessitated by the Gulf's gradually sloping coastal shelf. It's necessary to walk about 1/2k from shore to reach shoulder-deep water.

If you choose at this point to return to Merida, it is but a short 36k ride south. Or, after a day of lying around in the sun, you can continue east, as we did, to Dzilam de Bravo.

The abundance of empty summer houses is largely confined to the countryside west of Progreso. To the east the city merges seamlessly with the suburb of Chicxulub Puerto then again opens into expanses of field and marsh. This 51k stretch is frequently buffeted by strong northeasterly winds, which can have an impact on your daily distance. For some it may mean a great workout; for others, a test of will.

We went as far as Chabihau and spent the night at the **Hotel Rita Isabel** where, for an astounding 1800p per room ($.85), we were provided hammocks and cool showers. Chabihau is not much of a town and our expectations for a decent dinner were slim indeed. The Rita Isabel's manager directed us across the plaza to what looked like a shut-down *biergarten*. Inside, the senora was busily preparing her family's dinner. She invited us to sit at one of the dozens of empty tables which filled the room, and served appetizers while she prepared our dinner.

Dinner, when it arrived, consisted of black beans, rice, home-made tortillas, a rich, spicy salsa, marinated onions, fresh vegetables, and fish. As she placed a humongous fish in front of Eric, the woman said, "Aqui es suyo."

Ricky, less practiced in Spanish, hitched her chair a few inches closer and was met by the territorial slashing of Eric's fork.

"*Your's* is coming."

A moment later the senora returned with another fish. The quantities of food were truly amazing; we couldn't finish our servings. Everything was wonderfully spiced and cooked to perfection. The cost of this outstanding meal, which included a couple of beers, was an incredible 9,500p. ($4.33). We were told that if the fish had been smaller we would have been charged less.

Our bellies full, we retired for the night to our gently rocking hammocks.

The following morning Eric arose at 5:30. Just outside our door he yelled, "Holy Jesus! Holy Jesus!" Slight pause, then, "Holy Jesus!"

"Eric, what is it?"

"Holy Jesus! There's a scorpion on my shirt!"

Ricky jumped up, wrapped in a sheet, and rushed outside. Eric's shirt lay on the ground. A large black scorpion clung to the breast area.

"I must have touched it three times before I realized . . . Holy Jesus!" The adrenalin was pumping.

There are few creatures Ricky is willing to kill but as far as she's concerned the scorpion is the devil incarnate. She photographed it before Eric sent it back to hell.

Dzilam de Bravo

Dzilam de Bravo is perhaps best known as the (contested) final resting place of the pirate marauder Jean Lafitte. A headstone placed by the Mexican Explorer's Club commemorates Lafitte, his infamy forgiven, his notoriety mellowed by the passage of time. The dubiously authentic tomb now adds a larcenous note of glamour to this otherwise quiet maritime village.

There is a natural breakwater at Dzilam de Bravo, an extensive reef whose shoals temper the agitated sea. The port is a good debarcation point for visits to the nearby **Bocas de Dzilam de Bravo,** a flamingo colony preserve. It can only be approached by boat. For information about the launch schedule inquire at **Los Flamencos Hotel and Restaurant** on the main street of town.

If you spend the night at Los Flamencos, keep in mind that the low exterior wall provides only minimum security for your bike. It should be kept in your room. We have done this, without exception, every night we have slept indoors in Mexico. Los Flamencos, with its swimming pool, firm mattresses and only moderately run-down interior, is a bargain at 5,000p ($2.40) for two.

From Dzilam de Bravo the road turns inland. While not wildly fascinating, the route goes through towns that are as typical of Yucatecan life as they can possibly be. These townfolk don't see many tourists, either Mexican or foreign. Most people pass through the area quickly, by bus, on their way to somewhere else. For that reason, if no other, the 100k return to Merida is pleasurable. It should be noted that, in any season other than late fall to early spring, the area is oppressively hot. But in winter your ride will be assisted by prevailing easterly winds.

Miles and miles of henequen stretch before you. The heavily armored plants thrive beneath the Yucatan's blazing sun, growing in the region's inhospitable, alkaline-rich soil. The harvest resembles hand-to-hand combat, unchanged by modern farming techniques. Peasants with bone-handled machetes gather the long, spikey, resilient leaves, stack them one by one, and cart the fibrous bundles off to mill. Enroute, they pass the fallen remains of abandoned *haciendas.*

For decades henequen formed the economic backbone of the Yucatan. Under the crushingly oppressive regime of General Porfirio Diaz (1876–1911) the *haciendas,* relying on slave labor, flourished. While peasants toiled under brutal conditions, the owners of the *haciendas* grew rich sating the voracious appetite of the world's henequen market. Change, when it finally came, was the result of external forces. The demise of sailing vessels and the invention of synthetic fibre struck the industry's death knell. Today production is only modest and, despite a more democratic government, time has brought little financial improvement to the peasants who tend the crops.

Huevos Motulenos

The **Motul Motel** is the only place in Motul that is open year-round. It's located just off the plaza, behind the Banco Atlantico. Rooms downstairs cost 7,000p ($3.30), upstairs, 12,000p. The rooms are somewhat clean and have fans and TVs. Security is good, the mattresses soft, the management indifferent. It isn't the sort of place to go out of your way for, which pretty much sums up our feeling about Motul.

Oh yes. . . . Since you'll see it on the menu everywhere, you should know that Motul is the birthplace of the Yucatan's famed *huevos motulenos,* an interesting concoction of eggs, ham, peas and sauce, poured over a fried tortilla.

After five days in the Yucatecan outback, we returned happily to Merida, in time for the start of *Carnaval.*

ROADNOTES

WHAT'S AHEAD: Level riding on lightly travelled roads. Cycling on the unpaved 27k stretch between Sisal and Chuburna is hindered by mud and sand but is generally passable on both mountain and standard touring bike.

Kilometer 0	Main plaza, Merida.
	One-way streets around plaza, closed to traffic on Sundays and (frequent) special occasions. Follow Calle 61 west to Calle 82. Turn right. Continue one block north. Turn left. Go two blocks west to Av. de las Itzaes. Turn right.
2.3	Intersection of Av. de las Itzaes and Calle 59-A. Turn left onto 59-A. This leads northwest, away from Merida. Road remains four lane, traffic diminishes.
6	Road narrows to two lanes.
11	Caucel. Sodas and junk food.
16	Ucu. Sodas and junk food.
29	Hunucma. Restaurants.
53	Sisal. Road leads straight to the sea. Okay to camp on the beach and it is possible to rent a room for the night in a fisherman's home. **Los Consarios Restaurant**— snack bar fare, beer and ceviche. **El Paso del Pescador** will probably open by the time you read this.
	Turn east (right) on the street fronting the plaza. Pavement becomes dirt after 1k and continues for the next 27k. Confusing road—keep your friends in sight. Possible to camp anywhere along here, but there are no facilities whatsoever. Fill water bottles, buy juice and food before leaving Sisal.
66	Abandoned beach house. Surprisingly clean, a good emergency bivouac. Half-way point to nearest pavement.
80	Chuburna. Civilization! Pavement begins. Restaurants and lodging.
88	Chelem. Awesome tract of vacation homes and guest houses. Heavy traffic during summer months and for *Semana Santa.*
92	Yucalpeten. Sign for Progreso and right hand turn over causeway. The turn comes before the Naval station.
97	Progreso. Restaurants, hotels, good beach, shops and market. Major north coast center. Bicycle shops.
101	Chicxulub Puerto. Eastern suburb of Progreso.

137	Telchac Puerto. Coconut-lined landing strip layout. Sodas and junk food only.
152	Chabihau. Smaller than Telchac Puerto, but has more tourist facilities: one hotel, one or sometimes two restaurants, beach.
163	Sta. Clara. Tiny town with one restaurant.
176	Dzilam de Bravo. Hotels, restaurants, beach. Pirate Jean Lafitte's tomb. Debarkation point for boats to flamingo colonies. Bicycle shops.
189	Dzilam Gonzalez. Sodas and junk food. Bicycle shop near the square.
201	Hacienda San Francisco. Possible to visit.
202	Dzidzantun. Sodas and junk food. Bicycle shop called "Pedal Loco." Weekend cinema.
209	Yobain. ("Spiny Lizard" in Maya). Sodas and junk food.
216	Sinanche. Sodas and junk food.
225	Telchac Pueblo. Sodas and junk food. Turn left beyond plaza for Motul.
235	Motul. Hotel, restaurants, excellent market, fast food stalls. Movie theatre.
248	Intersection for Mex 80. Turn right for Tixkokob.
251	Tixkokob. Excellent dining at **Gran Mansion.** A hammock production center for the Yucatan. Good swimming in nearby *cenotes.*
257	Tixpehual. Sodas and junk food.
272	Main plaza, Merida.

TOUR 2

THE PUUC HILLS: RUINS, CAVES AND CENOTES

ROUTE: Merida—Uxmal—Oxkutzkob—Ticul—Telchaquillo.
DISTANCE: 280k.
RIDING TIME: 4 or 5 days.
DIFFICULTY: Easy to moderately easy.
TERRAIN: Flatlands and rolling hills.
BEST TIME: November to mid-March.
ATTRACTIONS: Exquisite Maya ruins seldom visited by tourists, charming country towns and a remarkable cave.

We had to get out of Merida. Our *casa de huespedes*/guesthouse, only a quarter-block from the main square, proved a too-good vantage point from which to enjoy *Carnaval.* Instead of observers, we found ourselves full-time participants. The morning quest for a cup of coffee became a tactical maneuver through the crowds. Police regulated the flow of pedestrian traffic from every corner.

The streets were clogged with cars. Drivers impatiently leaned on their horns, idling cars emitted a choking perfume of exhaust. On the parade route, which passed our door, ornately decorated diesel-driven floats crawled by in an unsteady rhythm. Blaring sound tracks competed with one another while sequined dancers gyrated to the dissonant sound. The fun was scheduled to go on for eight long days. On the third, we headed for the Puuc Hills.

Leaving Merida

From the main plaza in Merida, proceed west on Calle 69 to the Av. de las Itzaes. Turn left and continue south. From there the roads are clearly marked. You want to follow Mex 261 for Uxmal.

Merida's urban sprawl extends 18k, to the limits of Uman, where the highway narrows from the six- to a two-lane road. Traffic, which has been heavy, diminishes to somewhat busier than expected. But as you pedal south, it continues to drop off.

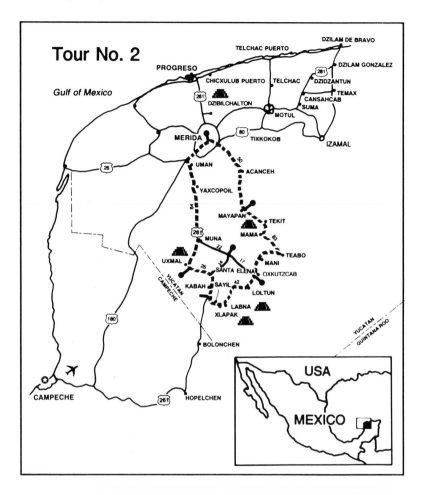

The Hacienda Yaxcopoil

Fifteen kilometers south of Uman, the **Hacienda Yaxcopoil,** formerly a 22,000-acre henequen plantation, is a must-see. Even today it is almost all there is to the town of Yaxcopoil and is clearly visible from the highway. To ensure your not missing it, screaming yellow billboards announce the approach. Admittance to the hacienda museum is 1,000p ($.45). A flyer with a well-drawn map of the hacienda layout is included.

Framed by a 17th-century Moorish double arch, Yaxcopoil is one of the few haciendas of such magnitude which have remained intact throughout Mexico's long periods of political turbulence and social change. It is still owned by an heir of Don Donanciano Garcia Rejon, who acquired the hacienda in 1864. The main house is divided into drawing rooms, an office and a chapel. Original furniture and minutiae imported from Europe, the opulent trappings of a blessed life, fill the gorgeous, airy, high-ceilinged rooms. Outside, gardens, corrals and orchards surround the living quarters. There is a swimming pool in the backyard. A long concrete irrigation ditch connects house and factory. Across the yard stand the machine shops, the plant and the storage rooms for the processed henequen. Even the facades of the workshops are beautifully stylized.

Haciendas were self-contained units which created and sustained the town around their perimeters. There is something perturbing in the silence which now shrouds the property. It seems to mark more clearly than the functioning plantation could have, the contrast between lives of bounty and those of poverty, between vitality and simple necessity. What was it like to grow up in such a place?

There's little drama between Yaxcopoil and Muna, just the open vistas, great road and lack of traffic that make the Yucatan so ideal for pedaling. Beyond the Abala turn-off, almost midway to Muna, the road becomes indisputably hilly—for which the region is named the Puuc Hills.

Camping and Lodging in the Puuc Hills

A few recommendations about making plans to see the Puuc Hills: Between Muna and Oxkutzkob, a distance of 86k traverses areas where you will probably want to tarry. But there is a dearth of affordable places to eat or sleep. A night at Club Med's **Villa Arqueologica,** for instance, costs around 100,000p ($45), room only. Between Uxmal and Oxkutzkob there are virtually no stores at which to buy supplies. If you have not already stocked up in Merida, Muna offers the last chance to do so.

This area is resplendent with cultural and scenic beauty, more than we could hope to treat thoroughly in a 19-tour guide to Mexico, and more than you could possibly see in a single day. For that reason plan to see Uxmal one day and the four smaller sites the next. Even then expect to start early in the day. If you hope to take in the cave at Loltun as well, your day will be crammed full and unsatisfyingly hurried. The last tour of the day at Loltun is 3:30.

But there is no need to rush. The management at Sayil, Xlapak, and Labna permit camping adjacent to their parking lots. At Loltun we met a family in a camper who, at the suggestion of the groundskeeper, were spending the night. The added bonus of a really good restaurant at the cave encourages one to take advantage of a leisurely bicycle/camping tour.

About 5k north of the Uxmal ruins, is **Rancho Uxmal,** the area's most affordable lodging (25,000p, $12, double occupancy. The rooms are dingy). Rancho Uxmal's decrepit driveway and dark jungle atmosphere probably discourages potential business. We did, in fact, eat a decent enough meal in their *palappa*-style restaurant and the price was reasonable (7,000p each) given the scarcity of choice. For 1,000p per person you can hang a hammock for the night under a rickety looking *palappa* just off the driveway. Although intent on camping, we declined to stay here. Twenty feet from the *palappa* a disused swimming pool was teeming with mosquitoes. In our hammocks, like chickens skewered on a rotisserie, we'd have been vulnerable from every direction.

Uxmal has few hotels and they fall within the luxury category. Club Med's **Villa Arqueologica** is adjacent to the Uxmal ruins, less than a five-minute walk. It has a beautiful swimming pool and the management is tolerant of non-residents using the facilities. Our bikes conspicuously parked near the hotel entrance, we whiled away a few hours poolside, drinking beers.

The other luxury hotels, which we did not investigate, are the **Hacienda Uxmal** and the slightly less expensive, purportedly much less comfortable **Hotel Mision Uxmal.**

Uxmal

The ruins of Uxmal are utterly magnificent. Popular legend about a sorcerer-dwarf who built the main pyramid is still invoked today to explain the building's unusual form. A cross be-

tween a circle and a square, or an oval and a rectangle . . . we really don't know what it is. You figure it.

Entry costs 1,750p ($.75). Closing time is 5 p.m., but at 9 p.m. there is a sound and light show, which costs an additional 1,750p. It's probably the sort of thing everyone should put themselves through once. Judging by the crowd's response, lots of people loved it—garish colored lights illuminating the beautiful ancient city, a sound track imploring the Maya to "come to Mani." For us a full moon and some restrained indigenous music would have better enhanced the night. After the performance we headed for the jungle.

Campers take heart. The aridity which the Maya found a survival challenge is a boon to your own. There is no natural standing water for mosquitoes to breed in. The surrounding jungle is thick but not impenetrable and rates high for sleeping out—if you remember to bring *sogas,* hammock ropes.

We camped near the ruins of Uxmal, but because we hadn't read our own book, spent an uncomfortable, buggy night on the ground. We didn't look for a campsite while it was light and ended up crashing by the side of a driveway. Twice, night watchmen came by and asked us to move. We were exhausted and they were less than emphatic so we didn't get up (and go where?), but instead anxiously lay there awaiting the Federales. At 3 a.m., hundreds of ants did what the night watchmen had been unable to do, and we moved from the dirt to the sidewalk in front of the museum entrance. At 4 a car pulled up and, mistaking us for caretakers, asked if there were any rooms to rent. At 5, conceding defeat, we rose.

Because breakfast hadn't merited forethought either, we primed our bellies (no supper the night before!) with a 14k "wake up" ride to Sta. Elena.

The cathedral in Sta. Elena is visible for miles. Built high on a hill, the crumbling, unadorned, box-like structure overwhelms the timorous town which sprawls in supplication at its base. Everything here is decrepit. The plaza is littered with garbage and broken glass. Stores were few, restaurants did not exist. The stalls in the marketplace sold only a few pathetic vegetables. The town is a sad contrast to the many other small, lively villages of the Yucatan. In the bleak light of an overcast morning, Sta.

Elena is a strong contender as the ugliest town in all of Mexico. If you've come in frustrated search of breakfast, the town wins, hands down.

More Great Ruins

Pedaling away from Sta. Elena—the faster the better—you enter serious hill country. Nine kilometers of rolling terrain bring you to Kabah, the first of four tightly clustered archaeological sites. One bus a day goes roundtrip from Merida and stays at each site for a maximum of 45 minutes, but because there are no overnight facilities these ruins do not yet receive much tourist attention. Take advantage of this solitude while you can—it surely won't last!

Kabah is dominated by the Temple of Codz Poop, a broad structure which celebrates the rain god "Chaac." Hundreds of Chaac's hooknosed images peer outward. Across the empty highway, shielded by unexcavated pyramids, is Kabah's beautiful false arch. From it a foot trail leads into the forest, suggesting that a more historically authentic route may offer mountainbikers the chance to ride directly to Uxmal from Kabah. Archaeologists say the footpath follows the route of a pre-Columbian thoroughfare which did just that. We think it represents the Kabah citizenry's desire to bypass Sta. Elena.

Five kilometers south of Kabah, a stack of roadside directives urge you to turn left for Sayil, Xlapak and Labna. Few tourists do. The recently paved road is a beauty, gently tracing a sinuous track over crest and swoop. A delightful, steady breeze, blows down from the hills.

One can easily spend hours wandering through the reconstructed buildings at Sayil. Almost the only people you will meet are the field teams for "Projecto Sayil," archaeologists connected with the Universities of New Mexico and Pennsylvania. They will generously share their knowledge and invited us to visit them at their Ticul headquarters.

The ruins of Xlapak, another 5k, seem humble after the magnificent collonades of Sayil's Palace. Three fallen structures reflect nature's patient effort to reclaim the planet. Tiny portions of friezes lie scattered in a tangle of rock and vegetation, a daunting starting point for the fanciful art of archaeological recon-

Ruins at Sayil

struction. The scene gives real meaning to the word "ruin." The comparison between Sayil and Xlapak is a study in the challenge and accomplishment of restoration.

Labna, just minutes and 4k away, has the finest examples of Puuc architectural style. This site is best known for its arch, an intricate mosaic of carved stone. While smaller than the ruins of Uxmal and Chichen, the exquisite detail of these monuments and the utter tranquility of their surroundings makes this visit powerful and fulfilling.

The Cave of Loltun

Eighteen kilometers of deleriously vacant highway now spread before you. At Loltun, the extensive cavern once used by the Maya as a source for clay and a place of worship seems poised to become the first major Puuc Hills tourist attraction. It is the only site along this route with newly constructed permanent buildings. The parking lot is gravelled, the grounds carefully tended.

The cave itself is pretty awesome. Five hundred meters of underground chambers have been thoughtfully lighted and guided tours (the only way you are allowed into the labyrinthine passage) depart every 90 minutes from 9:30 a.m. It is a dream world of bizarre shape and gorgeous, muted color. Artifacts found in the cave, grinding stones and vessels, have been catalogued and replaced. Altars are tucked into niches. On some walls the guide points out paintings, and handprints, the signature of the artist. He explains the ceremonial function of certain chambers and invites you to pound on two columns of stalactites which were used in religious celebration. The deep tones resonate throughout the cave.

The tour culminates with a long climb through a spectacular double cenote. An excellent restaurant sits at its edge. After the muggy heat and moderate tempo of the walk, a cold beer is a crowning toast to a glorious day.

Beyond Loltun the road widens. A painted centerline, the first in many miles, heralds the appearance of light traffic. To the north a geologic fault marks the edge of the Puuc Hills uplift. About 2k before Oxkutzkob that rarest of species, the long Yucatecan downhill, ushers you into town.

Puuc Towns

Depending on how you choose to break up your tour of this region, the towns of Oxkutzkob and Ticul offer good options for dining and spending the night. They are two of the most pleasant towns we saw in the Yucatan.

Oxkutzkob, the citrus growing center for the region, is a peaceful town where pedicabs have replaced motorized taxis. Orchards stretch for miles in every direction. Snaking between the acres, a marvelously crafted irrigation ditch brings water to the arid fields. In town a thriving marketplace hums with commerce. Scents of orange and tangerine waft in the air. Food stalls are plentiful—it's a wonderful town for street grazing. In addition there's the restaurant **La Cabana Suiza,** two blocks west of the market. Its owners are gracious and the food delicious. Vegetarians beware, however; their fabulous black beans are made with lard.

We found an okay hotel on the western side of town, the **San Carlos.** Well, let's qualify that. Eric thought it was okay and adequately clean. Ricky thought the place was yucky. Maybe it was the guy taking a pee against a coconut palm in the front yard that did it. We all have our limits.

We might have fared better had we known about Sr. Vicente Chable Canul, a guide at Loltun who lives in Oxkutzkob. His address is Calle 43 #95, between Calles 48 and 50. Sr. Chable has space in his backyard for several tents at a charge of 2,500p per person. He is available on weekends as a guide to the entire Puuc region.

We were quite taken with Ticul, a lovely town with one major drawback: Its motorcycles are plentiful and their drivers tear ass down narrow streets, past open cafes in an apparent effort to dissuade tourism. If you can get beyond the noise, however, Ticul has several good restaurants. It is the home of the first (of three) **Los Almendros** a well-known Yucatecan establishment. The **Cerro Inn,** a clean, spare hotel with firm beds, hammock hooks and fans in every room, and a spacious camping area in the yard, also has a restaurant on the premises.

We chose to spend the night at **Conchita's,** however. Conchita rents rooms in an old house which has been in her family for generations. The rooms are clean and spare and, as everywhere in the Yucatan, have hammock hooks. Rooms vary in price between 2,000p and 3,500p. Some have hot water.

The next day we took a good look around town. Most shops were closed because of *Carnaval*. Ticul is a ceramic craft center and it is fair to say we did not see even one piece of work for which the town is known. But we did see "The Shoe." Ticul is a shoe manufacturing center and a shoe, an enormous, clunky, high-heeled shoe, cast in concrete and painted sludge brown, is the focal point for one of the town's smaller squares.

And we saw the baseball game: This was obviously a town with a sense of humor. Both teams were dressed in drag. Skirts, bonnets, falsies, even a "pregnant" fellow. We have since seen this spoof in other towns but it remains a surprising and funny sight, especially in light of machismo and an otherwise serious attitude toward the sport of *beisbol*.

No characterization of Oxkutzkob and Ticul more aptly describes these towns, however, than their bicycle taxis. Hundreds of them occupy the streets, forming a monopoly of the internal transit system. Trucks and busses handle the larger, longer hauls, but few cars pass through town. Women on their way to market, children on their way to school, laborers on their way to work, all utilize the three-wheeled taxis. Need to transport your pig across town? Hail a bicycle taxi! It makes for a charming and agreeable atmosphere. Bicycle taxis have been used extensively for only the past ten years, a positive trend.

The Colonial Route

From Ticul head east to follow the "colonial route," a string of tiny villages dominated by colonial-era churches. Frankly, we've never determined what makes these towns unique. Creaky stone churches are everywhere.

At the small town of Dzan the road narrows and barely permits the passage of two vehicles. Watch for squeeze plays.

Mani, the city named on the soundtrack of the Uxmal light and sound show, is famous as the site for one of the great follies of eclesiastic rule. It was here, in 1562, that Bishop Diego de Landa burned the Maya codices in front of the huge church. Only three of the ancient texts survived unscorched. These days the building offers cool relief from the blistering sun.

Leaving Mani, the road becomes a bona fide two-way. At Teabo there is the **Posada de los Presidentes,** the first restaurant in the 26k from Ticul. A left-hand turn behind the plaza leads north to Chumayel where the terrain once more begins to roll.

Chumayel is a hammock-weaving center. If you are interested in buying one you can probably find a hammock dealer who will invite you to his house where, likely as not, his wife will be weaving. They will both participate in showing you their stock, discussing quality, size and price.

Between Mama and Tekit the road breaks into a washboard of short, steep, rippling hills. This brief stretch is pure joy, for some of us. Beyond Tekit the hills gradually disappear and, by the time you reach the ruins of Mayapan, the terrain is almost flat again.

The ruins of Mayapan shouldn't be confused with the town of Mayapan, 50k to the southeast. We spent the night in Telchaquillo, 2k north of the ruins, in a small house belonging to Sr. Fausto Uc Flores, local administrator of the Mayapan ruins. There are no restaurants in Telchaquillo, but groceries are available in either of two stores on the town's main street.

Mayapan has seen little archaeological reconstruction, and the dense jungly turf gives no indication of the extent or former grandeur of this capital city. The ruins stretch for miles. It is thought that at least 3,000 structures have been hidden by time and nature. There is no admission fee to the ruin site, and no refreshments are available. It is possible to camp there.

The Chaksikin Cenote

The real treat for us, however, was the Chaksikin cenote. Moises Uc, Don Fausto's son, led us the 1/2k through the jungle, past grazing cattle and horses, to a small hole in the ground. There, he dropped a very long rope and we lowered ourselves through the shaft. Slippery. Bats and swallows resented the intrusion. At the bottom of the 20-foot-deep hole lay an underground lake of the most incredible clarity. Eric stripped and dove in. The water shimmered in the gloom, extending far down the unexplored passage. He yelled. Echoes bounced off the walls. A few distressed swallows rapidly flew back and forth.

Don Fausto's house is available as an overnight rental for bicyclists for 2,500p. A stay there should be governed by the principle of being a guest in someone's home. Moises' services as a guide are available for 3,000p. Everyone knows where Don Fausto lives and you can ask directions at the grocery stores.

Henequen fields reappear north of Mayapan. In Tecoh there is another cenote/swimming hole which will take some effort to find. You will need to ask directions frequently but it is worth the effort.

By now you are really rolling along toward Merida. Another 45k or so remain to be covered, but towns increase in size and frequency and the usual preoccupation with where to get the next drink diminishes. Acanceh has three restaurants; Tepich, a pathetic ghost town of the henequen industry, provides only junk food. At San Antonio Tehuis henequen still reigns and from the road you can view a functioning processing plant. Traffic has really picked up by Kanasin, a large town with restaurants and a *panaderia.* Two kilometers beyond town, railroad tracks cross the highway at a treacherously high angle and warrant caution.

The highway widens and the peaceful bliss of the last few days rapidly dissipates. Seven kilometers beyond Kanasin you cross the *periferico* and Merida looms. Navigating through the city's grid of one-way streets is surprisingly simple. The road you're travelling merges with Calle 65, whose halting traffic escorts you to within a block of the *zocalo.*

The celebration had ended by the time we returned to Merida. We headed for our favorite *casa de huespedes,* showered, broke out the maps and began plotting our next foray.

The Caribbean beckoned.

ROADNOTES

WHAT'S AHEAD: The flat country around Merida extends nearly to Uxmal and the gentle hills of the Puuc region. There are hotels in Uxmal, Ticul and Oxkutzkob. Since lodging near Uxmal is fairly expensive, those on a budget may prefer to camp nearby. Scout it out before dark!

Kilometer 0	Merida's central plaza.
	Proceed west on Calle 69 to Av. de las Itzaes. Turn left and proceed south past airport. Follow signs for Uxmal.
18	Uman. Road splits. Follow Mex 261 left for Uxmal. Uman is a large town with several restaurants and an interesting church.
33	Yaxcopoil. Former henequen plantation, now a museum. Costs 1,000p ($.45) for self-guided tour. Quite interesting. Refreshments available.
45	Left turn sign for Abala. Continue straight. No services.
64	Muna. Large town with several restaurants and stores. Last chance to stock up on supplies until Oxkutzkob. South of Muna the terrain becomes hilly.
75	Rancho Uxmal. Restaurant, hotel and gift shop with camping area. Mosquitoville. Best to keep going.
80	Uxmal ruins. No town. Snacks only at the ruins. Panniers can be stored at the museum entrance for 900p ($.40). Bikes must be left in the parking lot. Bring a lock. Three nearby luxury hotels.
	Villa Archaeologica, a Club Med facility. Expensive (95,000p, $45) and very nice. Bar patrons can use the swimming pool.
94	Sta. Elena. Ughhh! A town so ugly only its patron saint could love it. Sodas and junk food—barely.
103	Kabah. Impressive ruins. Temple of Codz Poop. Across the road an archway marks a probable pre-Columbian thoroughfare between here and Uxmal. Only a footpath remains but it may be possible to bike the 20k.
105	Sign for Sayil, Xlapak, Labna. Turn left.
110	Ruins of Sayil. Refreshments. Management allows camping, no charge.
115	Xlapak. Smaller ruins, less ambitious reconstruction. No fee. Management allows camping, no charge.
119	Labna. Refreshments. No admission fee. Management allows camping, no charge.
137	Cave of Loltun. Tours every 90 minutes beginning at

9:30 a.m. Don't miss it! Excellent restaurant on the premises. Management is sympathetic to campers. Also, Sr. Vincente Chable Canul works here, has space in his yard in Oxkutzkob for campers, 2,500p ($1.10) per person.

147   Oxkutzkob, citrus capital for the region. Great market, small restaurants, hotel, two movie theatres, bike shops. Bicycle taxis monopolize the town's transit system. A charming town. Camping at Sr. Chable's.

The Cerro Inn, Calle 23, 2k from *zocalo*. Clean spare rooms with firm beds, hammock hooks and fans. Two beds, 12,000p ($5.20). Singles, 8,000p ($3.50). Camping is okay in the spacious yard but there are no shower facilities. 2,000p per person. A trailer park is under construction.

152   Yohtolin. Hacienda and nearby caves allegedly worth exploring.

167   Ticul. Several hotels, home of the original "Los Almendros" restaurant. Bike shops. A pleasant town except for the incessant rev of motorcycles. Depart for Dzan from intersection of Calle 24 and Calle 25. One block east of the church cross railroad tracks and continue east. Road narrows and barely permits passage of two vehicles. Watch for squeeze plays.

173   Dzan. Sodas and junk food. Narrow road continues.

181   Mani, site of Bishop Diego de Landa's burning of the Maya codices. Coming into town, road splits at raised concrete patio dedicated to Benito Juarez. Bear left and then right for the *centro*. Leaving Mani the road becomes a bona fide two lane.

193   Teabo. Pass the restaurant **Posada de los Presidentes.** Left hand turn behind the plaza goes north to Chumayel. Terrain begins to roll.

197   Chumayel. Sodas and junk food. Town known as hammock weaving center.

206   Mama, also known as "Mamita." Sodas and junk food. Halfway to Tekit begin washboard-like range of short, steep, rippling hills. A real rollercoaster.

213   Tekit. *Loncheria* **San Antonio de Padua** near plaza, otherwise sodas and junk food. Hills gradually disappear toward Mayapan.

230   Ruins of Mayapan, not to be confused with the town of Mayapan. Former Maya capital city. No admission, no refreshments, camping okay.

Sidetrip: Hire a guide to take you to the cavelike Chaksikin cenote, a half-kilometer walk. Bring a long rope and a flashlight. 3,000p ($1.30).

232   Telchaquillo.

Don Fausto's. Lodging at Don Fausto's house. Hang a hammock in his living room. Shower and toilet across the backyard. A warm and accommodating family. 2,500p ($1.10) for the night. Ask for directions to Don Fausto's at either of the town's two grocery stores.

243   Tecoh. Sodas and junk food. Sandwiches for sale in the farmacia.

Sidetrip: Tecoh has a cenote that's ideal for swimming. To find it be prepared to ask directions frequently. It's less than 3k and worth the effort.

251   Acanceh. Fair-sized town with three restaurants.

259   Tepich. Henequen industry ghost town. Sodas and junk food.

266   San Antonio Tehuis. Functioning henequen plantation.

270   Kanasin. Large town, restaurants and *panaderia.*

272   Caution! Railroad tracks cross the road at a high angle.

277   Cross Merida's *periferico,* the highway which encircles the city.

280   Main plaza, Merida.

CHICHEN TO THE SEA

ROUTE: Merida—Chichen Itza—Coba—Tulum—Cancun.
DISTANCE: 439k.
RIDING TIME: 8 days + beach time.
DIFFICULTY: Easy pedalling; a few long hauls.
TERRAIN: Flat, flat, flat.
BEST TIME: October to May.
ATTRACTIONS: Hammocks, *cenotes,* ruins, and maybe the world's best beaches.

The most popular tourist destinations in the Yucatan Peninsula lie east of Merida. Two of the greatest Mayan archaeological zones, intriguing *cenotes* and traditional towns mark the land between the capital city and cosmopolitan Cancun. Yet these attractions are only part of what makes this a great cycle tour. There's nothing like a sun-drenched cross-peninsula ride to heighten the anticipation of the Caribbean's sparkling water, soft carbonate sands and shady palm groves.

Most tourists take Mex 180 from Merida to the Caribbean, the newest and most direct road east. Unfortunately, with Cancun growing like a nuclear reaction it's also the busiest road on the peninsula. Traffic volume, while only moderate in comparison to U.S. highways, includes a high percentage of busses and trucks. By mid-morning, the speedy traffic builds to a density that, combined with numerous view-obstructing dips in the road and lack of a shoulder, present considerable danger to the cyclist.

A Road Less Travelled

Slightly north of Mex 180 is Mex 80, an older, less trafficked road. It is more scenic and topographically diverse, and it passes through far more interesting communities than the main highway. Reaping these advantages adds a mere 22k to your first two days of riding and makes Mex 80 unequivocally the best biking route to the Caribbean.

Tixkokob, 24k from Merida, is the headquarters for Merida's hammock trade. Compared to the high sales pressure in Merida's

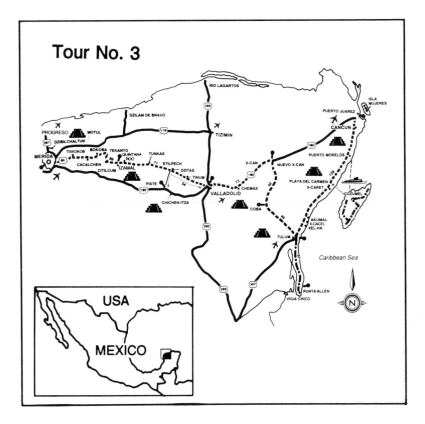

Tour No. 3

plaza, where even a hammock worn amulet-style around your neck will not thwart the hard working hammock salesmen, the scene in Tixkokob is relaxed. Though hammock size and quality are often better in Tixkokob than in Merida, it has been our experience that price savings alone don't warrant the trip. Personal association with the weaver, however, and the knowledge that no middle man is reducing the artisan's profit, instill your purchase with a value that no big-city distributor can match.

There's an excellent restaurant on the main street of Tixkokob called the **Gran Mansion.** After lunch you can detour 2k south to "Yaxshua" *cenote* where, reportedly, the swimming is excellent. Choose a rock to lie on and digest your meal like an iguana under the hot Yucatecan sun.

Eric wore his latex riding shorts in the Yucatan for the first time since crossing Baja. The form-fitting elastic brings outright guffaws in most parts of Mexico. To our surprise, wearing the skintight clothing here had no effect on his reception. Children waved and young girls called "buenos dias." Surging afternoon heat induced him to further test the limits of local mores. Off came his shirt. Unescorted mothers in blazing white *huipiles* still greeted him warmly.

If anything, people seemed more alarmed to see a woman cycling than offended by a bearded, half-naked man on a bike. While Eric postulated that the refreshingly blasé response represented a cultural adaptation to the heat, an aghast Ricky, in long-sleeved cotton blouse and pants, sweated on.

The towns which lie east of Tixkokob are tiny and traffic diminishes to almost nothing; it's only you and the stone-bordered henequen fields. Every so often the horizon is broken by the appearance of homes, speed bumps, a pop-stand, and finally, the plaza. The villages are simple and bare, dominated by brooding churches of aircraft hangar proportions. Quonset hut design and reinforced walls lend a bomb-proof bearing. In Bokoba the heavy eclesiastic air is leavened by the adjacent ballfield. Its lush, immaculately groomed field upstages the church and suggests that Bokobians enjoy *beisbol* as much as worship.

Just when these little towns have all begun to look alike you arrive in Izamal, the "Yellow City." Izamal's architecture is best described as inspired bizarre. Long colonnades of peeling mustard-yellow arches ring the plaza. Surrounded by scalloped walls, the traffic flows into a second plaza where the outlandish motif doubles in height. Ramps lead behind curved pillars to an enormous church and the largest courtyard in all of Mexico. The arches are structurally intact but the yellow paint which covers everything is badly faded.

A long horse and buggy queue is parked in front of the double tiers. For a small fee these equine taxis will take you on a tour of town and to Izamal's impressive double pyramid a few blocks away. The ruins are massive, as disproportionate to the small town as the monstrous church. Atop several flights of stairs is a shaded grove the size of a small city park. It's only after clambering to this elevated plaza that you spy the second pyramid, hidden from street visibility. From the top of this second structure there is a breathtaking view of the outlying countryside. Is it possible that the vague dimple on the horizon is Chichen Itza's towering El Castillo pyramid?

Because Chichen is still 74k we suggest spending the night in one of Izamal's three humble hotels. This will facilitate an early start in the morning and allow a full afternoon's viewing of the Yucatan's most famous ruins.

Miles before Stilpech its tiny church steeple beckons you to an otherwise nondescript town. Stilpech appears to have not quite emerged from beneath Izamal's long shadow. Its buildings are painted a familiar shade of leftover yellow. Only sodas and junk food are available here.

In Tunkas, the municipal building adjacent the plaza has a spigot where you can obtain potable water.

From here, the road narrows to a single lane and develops relief. Henequen fields yield to primeval forest. The road bucks and sways under a canopy of branches.

There's a good beer hall on the left on the way into Dzitas. Freshly painted in red and yellow, the only name it bears is "Salon Familiar." The invitation isn't as democratic as it sounds. As with all cantinas, the sign really refers to the "family" of men. If you're a thirsty woman in search of one of their 700p ($.30) "Superiors," ask if they will serve you—and don't take it personally if they refuse.

Chances are you missed the turn for Chichen on the way into Dzitas. It is unsigned, intercepts the road at a high angle and is easily overlooked. Doubling back from the beer hall though, you can't miss it. Go .3k and veer left.

Piste, 18k south, is something of a service community for nearby Chichen. Prices for food and lodging are more reasonable than at the ruins. Unless planning to spend the night in Valladolid, another 40k beyond Chichén, secure a room in Piste before viewing the ruins.

If you do plan to ride to Valladolid later that day, check your panniers in the locker room at Chichen (900p/$.40) but bring a lock for your bike, which must remain in the parking lot. The strength of the sun at Chichen is almost as impressive as the archaeological reconstructions, so it's good to know there is a Club Med pool nearby. As with their facilities at Uxmal and Coba, use of the pool comes with the price of a beer (2300p/$1.05).

Before leaving Club Med's poolside haven get out your map.

The most tempting route to Valladolid and a large part of the only route to Coba are heavily trafficked. Three options occur to us: Spend the night in Piste and cycle to Valladolid ahead of traffic in the morning; use the bus to skip the Chichen—Nuevo X-Can section of highway; or bike back to Dzitas and resume travel on the paved one-lane through the towns of Tinum and Uayma to Valladolid (and then bus to Nuevo X-Can). In our opinion, any of these options is preferable to playing chicken with thousands of Cancún-based sightseers on Mex 180's non-existent shoulder.

The Road from Chemax to Coba

Many maps suggest that these logistical considerations are unnecessary. A dirt road of unspecified length is indicated to link Chemax with Coba. It would cut 70k off the roundabout route via Nuevo X-Can if it existed. But it doesn't. In the early 1980's when the opposition National Action Party (PAN) elected one of their own to local government, the ruling PRI refused to allow the delegate to be seated. Outraged PANistas seized the Palacio Municipal and three PANistas were killed in the ensuing melee. Years later the community is still polarized, the Palace remains under heavy armed guard and government controlled funding for projects such as highway construction ceased long ago. The once-projected road from Chemax to Coba stops dead 8k into the jungle.

We investigated the Chemax to Coba link and this is what we found. From the point where the road ends, a narrow foot trail continues for 20k through terrain that the locals describe as "monte" or mountainous. At times the rocky path promises to improve, but it never does for more than a few feet. Travel here is more akin to navigating the boulders of a dry riverbed than cycling. If carrying gear, take some advice and don't even try it. You'll end up pushing, pulling and carrying your bike for 18 of the 20 kilometers. Eric broke several teeth on his chain ring researching this route.

X-Can is an unappealing town which seems to have admitted its own failure. But they've made the most of a bad deal and it's a good place to stock up for the 50k ride to Coba.

A sign marks the turn for Coba and Punta Laguna. The road narrows and in winter is enclosed by thick hedges of yellow wild-flowers. Tall trees cast protective shadows and the absence of traffic allows you to scan the tree tops for jungle birds and howler monkeys. Twenty-seven kilometers from the turnoff, a small hand-lettered sign and three huts are all that indicate your arrival in Punta Laguna. Sr. Serafio Canul lives here. Twenty years ago, while working his chicle grove, he discovered a small set of ruins. At his own expense Sr. Canul travelled to Mexico City to bring the site to official attention. Authorities made him the site's custodian and over the years he has constructed paths to the modest buildings and foiled at least one grave robbery. Sr. Canul is an excellent guide. The ruins are quite small but the trails he leads you over are his age-old stomping ground. His extensive knowledge of local flora includes both medicinal and edible plants. He points out the scars on the chicle trees he once tapped, now grown beyond reach. He gives you a piece of the gummy white sap to chew while pointing out other fruit trees—zapote, mamey, poisonous species that cause a rash and another tree whose bark is the antidote. There are several lakes nearby and the tour concludes with a visit to a *cenote*. Swimming is possible and, if you're prepared to deal with the mosquitoes, camping is free. Serafio's in-depth services should be adequately compensated. We gave him 3,000p ($1.40).

The Ancient City of Cobá

Another 20k south are the ruins of Coba. The ancient city is so huge it took aerial surveys to recognize its extent. Vegetation covers an estimated 6,500 buildings and disguises them as abrupt hillocks strewn across the plain. The site is a wonderful counterpoint to your recent visit to Chichen. Depopulated instead of over-run with tourists, overgrown with jungle instead of manicured, and dotted with swimmable lakes, it offers things that Chichen Itza cannot. Coba is cloaked in untouched authenticity. Wandering its thick forests, seeing unexcavated remnants projecting from countless hillsides, you get the feeling that reconstructive efforts have lagged not for lack of funding but out of simple awe before the task.

To fully appreciate Coba, you may want to spend an extra night in the miniscule town of Coba. For one thing there's another Club Med. For another, there's inexpensive lodging available. The **Hotel/Restaurant Isabel** has four rooms that rent for 6,000p ($2.67) a night. Beds are firm and there are hammock hooks. The palappa-style roof occasionally rains organic debris and if the room has not been used recently, a fine dusting of thatch may cover the bed. The management is responsive to the need for fresh coverlets. Toilet and shower facilities are around the back and are shared with diners. More exclusive arrangements can be had a block away next to the **Bocadito Restaurant.** Comfortable rooms with private baths rent for 15,000p ($6.80). The Bocadito has excellent dining at very fair prices.

Continuing south, the road becomes little more than a gash through the jungle. Several tiny settlements offer few services and a depressing look at how quickly the forest is disappearing. Wide tracts of forests have been cleared for corn fields. The sacrifice seems to have won people little in return, however, for the fields appear to be of questionable fertility. Their huts are miserable.

In Francisco Uh-May we met a successful hunting party. A juvenile buck, his neck broken and head tied back for a handhold, was slung over the shoulders of a small man who stumbled under the weight of this minimal load. We spoke with the festive group and feigned excitement at their good luck but we were filled with a feeling of dread. There's nothing more natural than for forest dwellers to hunt; it certainly beats razing the forest to farm. But the immature buck, weighing down the undernourished hunter was unsettling.

Tulum by the Sea

Twenty-four kilometers of forest give no hint of the approaching sea. Abruptly, the road intersects the coast highway, Mex 307. The junction lies midway between the fast growing community of Tulum Pueblo, 1k south, and the seaside ruins of Tulum, 1.5k north, on which the town's economy relies. Tulum Pueblo forsakes typical plaza-centered design for the style of an American interstate highway. Restaurants, groceries and a long-distance dialing facility line the road.

The Tulum ruin's archaeological merits are considerable and include highly detailed murals and patches of original paint that have withstood centuries of weathering. Several building entranceways have large depictions of "God Descending," cited by Erich Von Daniken as evidence of the Maya's contact with extraterrestrial "ancient astronauts."

What puts Tulum on most people's map however is its location, dramatically perched on a bluff overlooking the palm-lined Caribbean. Miles of under-utilized beach stretch in both directions. Nearby, a string of camping/cabaña facilities extends along 20k of coastline and serves a diversified group of beach-worshipping ruin fanciers. They offer a wide spectrum of prices and services. **Don Armando's** and the **Santa Fe** have restaurants which serve good food at very reasonable prices. Their young international clientele has made Tulum a major stop on the Gringo trail. Cabañas rent for around 9,000p ($4). If you plan to join this sandy little enclave remember to bring a lock for your cabaña door.

Exchange rates at the Santa Fe are posted in marks, francs, Swiss francs and Canadian dollars. Beers are a reasonable 1200p ($.55). On the downside, facilities are rustic—outhouses and bucket baths. Apparently not many are dissuaded by these considerations. Space is tight during the winter months. Unless planning to camp, (2,000p/$.85) arrive early for a cabaña rental.

Facilities become more plush with increasing distance from the ruins. Five kilometers south, **Cabañas Tulum** is fancier with prices to match (33,000p/$15). At the far end of the spectrum **Boca de Paila**, 24k away, offers exclusive surroundings, powerboats and private fishing tours.

Some people stay in Tulum for months. The convenience of town, the good beach, everchanging crowd and cheap cabaña rentals discourage many from discovering other, even better, retreats to the north.

Tulum is within an hour's drive of the Xel-Ha lagoon, first of several worthy stops in the FideCaribe National Park. Although it is only 13k to the lagoon, an early start is essential. By 11 a.m. tourbusses fill the beach to capacity. The fish, a remarkable array of saltwater species, are accustomed to people and even hundreds of splashing swimmers don't chase them off. Reef life can be observed throughout the afternoon.

When the crowd gets too thick, head for the Xel-Ha ruins, only one kilometer away. Several reconstructed buildings are scattered around the shady wood. Nearby jagged rocks and dense vegetation protectively surround the "Jaguar" cenote, a deep pool of clear, inviting water. The beauty and peace are yours alone.

Be aware of the time however; as the afternoon wears on, traffic on Mex 307 picks up.

Coast traffic is clearly patterned. In the morning, vehicles fill the southbound lane for destinations like Tulum and Xel-Ha. In the late afternoon the flow reverses, heading north to Cancún. If heading in this direction, cycling is best concluded before 2 or 3 p.m.

Five kilometers away, and still within the confines of FideCaribe National Park, are the X-Cacel and Chemuyil campgrounds. Both are administered by the Federal Park Commission. Signs indicate the turns for each. The sign for Chemuyil is less than humble. Faded peeling letters proclaim, in both Spanish and English, "The Most Beautiful Beach In The World."

"Oh, come now," you say. A nasty potholed drive to the Chemuyil gate may increase your skepticism. After paying 1500p ($.66) to enter (the fee includes camping), expectations are further reduced by the sight of an RV parking area surrounded by dead or dying palm trees.

Only after mounting the stairs do you get a mesmerizing view of the crescent-shaped bay. Waves splash over a barrier reef into the calm, protected inlet. A thriving grove of coconut palms shades the beachfront campground. The sand is glistening white and brilliant against the water's edge. The most beautiful beach in the world? Maybe not, but Chemuyil is surely the most beautiful beach in the neighborhood. Around here, that's talking.

The camping facility of X-Cacel is similar to Chemuyil and prices are identical. Both offer cabaña rentals, have immaculate shower facilities, and each a somewhat pricey bar and restaurant.

Chemuyil's RV area has been hard hit by the coconut blight. As a result most RV campers seem to choose X-Cacel, where the RV lot has suffered less damage. We prefer Chemuyil. The cabaña and camping areas are still thick with palms, there are fewer people and it is closer to the markets of Akumal.

Five kilometers north, Akumal was once an exclusive resort. A fortress-like checkpoint breaches the massive walls that guard the beach. On any given day, a perfectly normal marketplace and busy laborers outside complete a feudal scene. Ignore the sensation that you're crashing a party, cross the drawbridge . . . uh, gate, and cycle on in.

There is excellent snorkeling in Akumal's bay. Even finer, idyllic conditions exist at nearby Yalku lagoon. Access is via a 2k dirt road that is technically private and usually guarded. Entry may require some bluffing. Feigning a Texas drawl, we claimed to be guests at a local condominium, "Casa de Guerra" ("Stamos day Casuh day Gayruh"). Hey, it worked for us.

Playa del Carmen

Playa del Carmen, "Playa" to the locals, has a sharply split tour-ist population. Cruise ships anchor nearby and deposit loads of well-to-do tourists, and a busy ferry transports vacationers from nearby Cozumel Island. The other half is the Tulum crowd, budget-minded travelers drawn to the magnificent beach and moderately priced cabañas.

Tiny Playa's narrow streets are clogged with shoppers and back-packers. The scene is a bit like summer's end when suntanned parents and vagabond children mill through the airport in search of one another.

Cozumel, Mexico's Largest Island

Cozumel, the largest island in Mexico, has excellent, lightly used roads and, many believe, the finest diving in the country. If you're carrying a mask and snorkel, Cozumel is a worthy detour.

Two ferries sail between Cozumel and Playa. The larger boat, *Mexico,* is a hydrofoil which crosses the sound in only half an hour. Conveying bicycles, however, is by whim of the captain. The boat has no lounge and passengers are pretty much confined to narrow rows of seats. Tiny portholes give it the atmosphere of a DC-10. Worse yet, projection screens fore and aft subject passen-gers to continuous-loop black and white animated cartoons. In English.

Passage is more likely achieved on the smaller ferry, a boat de-signed for cargo as well as passengers. Although the 1500p (.65) freight charge for your bike wipes out any cost savings over the *Mexico,* you are assured its passage. Besides, it is a pleasant open-air voyage.

Nearly all of Cozumel's world-class hotels are clustered on the northwest corner of the island, creating endless primitive camp-ing opportunities along the remaining miles of untouched coast-line. Permission to camp is required from the local SEDUE, Mexico's environmental protection ministry. If staying for no more than a few nights, approval is automatic. The second-floor office is on the main drag in front of the pier, two blocks south of the naval station.

Stock up on supplies and water in town before heading out in either direction for the 73k loop. We want to emphasize that only a few expensive restaurants dot the island's long periphery and your enthusiasm at so much wilderness coexisting with big-dollar tourism will be dampened if you haven't brought enough groceries.

Rideable dirt roads at the far ends of the island lead to light-houses. Visiting them will add 64k to the round-trip total. The lighthouses are manned by military detachments which can provide you with fresh water, but camping is not permitted on their grounds.

If continuing north from Playa, there are two options at this point. You can ferry back to Playa and visit Punta Bete where, we hear, beach camping is terrific. Or you can bypass this section of Mex 307 by taking the ferry directly to Pto. Morelos.

Pto. Morelos is not graced with Playa del Carmen's expansive beach. As a result, tourism has not caught on yet. Low prices and a tranquil atmosphere prevail. With Cancun only 34k away, however, the t-shirt shops can't be far behind.

The "Miracle" of Cancun

Hunger for new experience and the desire to immerse oneself in a foreign culture is universal, which is why millions of Mexicans love Cancun: its address is the only thing Mexican about it. Cancun may be the ultimate display of Latin hospitality, a city designed to please Americans who don't like what its host had to offer. Flashy discos, foreign restaurants, nightclubs and a big city pace are unusual for most of Mexico. A 20-mile strip of exclusive hotels is—gracias a Dios—rare anywhere. If your taste in interior design runs to neo-Mayan hotel lobbies, you like your pools measured in acreage, and the last thing you want to have to do is speak Spanish, Cancun is your kind of town. Like any good city, though, it offers alternatives to the norm. Even on a budget, it can be your kind of town too.

A commitment to clean, safe, affordable lodging for Mexico's youth led to the creation of a federal chain of hostels called CREAs. Although they are found throughout Mexico the one in Cancun is in a class all its own. Its 612 beds are more than the local hospital accommodates. There is a camping area and a swimming pool. A night costs 12,000p ($5.40), a good deal anywhere in Cancun. But finding it in the classy hotel zone makes it a real bargain. With your bike safe in the CREA security room you are free to explore Cancun.

Mexico's more than 7,000k of coastline are nationalized, assuring democratic and equal access to peon and bike tourist alike. Unrestricted use of the beach is a fine example of populist revolutionary spirit resisting betrayal to special interest groups. Grab a city bus for the Sheraton, take a stroll through the lobby, past the pool, and exercise your right to enjoy the clean white sand as much as the $180-a-night guests.

The miracle of Cancun has sparked migrations from all over the country. Ambitious university graduates find better paying jobs as waiters in Cancun than as industrial engineers. Following the 1986 Mexico City earthquake thousands of people relocated here. Most live beyond the central district and, for bargains in dining, the outskirts of town are where to go. Our candidate for best deal is **La Poblanita** on Calle Lopez Portillo underneath the "Cine Maya" marquee. Behind the lines for the theatre La Poblanita's tables spill out onto the sidewalk. The Ramirez family specializes in beef and pork chops "distrito federal," marinated in lime juice and grilled over an open fire. Two big chops served with tortillas, beans, *chilaquiles* and a drink are 3,000p ($1.33).

Isla Mujeres, A Pleasing Alternative

Five kilometers beyond Cancun, Pto. Juarez is the debarkation point for the Isla Mujeres ferry. The island has long enjoyed a good reputation among budget travellers but, with the closing of the Poc-Na hostel and the disappearance of other camping/cabaña facilities, those days are over. Even so, a beautiful road encircles the island and the nearly deserted western shore offers camping opportunities. For the discreet, that is. Though we've yet to see it enforced, official policy prohibits camping.

Restaurants in Isla Mujeres are reasonable, if no great bargain. The market is typical and offers rock-bottom prices. The mixed crowd attracted to Isla Mujeres and the slow pace of island life make it a pleasurable alternative to Cancun.

For the sake of continuity it's tempting to cycle from Pto. Juarez back to Valladolid and Merida on Mex 180. In the name of research we yielded to this temptation and it's nothing we'd recommend. The Cancun–Valladolid stretch is just too heavily trafficked and is not sufficiently interesting to warrant the trouble. We suggest you save some time and effort, and take the bus.

Low cost flights from the U.S. and Europe have made Cancun a favorable port of entry and many people will elect to begin travel here. If you are biking the Caribbean coast highway north-to-south instead of as described, remember that you'll have lots of high-speed company by 10 a.m. Try to schedule your riding accordingly. Southbound traffic slackens by late afternoon and that's when you should shoot for mileage.

Southbound cyclists who reach Tulum may want to continue on to Punta Allen. Fifty seven kilometers of sandy, unpaved road practically guarantee a little solitude. Tangled fishing nets and discarded boat parts along the shore attest to this as a working man's beach.

For tourists, Punta Allen is a do-it-yourself challenge. The only lodging is on the beachside property of Sonia and Armando. Their half-dozen cabañas rent for 33,000p ($15) a night and include mosquito-netting. Campers are generously accommodated in the yard and receive full shower privileges for 2,000p ($.90). Make note of that mosquito netting. Unless a stiff wind is blowing—something on the order of a small craft warning—the buggers from nearby Emiliano Zapata Bay are impossible.

Seafood lovers may also want to make the trip to Punta Allen. Lobster, frequently in short supply elsewhere, is almost always available through the local lobstermen's cooperative. Since most crustaceans are bound for export, prices at the resorts are pegged to the U.S. market. One succulent tail goes for upwards of 30,000p ($14) in Cancun. In Punta Allen, the same tail, "al gusto"—as you like it—costs 9,500p ($4.50).

From her house, Sonia operates one of the two very informal restaurants in town. If she isn't cooking that night, she'll send you over to her neighbor Candy, who probably is.

On the mainland across from Punta Allen a nature preserve has been created to protect the toucan. For 22,500p ($10) Armando will boat bird-loving bikers to the preserve where, if you are lucky, you may see this beautiful endangered species.

Toucan

The toucan's nature preserve and FideCaribe National Park guarantee some ecological status quo in this region of Quintana Roo. But not too much. In his electoral campaign of 1988, ruling party candidate Salinas de Gortari has called for construction of a four-lane highway between Cancun and Tulum. Gortari's plan calls for development of Tulum as the next major Caribbean resort.

Cyclists heading on to Belize and Central America will want to consider Armando's shuttle as well. An unpaved road, reportedly in better condition than the Tulum–Punta Allen road and over-hung with palm trees, connects Vigia Chico to Felipe Carrillo Puerto. From what we hear it sounds like a terrific way to beat the crowd on Mex 307.

Of all the Yucatan, the Caribbean tour includes the most famous archaeological ruins and the best recreational opportunities. For people with a limited amount of time this is probably the most all-encompassing and gratifying tour on the peninsula.

ROADNOTES

WHAT'S AHEAD: Travel on older, quieter Mex 80 instead of busy Mex 180. Lodging is available in Izamal, Chichen Itza, Piste, Coba and the Caribbean coast. Terrain is level, towns occur frequently, water is easily obtained along the way. Beware of the alleged Chemax to Coba shortcut depicted on the AAA map. It does not exist.

Kilometer 0	Merida's central plaza. Follow Calle 63 east to "T" near Calle 24. Follow signs to turn left, then right. Cross railroad tracks and turn left, proceeding north until Mex 180. Take a right. Mex 80 branches at Pemex station. Bear left.
15	Tixpehual. Sodas and junk food.
21	Tixkokob. **Gran Mansion** restaurant, Yaxshua cenote.
36	Cacalchen. Sodas and junk food.
44	Bokoba. Sodas and junk food.
52	Tekanto. Sodas and junk food.
58	Citilcum. Sodas and junk food.
69	Izamal. Lovely town, restaurants, market, largest church plaza in Mexico. **Kabul, Canto,** and **Toto** hotels on the streets bordering the plaza. All are simple but safe and inexpensive, approx. 8,000p/dbl. ($3.50)
75	Stilpech. Sodas and junk food.
98	Tunkas. Sodas and junk food. Potable water is available at the municipal building. Road narrows to one lane.
112	Quintana Roo. Sodas and junk food.
123	Dzitas. Watch for right turn for Chichén at entrance to town. Good cantina, sodas and junk food.
141	Piste. Many restaurants and hotels. **El Paso** hotel. In the middle of the strip. Rooms are 20,000p/dbl. ($8.70) but bargaining has yielded results here.
143	Chichen Itza. Site opens 8 a.m., closes 5 p.m. "Sight and Sound Spectacular," in English begins at 9 p.m., Spanish at 7. Several luxury hotels.
145	Balancanchen Cave. High tech—paved, electrified and wired for sound. Botanical garden outside is at least as interesting. !WARNING! It is not 12k to Balanchanchen as indicated on many maps, it is only 2k. If you are on foot don't get suckered into an *expensive* cab ride for a distance you can easily walk.

155	Turn for Chankom, go straight. Chankom was the subject of an important study of modern Maya society detailed in *A Mayan Village* by Robert Redfield and Alfonso Villa Rosa.
161	Kaua. Sodas, junk food and souvenirs.
174	Cuncunil. Sodas and junk food.
179	Dzitnup cenote. 2k detour, 1,000p ($.45) entrance fee. Subterranean swimming.
183	Valladolid. Hotels, restaurants, bike shops, movies. One of the Yucatan's largest and most pleasing cities.
213	Chemax. Bus station adjacent plaza offers chance to skip busy road ahead to Nuevo X-Can. The road to Coba does not exist. Check out the militia guarding the palace—those are tear gas canisters on their hips, not grenades.
249	X-Can. Sodas and junk food.
257	Nuevo X-Can Sodas and junk food.
284	Punta Laguna. Ruins (tiny), lakes, cenote. Inquire with Sr. Serafio Canul for tour of area and camping.
303	Entrance to Coba. Ruins, lakes, jungle, all 2k to the right. Several hotels and restaurants.
	Isabel restaurant and hotel. Simple rooms with double bed and hammock hooks, 7,000p/dbl. ($3). More luxurious facilities at the local **Villa Archaeologica.**
3212	Francisco Uh-May. Sodas and junk food.
325	Marconio Gomez. Sodas and junk food.
345	Junction with Mex 307, the coast highway. Turn right for Tulum Pueblo, 1k, left for Tulum ruins and beach. For Punta Allen, cross Mex 307, go straight 2k to beach, then right 57k on dirt road.
346	Turn for Tulum ruins, 1k. Cabana facilities begin .5k beyond ruins.
	El Crucero hotel at the turnoff is the cheapest hotel in the area. Clean rooms rent for 15,000p/dbl. ($6.50). Cabana rentals on the beach.
358	Xel-Ha lagoon. Snorkeling, refreshments, restaurant.
360	**La Esperanza** restaurant. One of the few non-tourist restaurants on Mex 307. Good food, entrees 4–6,000p ($1.80–$2.70).
362	X-Cacel. FideCaribe National Park. Great beach and campground, 1500p ($.65). Pricey bar and restaurant on premises.

365	Chemuyil, also within the confines of FideCaribe National Park. Camping, 1500p ($.65). Pricey bar and restaurant on premises.
370	Akumal. Formerly private resort. Dive center. Produce market, grocery store, liquor store. Very simple restaurant outside the gate.
407	Playa del Carmen. Continuous ferry service to Cozumel. Restaurants, hotels and cabanas.
	CREA youth hostel offers the best deal in lodging (4,000p) but is a hike from the beach.
439	Pto. Morelos. Less frequent ferry service to Cozumel. Restaurants and hotels.
	Cozumel. Permission to camp on the island's beaches can be obtained at the SEDUE office, south of the ferry dock and two blocks beyond the navel station. The office is on the second floor.
473	Cancun. Restaurants and hotels.
	CREA offers best lodging deal, 12,000p ($5.20) for a bunk, 2,000p ($.85) to camp.
478	Pto. Juarez. Ferry service to Isla Mujeres. Restaurants and hotels.
	Isabel hotel across from the ferry has rooms for three for 20,000p ($8.70).

ALONG THE GULF IN YUCATAN

ROUTE: Villahermosa—Frontera—Cd. del Carmen—Champoton—Campeche—Hopelchen—Uxmal—Merida.
DISTANCE: 652k.
RIDING TIME: 7–9 days.
DIFFICULTY: Easy cycling, long distances, enervating climate.
TERRAIN: Flat.
BEST TIME: Fall through Spring.
ATTRACTIONS: Pleasant countryside, great birdwatching, excellent seafood.

The Gulf is Mexico's most overlooked coast, a 2300-kilometer Sheraton-free zone stretching from the Texas border to the top of Yucatan. Its slender beaches have neither the Pacific's powerful combers nor the Caribbean's transparent blue water. The temperature is hot, the humidity, high. There is more swamp than swank and mangroves outnumber motorists.

But for all that, one of Mexico's greatest faunal preserves lies along the Gulf's southeastern perimeter. In the steaming lowlands where the Grijalva and Usumacinta rivers dump their waters into the Gulf of Mexico, is a world still inhabited by a stunning profusion of jungle mammals, reptiles, and birds. The remnants of Olmec civilization, regarded as the mother culture of Mexican civilization were discovered here, and it is also where the history of the New World begins.

How fitting, then, that this link to the past is one of Mexico's keys to the future. The petroleum fields of Campeche Bay, Mexico's largest, have transformed somnolent fishing villages into fast-paced refinery towns.

But Mex 180, between the cities of Villahermosa and Campeche, shows the Gulf of Mexico at its best, a shifting tableau of gentle surf, lowland thickets and tropical ranchland. Opportunities to swim occur often. The seafood is marvelous. The route is the path of least resistance from central Mexico to the Yucatan peninsula

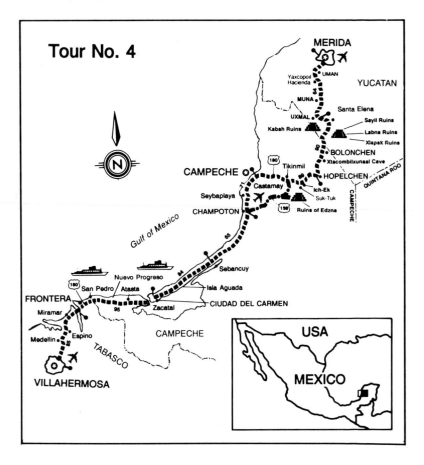

and the Caribbean. At Campeche the route turns inland on Mex 261, to visit several fascinating Maya ruins.

Villahermosa

This ride begins in Villahermosa, capital of Tabasco. Low in latitude and elevation, inland from the moderating effects of the Gulf, the city registers high on the misery index. Nonetheless, tourists brave oppressive heat and humidity to visit Villahermosa's two museums. The *Museo de Tabasco,* on the southeast corner of the plaza, cloisters a marvelous collection of Olmec, Maya, and other pre-Hispanic artifacts.

Museo de La Venta is an open-air exhibit situated on the banks of the placid *Laquna de las Illusiones.* The world's largest collection of Olmec art is housed within the park confines, and what a treat this place is! Leave your bicycle at the information desk, and bring mosquito repellent.

The ancient La Venta ruin is considered one of the most important archaeologic finds in North America. Monstrous basalt sculptures, weighing as much as 30 tons, were discovered at the site, impressive in part because the nearest quarry was 100 miles away. Following discovery, the colossal figures and altars were transported to Villahermosa's La Venta Park and reassembled as they were originally found. Trails weave past crocodile ponds, the

Olmec Head, La Venta Park

arboretum bursts with vivacious, colorful orchids and resonates with the sound of tropical birds. Keep an eye open for leafcutter ants marching in twin rows, one bound for the field, the other staggering home burdened with clippings.

Villahermosa to the Gulf

La Venta is located on a divided highway which heads out of town. Turn right on leaving the park and left at a sign for Cd. Industrial. A curtain of industry rims the city, gradually transitioning to marsh, forest and range. Small settlements appear regularly.

La Selva, a thatched-roof pavillion at k 20, is an invigorating place to break. Their cooler is stocked with icy Dos Equis lagers and a dip in the pool costs 500p.

Rolling along, the ground gets increasingly mushy. The road parallels a lagoon, where men and women dangle bags of fresh shrimp for inspection by passing motorists. The large crustaceans are the specialty at the excellent *Parador Espino,* k 36. Their patio extends over an estuary. Enjoy a swim while the kitchen prepares you a big platter of food.

The terrain again dries up a bit now. Fat cows mow the range. Orange orchards appear. The land is flat and mileage adds up quickly. Clearings in the forest reveal drilling platforms, but there is little else to indicate the nearness of the coast. Dirt roads disappear into jungle and emerge on the Gulf shore. Camping is possible but the area is settled. Be discreet and ask permission whenever possible.

The Coast

A bridge at k 77 has replaced the old ferry to Frontera, where the confluence of the Usumacinta and Grijalva rivers pour into the Gulf. Frontera is *not* a quaint village. Fishing is an industry here. Trawlers float four deep next to riverside docks. If you must spend the night, there is a choice of places to stay, a movie theatre and lots of places to eat.

Teeming coastal marshes extend for miles east of Frontera. At squalid San Pedro, the border between Tabasco and Campeche, another ferry crosses the sluggish Rio San Pedro. Mex 180 follows a sandy spit that is the barrier between the Gulf of Mexico and the saline Laguna de Terminos. North of the highway, in an expansive, nearly impenetrable mangrove forest, is one of the largest water bird rookeries on the Gulf of Mexico. Wood storks, egrets, herons and ibises can be glimpsed from the highway. Jacanas, parrots, and turkeys call the swamp home, to name but a few who comprise this avian world. To observe it up close you will need the services of a guide and a launch. Inquire on the pier in Frontera, or at hotels in Cd. del Carmen which cater to sports fishermen.

Nuevo Progreso is halfway to Cd. del Carmen and a good bet for lunch. There's a wonderful, nameless restaurant adjacent the plaza. Three loquacious parrots out front make it easy to recognize. The *pollo encebollado* served here is extraordinary, and the price is right too, about US$1.15.

The road continues through the kempt hamlets of San Antonio Cardenas, Atasta and Zacatal. Ferries from Zacatal to Cd. del Carmen depart hourly until 6 p.m. Relax in a breezy cafe near the ferry slip while waiting for the next boat.

Cd. del Carmen

Massive oil reserves have turned Cd. del Carmen into a center for petroleum exploration. The city maintains a standard of living that is unusual in Mexico. As boomtowns go it is a pleasant surprise. Yet, it's no family town and women cyclists may feel slightly uncomfortable. The streets are full of men—derrick hands, tool pushers, and roughnecks, all oil field laborers either just returned from or about to leave for their two-week platform shift.

A shockingly high percentage of the women one does see in Cd. del Carmen are prostitutes, but there's none of the usual solicitation. Just as the town's wealth and civility are built upon a dirty, exploitative industry, these transactions maintain a wholesome veneer. In the plaza there is the usual evening promenade where young men shyly ask the working ladies out.

Restaurants and hotels in Cd. del Carmen are plentiful. Male cyclists may want to take advantage of the seamen's quarters at the *Hotel Alex.* A mere 3,000p opens the door to a dormitory bunk with fresh sheets, a locker, bicycle security, unlimited hot water and, best of all, frigid air conditioning. Elsewhere, rooms are about 12,000p.

Get an early start for Champoton, a long 149k (93mi) away. The road closely follows the beach for more than half the distance, so vivifying dips in the Gulf are not far off. Should the heat and distance prove too much, stop in Sabancuy, k 264. Pleasing in a sun-stroked sort of way, the town has one second-rate hotel, a cafe and supplies.

Champoton, is a far more appealing place to spend the evening, and there are a number of hotels to choose from. The town is historically footnoted for an event which occurred in 1517. An expeditionary force under Cordoba suffered an early defeat by the Indians. Murals around town commemorate "The Night of the Bad Fight," when fifty Spaniards lost their lives.

Sixteen kilometers beyond Champoton, at Haltunchen, there is a right turn onto Mex 188. The road starts into the Puuc Hills and the cycling, rather dull until now, actually becomes quite interesting. If you are planning to take the sidetrip to Edzna, one of Mexico's more underrated Maya ruins, keep in mind that it bypasses Campeche. There are no services. Carry extra food and water and be prepared to camp. The nearest hotel is Hopelchen.

Continuing up the coast, however, just beyond the Haltunchen junction, the *Siho Playa* hotel has a wonderful, large swimming pool which costs just 500p. It's a good place to refresh before the final 50k to Campeche. The road, pretty flat until now, turns to little rolling hills.

Campeche, a Fortified City

Mid-afternoons, the beautiful capital city of Campeche is hauntingly quiet. Your derailleur ticks loudly in the narrow, cobbled streets. One feels the kind of puzzlement discoverers of the abandoned Maya cities must have felt, but in this case, heat has banished the citizenry. The lone sign of life is the accordion music spilling from cantinas.

Towards dusk vitality returns to the city. The cultural center on the corner of Calles #18 and #59 provides a wonderful opportunity for evening entertainment. Their programs include indigenous music, poetry readings and plays, performed in an open-air courtyard.

Campeche was once encircled by thick walls, meant to protect the city from marauding pirates. Hexagonal in shape, only parts of the wall remain today. Fort Soledad, one of the original fortresses, has been restored and turned into an interesting archaeology museum. It includes stellae from nearby excavations, Maya and colonial artifacts.

Turning Inland

There are two routes between Campeche and Merida, and both leave the Gulf behind. We take the longer of these, Mex 261, three days pedalling time. This is our preference because of the numerous ruins and other sights along the way. The terrain is slightly hilly but coping with heat, more than ever, is the real challenge. Sunrise starts are essential.

Hopelchen is a wonderful town with only one hotel, *Los Arcos,* to accommodate its burgeoning bicycle touring trade. The only restaurant in town is in it. A few *loncherias* inhabit the plaza. On weekends the movie theatre awakens, and there is a stadium for a favorite Mexican pastime, *beisbol.*

"Hopelchen" is Maya for "five springs." One, still used, is located in main street and from the plaza you can watch the townspeople line up to fill water jugs. Mennonites from a nearby community also use the well, making this a good place to observe the taciturn newcomers.

Continuing north on Mex 261, you many want to detour to *las grutas de*—ready?—*Xtacumbilxunaal,* meaning "hidden women." The immense caverns are located on an *ejido,* or communal farm, about 4k from Bolonchen.

It is 80k between Hopelchen and Merida. Along the way are the phenomenal ruins of Uxmal, a provincial capital of ancient Yucatan's three city states, and those of Kabah. These sites and others are discussed in Tour #2, but a glance at the map will indicate more than one approach to the area. Choose what works best for you. Keep in mind that facilities around Uxmal are limited and rather expensive. Either be prepared to splurge or buy camping supplies in advance.

ROADNOTES

WHAT'S AHEAD: Flat riding, high humidity, and some long distances between towns. Plan ahead if you want to avoid camping, and be sure to carry water. It's hot! Luckily, there are plenty of opportunities to stop for a refreshing swim.

Kilometer 0	La Venta Park, Villahermosa.
3	Frontage road ends. Turn left on Calle Universidad, a divided highway.
8	Industry peters out, jungle begins.
16	Medellin. Refreshments.
20	Ocuiltzapotlan. Groceries, **La Selva** restaurant and swimming pool.
27	Begin following lagoon.
36	Espino. **Espino Parador** restaurant; swim in the river off their patio.
50	Grocery.
64	Signed detour for Miramar beach.
72	Carrillo Puerto. Numerous small *tiendas* along the highway.
85	**Frontera.**
	Casa de Huespedes Familiar, Hotel Chichen Itza, and the **San Agustin,** all on the plaza, offer budget lodging. Rooms are on the second floors. Doubles, 6,000p–8,000p.
111	San Pedro, squalid ferry port, marks state line between Tabasco and Campeche.
129	Nuevo Progreso. Good restaurant near plaza, look for three loquacious parrots. Groceries.
136	San Antonio Cardenas; neat, prosperous town. Produce and groceries.
149	Atasta. Groceries.
177	Zacatal. Ferry to Cd. del Carmen.
180	Cd. del Carmen. Full service. **Hotel Alex.** Private rooms are 14,000p/dbl. Seaman's quarters are for men only. 3,000p/per bunk. Spotless, air conditioned, great deal.
196	**Las Ruedas** restaurant.
197	Beach.
207	Sodas.
220	Bridge to Isla de Iguada. Dolphins!
223	Isla de Aguada. Toll bridge, bikes free. *Loncherias.*

264	Sebancuy detour, 2.3k. Cafes, groceries, fair sized, unexciting town.
	Hotel Posada Bella Vista. Pretty depressing, 10,000p/dbl. Stock up on food, not much available for the next 65k.
329	Champoton. Full service.
	Hotel/Restaurant La Cabana, Av. Revolucion #13. 9,000p/dbl.
343	Cd. del Sol. *Tiendas.* Turn for Haltunchen.
349	Villa Madero. Poor village, lots of good produce.
	Siho Playa hotel and restaurant. 500p to use the pool. Rooms 57,500p/dbl.
361	Seybaplaya. Several good beaches are accessible in the 20k east of Seybaplaya.
393	Campeche, full service.
432	Tikinmil, groceries.
438	Cayal. Groceries, water available in plaza.
455	Suc-Tuc, groceries.
466	Ich-Ek. *Loncherias,* groceries.
472	Roadside Maya ruin.
482	Hopelchen, full service.
	Los Arcos hotel and restaurant. Clean rooms, ceiling fans, private shower, 6,500p/dbl.
498	San Antonio Yaxcal. Wealthy ranch, no services.
514	Grutas de Xtacumbilxunaal.
516	Bolonchen. Nice town, cafes but no hotels.
542	Yucatan state line.
544	Signed detour for Sayil, Xlapak, Labna ruins. No refreshments or groceries for sale at any of them.
549	Kabah. Ruins, refreshments.
557	Sta. Elena. Strikingly ugly, good-sized town. Few groceries, no restaurants.
572	Uxmal, Maya ruins. See Tour #2 for more info.
652	Merida. See Tour #1 for more info.

INTRODUCTION TO CHIAPAS

Chiapas, the southernmost of Mexico's 32 states, defies preconceptions. The landscape encompasses towering, mist-shrouded, lush mountains, cool valleys, and steamy lowland jungles. An underdeveloped, poorly maintained highway system leaves much of the state geographically sequestered, which only heightens its appeal to the more determined sightseer. In fact, in all of Chiapas only four places warrant frequent stops by tour busses— Palenque, Agua Azul, San Cristobal de las Casas, and Tuxtla. That few tourists stray from the so-called "Gringo Trail" is a boon for the independent spirit. For cyclists, in particular, it means exhilarating paved and dirt road adventure and access to the more remote Indian villages.

Yet, despite the awesome beauty and shroud of tranquility, Chiapas is a troubled state; its tropical tableau can quickly turn from bedazzling to alarming. Scenes of environmental mayhem are everywhere—mutilated forest and ashen smoke-filled skies blot the view. Often, culprit and victim are one and the same. Impoverished campesinos, in an act which can only be described as self-cannibalization, raze and burn ever larger tracts of forest during the spring *quemazon* to clear the land for planting. Property titles are subject to dispute. Violent encounters—though often unreported—do occur.

But this is meant as a footnote more than a warning. We never felt personally threatened nor did we meet any other travelers who had been. Rather, we think, cognizance of these troubling issues can only deepen one's appreciation for this beautiful and threatened place.

The "Indigenas"

Chiapas is home to great numbers of indigenous people. Shielded by fortress mountains and camouflaged by the Lacondon Jungle, descendants of the Maya cling to a lifestyle that only grudgingly incorporates the unsolicited gift of Western progress.

The same geographic barricades that delayed the incursion of foreign influence for so long have restricted the circulation of ideas between clans as well. Separated from one another in their deep valley hamlets, language, crafts, and style of dress have evolved along similar but independent lines. A gathering of the tribes yields a *linqua cacaphonia,* and a gloriously vibrant display of exquisitely loomed regional clothing. Men wear shorts and straw hats, ribbons billowing. Women are in pink shawls, babies wrapped tight against their backs with striped *rebozos.* These are the markings that, at a glance, distinguish the people of San Andres Larrainzar, Pantelho, Zinacantan, and Bochil.

Within this festival of ethnicity, missionaries of various creeds have seen a signal flare. Mormons, Seventh Day Adventists, and

Zinacantecans Waiting For A Bus

Jehovah's Witnesses, to name a few, have descended upon Chiapas in droves. They have attracted legions of Indian followers, collectively called *evangelicos*. Converts in more than name only, their lives are being profoundly altered.

Many of the Indians one sees in San Cristobal are *evangelicos,* mostly little girls and women selling woven bracelets and shawls in the plaza while the men and boys tend to other, usually agrarian, jobs. Both boys and girls attend religious training, during which they learn educational basics. Attendance is mandatory, a stringent four to five hours daily. Sobriety is vigorously preached to the adults and many testify to its salubrious effect.

But advances in education and inroads against alcoholism must be weighed against the divisions these evangelical faiths create. Typically, the poorest Indians are the most willing converts; tensions run high between newly converted and traditional worshippers. Confrontations erupt into occasional violence and, of the approximately 15,000 *evangelicos,* many have been dispossessed and forced to resettle. Nuevo Palestine and Betania, two settlements near the city of San Cristobal, have grown quickly as a result of this displacement. This internecine conflict is just one more obstacle that prevents the Indians from collectively advancing their interests.

Environmental Concerns

Chiapas is endowed with an astounding diversity of plant and animal life. Sixty-six percent of all the bird species in Mexico live in Chiapas, as do 80% of the country's 1,200 kinds of butterflies (twice as many species as occur in the United States and Canada combined!). Forty-one percent of Mexico's plant species grow here. The last cloud forests in North America, as well as most of its remaining rain forests, are located in Chiapas. The state is the source for one third of the entire nations' water and three dams on two of its rivers, the Grijalva and the Usumacinta, provide 35% of Mexico's hydro-electric energy.

Older Chiapans can remember when almost all of the surrounding landscape was shrouded by trees and an abundance of wildlife flourished beneath the protective boughs. Today less than 15% of the original forests survive, and rapacious destruction continues at an alarming rate. In 1985 the *official* estimate of forest cut and burned was 62,500 acres; by 1986 the figure had risen to 347,500 acres and is increasing. Weather satellite images show "hot spots" throughout Chiapas. With deforestation, soil erosion begins. The nutrient-rich topsoil washes away, leaving the earth depleted and unproductive. Widespread destruction of trees results in lower precipitation, eventually affecting world-wide weather patterns.

Huge business concerns know well the bounty of the state's resources. In the early 1980's the oil industry sat poised to expand into the mountains of Chiapas. But dry holes and the global collapse of petroleum prices limited full scale exploration. Renewed efforts likely await the next major increase in demand. While this giant slumbers, other malignant concerns chip away at the teetering environmental balance. Fortunes are reaped in the illegal harvest of mahogany. In greedy pursuit of this fire-resistant hardwood, the forest is torched, causing reckless destruction of any vegetation and wildlife habitat which stands in the way.

Even the few preserves which have been created, such as Montes Azules and Marques de Canillas, are subject to illegal cutting. You can't help but wonder skeptically at the idea of someone quietly cutting down and sneaking off with a 90-foot tree, to say nothing of whole mountainsides of wood. Funding for land management is limited and enforcement of the law is weak. Often, officials are corrupt. In some instances, such as the Lacandon Rain Forest, Indians have sold the logging rights. This grievious situation, has resulted in the utter devastation of their ancestral lands.

The far reaching effects of this particular travesty have, in large part, gained worldwide attention through an organization called Na-Bolom, located in San Cristobal. Their work has resulted in an international effort to preserve the remaining Lacandon Rain Forest and to reforest areas of clear-cut, as well as to educate the Indians.

Economic factors for the vast majority of peasants dictate a concern for the present, not the future. Unimpeded, population growth has become a major threat to the environment. Expanding families, grouped into farming collectives called *ejidos* and no longer able to feed themselves on existing farmland, reach ever further into the jungle. Year by year terraced cornfields creep higher up mountainsides. To clear the land for crops the campesinos slash and burn, a practice which, like clear-cutting, destroys all foliation. Denied the protection of roots, the stripped hills begin to erode. Geologic bedding planes lie exposed, the rocks mimicking bleached animal bones. In the winter and early spring, as the land is prepared for planting, thousands upon thousands of acres are burned. Cinders blow across the road. Your eyes smart. A thick haze obscures entire mountain ranges for months. In recent years the rains often start late, precipitation is light, and water tables are dropping.

In the scramble for survival peasants must deal not only with their own growing numbers, inter-clan territorial disputes, and the shrinking response of nature. Wealthy landowners also compete for land. In the spring of 1988 near Villa Comaltitlan, for instance, two children were killed and twenty compesinos were wounded when police attempted to remove 180 families from national lands. The peasants had been granted an *amparo,* or legal immunity, by the National Supreme Court of Justice, and had occupied the land for eight years. Yet they were virtually powerless against the businessmen who wanted the land for coffee and soya production. This is not an isolated incident, nor is it peculiar to Chiapas.

Where the forest hasn't been cut, much of it has been drowned. Dams on the Grijalva have turned the once wild river into a recreational reservoir. Family outings along the treacherous cliffs on the Sumidero Canyon, whose sheer walls once plunged nearly 1,900 feet into a narrow valley, now overlook a tremendous body of water. Soon new dams on the Rio Usumacinta will allow tourists to launch upstream where previously only rubber rafts could float down. Construction of dams along the Rio Tacotalpa will cause the town and amber mines of Simojovel to be submerged. Hundreds of miners will be forced into unemployment. Tens of thousand of acres of farmland and forests will be destroyed, and with them precious wildlife habitats.

When the rains finally do come, the land turns green. Between the rivers and the remaining stands of jungle roll millions of acres of land, the deforestation attractively masked by tropical fertility. There are hillsides of corn, and cattle knee-deep in grassy pastures. Occasional jungle trees, relics of a recent past, dot the fields. Tall and singular, their sprawling crowns soak up the sunlight for which an entire canopy of leaves once competed.

Stories concerning the environment used to be granted cursory attention by the Mexican press. But now, having reached crisis proportions, reports about conflicts, drought, and water and air pollution compete with news about the national debt for headline space. Perhaps—just perhaps—it is not too late.

TOUGH TRIP THROUGH PARADISE

ROUTE: San Cristobal—Ocosingo—Agua Azul—Palenque.
DISTANCE: 222k.
RIDING TIME: 3 to 5 days.
DIFFICULTY: Difficult.
TERRAIN: Mountainous.
BEST TIME: Year round, but be prepared for some winter cold weather around San Cristobal.
ATTRACTIONS: Rain forest, small Indian towns, incredible waterfalls and good swimming, spectacular ruins.

The road from San Cristobal to Palenque winds through some of the most visually seductive countryside in Mexico. The mountains, at times so imposing they nearly shout their exhuberance, recede dreamlike and incomprehensible into a seeming eternity. Yet the hand of man is present everywhere. Cultivated second growth springs up where virgin forests have been slashed, forming a bizarre textural patchwork of green against the steep mountainous slopes. Livestock graze in recently created pastures, corn and beans adhere tenaciously to mountainsides, precarious foot trails lead to remote cabins. Whatever the repercussions of a disappearing forest, the pastoral beauty and visual magnificence of this transition—a far reaching environmental tragedy, in fact— is undeniable.

A Highway to Heaven

From San Cristobal's plaza take Calle M. Hidalgo to the highway and turn left. The road begins to climb almost immediately. After 8k the grade levels. Two kilometers further is the wooded entrance to *Grutas de San Cristobal,* a cavern rigged with electric lights and concert hall seating. A pleasant afternoon's adventure, but there is no time to tarry now. At the junction with Mex 199, another 2k, there is a sign for Palenque and the road, wonder of wonders, starts upward again. Get used to it. It's going to be a long day.

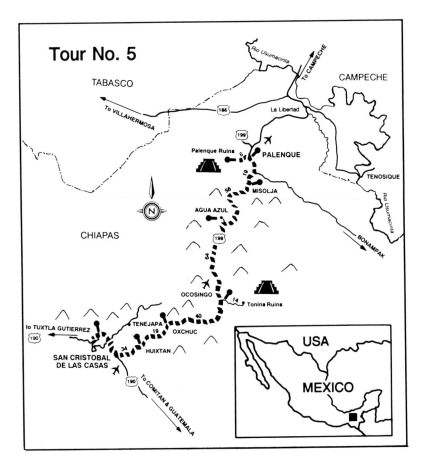

There's precious little level riding on Mex 199, a narrow, twisty route that was not designed with pedalling efficiency in mind. Its 2,000m elevation drop means little as you swoop down, only to climb back out of every valley between San Cristobal and Palenque. Thankfully, brevity tempers the challenge; riding days average a reasonable 75k. An early start the first day, more than anything, will determine whether you reach Ocosingo. It will be by far the toughest of the three days. Should it be a bit much, take heart; there is a surfeit of public transportation. Ricky hitched to Palenque by bus, taxi and truck and met Eric at each place we planned to spend the night.

Mex 199, the only paved thoroughfare between San Cristobal and Palenque, is virtually shoulderless. Yet there is a surprising paucity of traffic, welcome news indeed, since what exists tends to be fast moving and hugs the curves tightly. Not only is there livestock to watch for, people are everywhere, more often than not loaded down with cargo and children. The generally acceptable pavement is bone-jarringly rough in a couple of places. In addition, it occasionally funnels into one lane because of washouts; watch for signs marked *Deslave.*

Sounds like fun, huh? Well, it actually is once you have adjusted your senses to the pace and pattern of this particular route. The ride encompasses a lot of "sameness," a statement that normally triggers an impulse to bound in another direction. But in Chiapas this means an opportunity to indulge the senses, for what is extraordinary elsewhere is commonplace here. We won't belabor the chapter that follows with redundant descriptions of the countryside: it is, simply, gorgeous. Verdant, sumptuous, fecund. Deep river valleys, stunning waterfalls, and commanding vistas vie for your attention. Don't leave home without your bathing suit!

Ocosingo and the Ruins of Tonina

It was late afternoon by the time we met in Ocosingo, the largest town on the way to Palenque, and where we planned to spend the first night. Unlike most towns in Mexico, where the main street runs smack through it's center, Ocosingo's major thoroughfare forms one of its borders. The bulk of the settlement spills down the steep side of a narrow valley, effectively segregating intervillage commerce from internal affairs.

There are a remarkable number of hotels and restaurants in Ocosingo—odd given the absence of tourists. Ranching is its biggest industry. While the town hardly gussies up for travelers, genuine hospitality is the rule.

Ocosingo's plaza, the locus of social activity, is bordered by cafes, restaurants, and ice cream shops. On temperate evenings generations of families gather for the "promenade." The plaza fills with strollers—young couples, grandparents, children chasing about. In the midst of this a choreography of young people moves, the girls circulating in one direction, the boys in reverse, eyeing each other solicitously. Sweet, and oh so provincial.

It's no surprise that the ruins of Tonina, 14k from Ocosingo are practically unknown. The road is unpaved. There are no busses. Taxis, cornering the market, charge a whopping 30,000p for a visit. Mountain bikes are the perfect solution. Roundtrip riding time plus touring Tonina eats up most of the morning and effectively cancels all chances for making Agua Azul by nightfall. Rather than crazily rushing to see the ruins, or worse, deciding not to bother, consider spending a second night in Ocosingo. Start early because of the heat; bring water and food. Sodas are available at the site.

To get to the ruins, head southeast, downhill from the plaza on Calle 1 Oriente. The ride is mostly flat. One kilometer from town there's a junction. Turn left. An abandoned Pepsi shack marks a "Y" at k 4. Bear right. There's another left at k 10 and the hillside which the ruins occupy comes into view. A ranch house is at the site's informal entrance. Bikes can be left there.

The once mighty city of Tonina now moulders in the shadow of a working cattle ranch. A cowboy/attendant gallups over to unlock the cabin, which is a museum, office, and ticket booth rolled into one. All-business, he uses a slender tree branch pointer to emphasize the features of special interest on a plaster replica of the city. The orientation is brief; he drops the pointer and takes up the reins. "Sorry ma'am, no time for questions, there's bulls to be gelded," and he's gone.

One hillside dominates the excavations at Tonina. Seven terraces rise, in stepwise fashion, to a height of 200 feet. At each level the structures grow in size, paralleling the hierarchical arrangement of the ancient ruling castes. Beneath tin awnings are well-preserved glyphs, more intriguing than the crumbling buildings on which they are engraved. In the pasture, carved standing figures, faded stellae and circular stones of uncertain purpose lie scattered in the short grass, a small herd of cows their disinterested attendants. The best of Tonina's carvings have been removed and are jammed into the diminutive museum. Here you will find kneeling slaves and prisoners, stowed away, chockablock, like surplus tombstones in a mortuary annex.

The Cascades of Agua Azul

It's 66.5k from Ocosingo to Agua Azul and the ride involves enough ups and downs to render the overall drop in altitude unimportant. Refreshments are available at least every 15 to 20 kilometers, but what will really fuel your efforts are the glimpses of the technicolor blue Rio Tulija which feeds the cascades of Agua Azul. Drawing nearer, it is a bit reminiscent of an aerial view of L.A.'s swimming pools—the water is *that* shade of blue. At the signed turnoff for the falls you begin an incredible screaming descent. Savor it; the only way out is back up this very same road.

At first glance Agua Azul may be disheartening. RV campers and vans crowd the parking lot, the place is crawling with people, and the riverbank is studded with bathers, hawkers, food stalls and restaurants. But this need be only a brief interlude, for a short walk either upstream or down takes you far from the madding crowd. The further you go, the fewer people and the more beautiful the river with its hundreds of waterfalls. Find a mellow rapid in which to soak the kinks out of your butt while the dissipating light plays a symphony in shades of blue.

There are couple of things which will help insure a trouble-free visit. Signs along certain areas of shoreline warn of dangerous

Cascades At Agua Azul

undertows. Don't ignore them. In one place a group of five crosses commemorates the deaths of more than one hundred people. Belongings are another consideration. Leave your bicycle locked *inside* the big restaurant near the Agua Azul entrance and just keep a day pack. While the overall crime rate in Mexico is very low, Agua Azul is one of those places where tourists are a very easy mark. You're in the water, your clothes and money are on the shore just waiting for a hit-and-run artist to carry them off. The easy solution is to leave these things at one of the refreshment stalls or restaurants which dot the hillside. For a few hundred pesos someone will keep an eye on them and you'll gain a lot of peace of mind.

One or two restaurants near the entrance to Agua Azul offer crude sleeping accommodations, and in our opinion camping is the way to go. There are plenty of places which no one lays claim to where you can spread a sleeping bag for free. Or, spend the night in the front yard of one of the less frequented restaurants. It's best to ask permission and a small fee may be in order.

Leaving paradise is difficult and the 4.5k unmitigatedly steep climb to the highway may cause you to put it off awhile. But sooner or later, the choice is made. Palenque awaits.

It is 58k from the turnoff for Agua Azul to Palenque. At last gravity reigns. Mex 199 swoops down from the sierra, this time for good. The road crosses the Rio Tulija several times and there are swimming spots along the way, but the best is yet to come. At k 205 a sign indicates the 1.5k detour to Misolja: waterfall, lagoon, Eden. Few people know about Misolja. There is a restaurant on the premises and camping is strictly informal. Don't miss it.

The town of Palenque is an uninspiring place known only for its proximity to the ruins, another 8k away. There are plenty of hotels and restaurants and the kinds of prices one expects in a tourist town, high for what your money buys. On the other hand, at the **Mayabell** campground, 2k from the ruins, you can hang a hammock or roll out a sleeping bag for a fraction of the price of a hotel. A good, inexpensive restaurant with great music stays open late. Unguarded possessions have been known to disappear here, though. Play it safe by leaving valuables at the desk and loaded bikes locked in the store room.

"Magic" or psychoactive mushrooms thrive in the pastures around Mayabell. During the rainy season, when they are in peak abundance, it becomes something of a field camp for hallucinogen fans. Early rising campers search out the night-sprouting fungi near piles of cow manure, its favored medium. Local farmers, recognizing that the crop brings good money, frequently beat them to it. Late sleepers may prefer to purchase mushrooms, both for convenience and to avoid the zillions of endemic ticks. Just a reminder: These drugs are illegal.

The Magnificent Ruins of Palenque

The Palenque ruins are considered among the finest in the Americas. Surrounded by jungle, the city covers an area of 39 square kilometers. Only the central area of the city has been excavated and restored, itself a remarkable feat. An army of grounds-keepers constantly battles the encroaching vegetation.

Palenque's architecture reflects different periods of design, none more prolific than the 7th century. During the reign of Pakal, the "club foot king," there was a flowering of craftsmanship which resulted in carvings that are some of the best to be found in Mesoamerica. The most outstanding of these stucco bas-reliefs can be seen in the Temple of the Inscriptions. Inside, a narrow stairwell leads to Pakal's burial chamber, the first royal tomb discovered in North America. The fabulous jade-encrusted sarcophagus has been moved to the National Museum of Anthropology, but you can still peer into the crypt to see the intricately carved five-ton slab which was its lid. No one's moved *that* yet.

Within the confines of the site's entrance area, one cafe struggles to serve Palenque's many visitors. Late in the day, tourists hurry to expose the last of their film, bus drivers rev their engines impatiently, waiting for stragglers to appear. In the midst of this hullabaloo is a quiet group of Lacandon Indians. Garbed in knee-length white gowns, unkempt hair hanging to their shoulders, they look for all the world as if they just stepped out of a hospital observation ward. The Lacandons have a candor that is startling among Chiapans, for they are not shy in the least. They sit next to teepee stacks of bows and arrows, mementos for the tourists trade. Each arrow is decorated with brilliantly hued parrot feathers. Sales, regrettably, are brisk. Increasingly, parrots appear in hotel lobby cages and at the ends of souvenir arrows, more than in the jungle. It is, in fact, illegal to bring feathers or *any* wild

The Ruins Of Palenque, Temple Of The Inscriptions

animal parts into the United States (stipulated by the Feather Tariff Act and the Convention on International Trade in Endangered Species).

An Adventurous Detour

Cyclists looking for an adventurous route to Tikal, Guatemala, Maya civilization's greatest city, might want to consider a boat trip down the Rio San Pedro. In making plans, leave time for things to go awry such as missed connections, no room on the boat, and the like. Bring bug repellent and sunblock. And, Guatemala is *poor;* wear items of value, don't stash them in a pack on top of a bus.

Tenosique, the Mexican departure point, is 130k by highway from Palenque, and less by back roads. From Tenosique, cycle or bus the 33k to La Palma on the San Pedro river, where an open, flat-bottomed boat leaves daily for Guatemala. River time is 5 to

6 hours and costs around $10; the trip is a separate reality of jungle birds and basking alligators. When the boat docks in El Naranjo it is another 6 to 8 hours by bus to Flores, the junction for Tikal. The dirt road ought to be bikeable, though we haven't done it.

ROADNOTES

WHAT'S AHEAD: Mex 199, a major highway, is famous for breathtaking views, lousy pavement and enough twists and turns to send bus passengers scrambling for the dramamine. In places, landslides have pinched the narrow two lanes into a single corridor. Fortunately, traffic is light and there is usually ample warning of oncoming vehicles. Cafes and tiendas appear every 15 to 20k. This ride is difficult. Consider storing unnecessary gear in San Cristobal. Call us wimps but there are enough mountains between San Cristobal and Palenque to render the 2,000-meter drop insignificant.

Kilometer 0	San Cristobal. Calle M. Hidalgo to Mex 199, left. Begin climbing.
9	Top of first pass.
10	Signed right turn of **Grutas de San Cristobal,** campground and 1/2k of illuminated caves.
12	Signed left turn for Palenque. Resume climbing.
15	Top of second pass. Begin slow descent.
18	Restaurant **El Chivero.** Easy hills, equal parts up and down.
23	Signed turns for Chehil and Chenal. Road continues straight, begins gaining elevation.
25	Great view of farmland on the mesa.
27	Laera. No services.
28	Top. Begin rocket descent toward Huixtan.
33	**El Marchante** restaurant.
34	Grocery store. Easiest place to get supplies. Road does not pass through Huixtan.
25	Begin 5k climb.
40	Top. Road condition deteriorates; many washouts preceded by signs that say *Deslave.*
44	Chempil. Shack sells refrescos and snacks.
49	Begin 4k drop to Oxchuc.
53	Oxchuc, bustling Indian village. Cafes, tiendas. Begin 1.5k climb.
55	Top. Begin long descent.
68	El Coralito. Groceries.
69	Waterfall. Vegetation begins changing from alpine to tropical.
71	Bottom. Begin 2k climb to Abasolo.
73	Abasolo. Small village, restaurant **Ranchero.** Resume gradual descent.
78	La Florida, a small village off the road. Bus stop.

80	Xul-ha. Two good restaurants, **Los Arcos** and **El Bo-zal.** Road continues down.
87	Tremendous view of Ocosingo Valley. Descent quickens.
90	2k climb interrupts plummet.
92	Outskirts of Ocosingo. Turn right on an unsigned street opposite the grocery and go down a steep hill to the plaza.
93	Ocosingo's plaza.

DETOUR FOR TONINA (14k)

0	Head southeast from Ocosingo plaza, downhill.
1	Ranch. Left at signed turn for ruins. Road becomes dirt.
4	"Y" in road, signed right turn, abandoned Pepsi shack.
10	Turn left, ruins on cleared hillside to left.
14	Tonina.

95	Bottom of lush Ocosingo valley. Road follows creek.
100	Begin earnest 6k climb. Excellent swimming hole.
106	Top. Another range of mountains ahead.
107	Foot trail on left leads to a spring; treat all water. Road quality deteriorates.
115	Temo. Road splits. Signed right turn for Palenque. Road quality improves.
116	Bridge, swimming. Begin a series of 1–2k hills.
118	Rancho Tunapaz. Sodas and junk food.
120	Nameless popstands. Begin 2k drop.
121	Enter area of widespread deforestation.
122	Village with a supermarket.
126	Road straddles ridge, continues gradually down.
131	Paso El Macho. Cafes. Terrain levels.
145	First view of aquamarine Rio Tulija.
149	Chehil. Stores. Cross river and begin a 3k climb.
152	Top. Women selling fruit. Road starts down to Agua Azul turnoff.

DETOUR TO AGUA AZUL (4.5k)
Turn left; no directions necessary.

161	Yobchi. Marks bottom of 8.5k descent that began at Agua Azul detour. One small tienda.
163	Resume dropping.

168	Valley floor.
175	Rio Tulija. Swimming.
187	Santa Maria. Stores. Short climb leads to a 2k drop.
193	Begin 7k climb.
196	San Miguel. Big, but there are just a few stores on the road. Good artesian spring. Treat all water.
200	Top.
202	Signed left turn for Misolja, a marvelous waterfall and lagoon.

MISOLJA DETOUR (1.5k)
No formal campground but there is a restaurant on the premises.

209	Valley floor. Signed turn for Palenque, 10k.
211	Begin 3k drop.
215	Nututun. Restaurant and campground. Popular swimming hole. Begin roller coaster hills to Palenque.
219	Town of Palenque.

CHIAPAS: THE HIGHLAND DAY TRIPS

Okay, we confess: Chiapas is our favorite region in Mexico. Given a bike and a month in which to ride it, there's no other place we'd rather be. And there is no more pleasing base from which to explore the central highlands than San Cristobal de las Casas.

San Cristobal is an unusual tourist town and, in fact, it is the more unusual tourist who spends time here. Occasional caravans of chartered busses do squeeze up the twisted highway that is the city's tenuous link with mainstream Mexico, but their numbers are few. Most people come via public transportation, arriving singly or in small groups. Few guided tours here. The travellers you do see are hikers enroute to Guatemala, psychedelic mushroom gourmands from Palenque, importers scouring the region's fabulous textiles, and the rest of us, tending to be younger, more adventurous than average, and often travelling for extended periods of time. San Cristobal is a crossroads where North Americans are often outnumbered by other travellers. This internationality adds a cosmopolitan flair to the city's rustic atmosphere.

San Cristobal's attractions are low key. Pleasure is derived from everyday events. The gazebo in the main plaza provides a terrific vantage point from which to observe the goings-on. At dusk, as all over Mexico, the *zocalo* or plaza surges with a quite festive and ethnically impressive display. Weekend evenings there are food stalls and, sometimes, entertainment. Women ladle glasses of steaming fruit punch from bubbling cauldrons of guayaba, grapes, sugar cane and pineapple. Laced with *posh,* the local white lightning, and served with a scoop of cornbread, it is San Cristobal's signature aperitif. Nearby, other women serve *chalupas,* tasty tostadas layered with beans, cabbage, carrots and beets. Sprinkled with cheese and a fiery hot sauce, they sell for a pittance. A dozen or so make a scrumptious meal.

Daily, and during these festive evenings, one must ward off the *pulsera* children, little Chamulan girls who shake fistfuls of in-

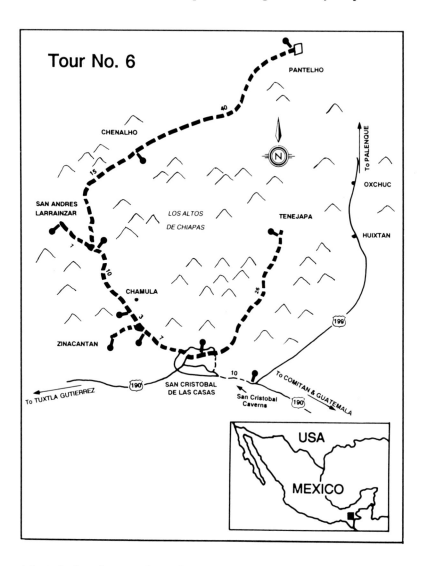

tricately hand-woven bracelets, urging you to buy. Despite all of our oaths, we eventually went from buying to wearing to getting lessons in how to weave them.

A Busy Corner Near The Market, San Cristobal

A few blocks away on Calle Cuauhtemoc, the **Cafeteria San Cristobal** serves the best cup of coffee we found in Mexico. Make a visit to the privately owned **Museo Zul-pepn** on Calle Guadalupe Victoria #17. The extensive butterfly and moth collection, and the local geology exhibits, prove both educational and fascinating.

For a crash course in local culture, a trip to Na-Bolom's museum and library is in order. Na-Bolom, and "Zoomat" in Tuxtla, are the two highest profile environmental preservation organizations in Chiapas. Populated by an international coterie of researchers and volunteers, Na-Bolom tends toward the self-righteous, but there's no denying the organization's valuable contributions to the environment and native people.

For the tourist, finding something to do at night in San Cristobal is a challenge. At **La Galeria,** you can hang out and play chess, read, or write letters, and at **Marguerite's** there's live music. But it all folds up around 10 p.m.

For a town that turns in so early, San Cristobal is slow to rise. At daybreak, activity is confined to the large open-air section of the market. You'll be hard-pressed to find a cup of coffee. Instead, have a steaming glass of *atole,* a thick vanilla bean and corn drink, delicious fortification against the morning chill. Around you, barefoot merchants set up stalls, rural shoppers throng the narrow aisles. Goats bleat, piglets squeal, women carry elbow-high bracelets of tied up chickens.

What at first seems a chaotic display of Indian fashion turns out to be strictly codified. Chamulan men wrapped in billowy black *chooks;* Zinacantecans in elaborately embroidered pink ponchos, the long, multi-colored streamers of their straw hats determining marital status; women from Bachajon in graceful, rainbow-striped skirts; the red armbands and scarlet chest patches of a group from Oxchuc.

A good place to help identify this local dress is **Sna Jolobil,** a weaving co-op whose purpose is the revitalization of Maya textile art. Sna Jolobil is located in the ex-Convent of Santo Domingo, not far from the market. Items are displayed by clan, making it easy to learn the unique styles. The store sells a wide array of weavings: blouses, belts, wall hangings. hats, sweaters, and much more. Prices range from mere pennies for a tiny embroidered purse to many hundreds of dollars for an exquisite tapestry.

With your interest in local ethnography whetted, it is time to check out the riding. San Cristobal is nestled into a region of Chiapas called *los altos,* the highlands, and for spectacular views and a test of aerobic capacity, you needn't go far. The *periferico,* a two-lane road encircling the city, is free of traffic and paved for most of its length. The urban waistcoat of industry that befouls most cities is strikingly absent here; the road climbs from paved streets to pasture to outlying hamlet. The *periferico* can be cycled in a few hours and provides a handy training course for longer, more demanding backcountry journeys that await.

Day Trip 1

SAN CRISTOBAL TO CHENALHO.

ROUTE: San Cristobal—Zinacantan—San Juan Chamula—Chenalho
DISTANCE: 36k.
RIDING TIME: Zinacantan and Chamula—1¹/₂ hr. each. San Andres and Chenalho—1 day each.
DIFFICULTY: Moderate to difficult.
TERRAIN: Mountainous.
BEST TIME: Year-round. Be prepared for cool winter weather.
ATTRACTIONS: Rural Indian villages and some tough, exhilarating riding.

The most accessible of San Cristobal's constellation of neighboring villages are San Juan Chamula and Zinacantan, only a few miles apart, and easily visited in one day. Cyclists travelling on mountain bikes can continue on to San Andres Larrainzar, Magdalenas, and Santa Marta (northwest of Chamula), and Chenalho and Pantelho (northeast of Chamula) for longer, more in-depth visits. The distances are relatively short but, no two ways about it, the riding is difficult. Should you choose to use them, second class bus service and *combis,* public transport vans, extend to even these out of the way communities.

Leaving Town

To begin, follow Calle Guadelupe Victoria west, downhill from San Cristobal's plaza. It merges into Calle Diagonal Ramon Larrainzar, a direct shot out of town. You roll over the final annoying speed bump, pass the last of the fender and autobody repair shops, and begin a strenuous ascent.

Women cyclists will find that in Chiapas, as in the Yucatan, encounters with aggressive males occur less frequently than in other parts of Mexico. Indeed, on these backroads *any* kind of encounter with men is unusual. Traffic is mostly pedestrian and predominantly female. Though Maya culture is somewhat macho-free in its dealings with women outsiders, the men are no sexual egalitarians. In these families it is they who wear the shoes. Literally.

The women are almost always barefoot. They march by on their way to town, groups of four or five portaging loads of firewood, cut flowers and produce. Leather thongs stretch around their heads to balance the backbreaking loads. Infants are wrapped to their bosoms, young children cling to their skirts. Modesty dictates women avoid the gaze of strange men but the taboo seems unnecessary; straining against the tumpline, each woman's eyes are fixed on the ground. If a man accompanies the group he strides along emptyhanded. Whatever his responsibilities, portage is not one of them.

The Left Fork

At k 7, near the top of a ridge dividing two valleys, the road forks. The left fork goes to Zinacantan, another 4k. The Zinacantecans are among the most extravagantly clad Indians in Mexico. Women and girls wear pink shawls embroidered with floral patterns shot through with tinsel. The men's ponchos are the same bright pink but display an extravagance that renders the women's drab by comparison; intricately stitched and decorated with fluffy tassels, they're really quite a sight. Flat straw hats with fluttering streamers adorn their heads.

If you have only a few hours in which to ride to one of the Indian villages, we recommend it be Zinacantan. The town is easily reached and its strikingly dressed people are especially appealing. Keep in mind that many tourists do come here, and Zinacantecans have wearied of the intrusion. The aversion to photography that is shared by most of the highland Maya is enforced by law, and is prohibited in the entire village. It may be tempting to flout the ordinance, but it's not only rude, you risk provoking righteous ire.

San Juan Chamula

To visit Chamula, return to where the road forked and this time continue north, following the edge of an over-grazed valley. Neatly delineated farms and orchards come into view, tight little cinder block homes that are humble in scale but have the orderly look of modest prosperity. After a short drop and an equally brief climb the pavement ends. Three giant crucifixes on a hill stand somber as Calvary and a billboard commands "Please Respect Our Customs." Welcome to Chamula.

It would be charitable to describe Chamula's response to tourism as indifferent. The plaza is stark, broad and dusty. Children panhandle aggressively. In the market people respond grudgingly. The women are cloaked in black except for their brilliant blue shawls, the only relief in an otherwise austere picture. Dressed in dark wooly ponchos and wide leather cinch belts, the men look somber and unapproachable. Suggestive of the town's militant atmosphere is the oft repeated tale of two German tourists who visited Chamula in the late 1970s. After ignoring requests to stop snapping photographs they were hacked to death *in the church.* The San Cristobal tourist office claims no knowledge of the incident, yet they are quick to advise people of the photography ban.

Despite this macabre history, Chamula's church is not to be missed—unless you are an ordained priest, that is. The schism between Chamulans and the Roman Catholic Church is such that clergy may enter the building only to perform baptisms. Services at other times bear little resemblance to Vatican-sanctioned procedure. Forest spirits are worshipped alongside Jesus and Mary. Coca-Cola is ceremonially imbibed. Burning "ocote" wood creates a smokey cloud, the sweetly resinous scent wafts through the chamber.

Religious fervor peaks during Semana Santa, Easter Week. Pre-Lenten activities include dancing, ritual fire-walking and the hypnotic sound of Chamulan music, a melodious whine of accordion, strings and mesmerizing chants. During Semana Santa the ban on photography extends to the plaza. To make the point unmistakably clear, the Chamulans have adapted the national custom of hanging effigies. Typically, the effigies assume the visage of unpopular world leaders or more shadowy threats such as the International Monetary Fund, but Chamula's "Judas" is different. The life-sized mannequin, suspended by its neck above the church door, looks like Joe Tourist. Dressed in Levi's, sporting wire rimmed glasses and a shoulder bag, all that is missing from the parody is a boarding pass for its flight home. At crotch level a camera dangles, the telephoto lens projecting through a patch of curly dark hair. It seems the Chamulans have a Freudian explanation for the shutterbug impulse.

Permits are required to enter the church in San Juan Chamula. They are available in an office on the plaza and, if carrying a camera, it's best to leave it there. At the church gate, nightstick-wielding guards see that neither cameras nor machetes enter the building's hazy interior.

So Long to the Tourist Crowd

Pedal north of Chamula and you shake the last of the tourist crowd. The road turns to stone and follows the rim of a valley where grazing sheep have clipped the sparse vegetation to bristly stubble. A supermarket warehouse unexpectedly appears, a reminder that what lies ahead is no standard wilderness.

Simple clusters of homes, know as *parajes,* populate these mountains. Although they've escaped tourist attention, the religion and soda pop industries have clearly taken note. The door-to-door knock of the evangelist and the throaty rumble of the Coca-Cola delivery truck are prevasive; you can't help but marvel at their distribution networks. No matter how remote, you bump into missionaries, and on at least one home in every *paraje* hangs a battered "refresco" sign. Little else may be available but you certainly won't die from thirst.

The first refreshment break comes at the *paraje* of Tzayaltetik. The owner's familiar black tunic is a reminder that this is still the *municipio* of Chamula, so his pleasant conversation is a surprise after the brusque indifference in town. He has heard of cannibals outside the highlands and asks whether that is the practice in your country. A burst of laughter from the rear of the store reveals his eavesdropping wife and mother. Are you being had? It's tough to tell.

The road, slightly improved, goes up and down through the *paraje* of Cruz Quemada before beginning to drop. At k 19.5, it flattens and an unsigned left marks the turn for San Andres Larrainzar. It is hard riding to reach San Andres. Tourists are an infrequent sight, rendering the populace much friendlier and happier to see them. A few cafes provide simple fare. The textile cooperative is open on Sundays only. The lack of a hotel necessitates making arrangements to stay in a private room, which can be one of the more gratifying aspects of backwoods travel. Continue north to the more distant villages of Magdalenas and Santa Marta and you are really on your own.

Returning to the fork of the unsigned turn for San Andres, the road continues north to Chenalho. At the lip of a huge valley a collection of homes mark the *paraje* of Temtik. There is a general store where you can carbo-load, and a local weaving school. The Tzoltzil-speaking children warn against taking photographs, then offer to waive the prohibition for 1,000p.

At this point the road becomes truly wretched and begins a steep descent into a populated valley. In the fields, sheep pick through the dry husks of last year's harvest. Wafting smoke indicates where land is being prepared for the new growing season. Lilies adorn the entrances of homes, and green *chilicayote,* barrel-shaped squash the size of watermelon, are planted in the yards.

Men pause from their labor to watch a bicyclist negotiate the steep gullied track. This kind of riding demands concentration; you scarcely glance around. Women sitting outside continue working without pause. Leaning on their haunches, they adjust the tension of their backstrap looms, and weave new *chooks* one careful thread at a time.

Three kilometers past Yaalchichen, signs point the way to remote *parajes* tucked among the hills. There is a 6.5k descent to the valley floor; cross a bridge and you arrive at the tiny bodega of Sr. Jesus Salvador Diaz, who has a stash of cold Superior beers. It's a piece of cake from here. The road improves and moseys along beneath the towering cliffs of Cerros Hualitz and Campanachen.

There is enough intervillage traffic to sustain a few guest houses and restaurants in Chenalho, and it is just large enough for the town's social stratification to be apparent. Indian men in white tunics sit in the shade of the municipal building weaving identical shoulderbags while squads of ladino youths scrimmage on the basketball court. Vehicles are almost non-existant. The buzz of activity is entirely human.

Staying the Night in Chenalho

Don Alberto Aguilar is Chenalho's hotelier. His spartan rooms cost 3,000p. Meals are available at neighborhood kitchens known as *casitas de asistencia* and of these, Dona Lichi enjoys a special reputation. Ask for directions to her home, where babyback ribs served with fresh avocados and homemade tortillas cost 2,000p.

The Zocalo *In Chenalho*

Seconds on beans and coffee are included and the Spanish lessons are free.

Chenalho is one of the friendliest towns in the Chiapas highlands and with prices so reasonable it is easy to spend some time around here. There's lots to explore. About 2k from town the Rio San Pedro disappears into a cave. Inside, the water is knee-deep and, according to veteran caver Mike Boone, neophyte spelunkers can safely splash around through a kilometer of flooded subterranean passage. From the avocado orchard foot trails lead to two villages near the mountain top where visitors are, at best, an infrequent occurrence. Go, be a sensation! On the opposite side of the valley is the "Campo Santo," a gaily colored cemetery. Gaudy upright vaults which look like telephone booths are next to the bare dirt mounds of the truly destitute.

From the cemetery you can survey the arrow-straight climb to Pantelho, a ride that is serious work. Beyond Chenalho the road degenerates to a whole new level of wretchedness. Should it prove too onerous, remember, there is a daily bus.

To return to San Cristobal, busses depart from Don Alberto's in Chenalho. There's little likelihood of missing it—the driver is Don Alberto's best customer. At 5 a.m. his revving engine wakes all but the dead.

ROADNOTES

WHAT'S AHEAD: This ride includes sidetrips to San Juan Chamula, Zinacantan, and San Andres Larrainzar, as well as suggestions for other nearby rides. An abundance of unpaved roads link the beautiful villages of the highland Maya in this, our favorite region in Mexico. The mountains are well settled; the only food and water necessary is what you'll consume between towns. Distances are short, the riding is tough and there is regular bus service. Opportunities to explore are limitless.

Kilometer 0	San Cristobal's plaza. Follow Calle Guadelupe Victoria west, downhill.
0.8	Calle Guadelupe Victoria splits. Bear right. Broadcast tower is dead ahead.
1	Another split, speedbumps, bear right.
3	Cross unpaved section of the *periferico*. Sign lists distances ahead, Chamula 9, Zinacantan 10, Pantelho 65. Road begins gentle climb.
5	**Restaurant Campestre.**
6	Nature preserve "**Pronatura.**"
7	Split for Zinacantan (left) and Chamula (right).

DETOUR FOR ZINACANTAN (4k)
Continue climbing ¹/₄k from signed turn, then down into the valley of Zinacantan, ultimately 3.5k further. Photography is banned by law in the entire village.

8	Paraje Ventana. Refrescos for sale, road starts down.
10	Begin 1.5k climb.
11	Turn for Chamula. Sign indicates right turn onto cobbled road. 100 feet beyond a better road parallels it.

DETOUR TO CHAMULA (.75k)
No directions necessary.

11	Road splits. Refrescos. No sign, bear right for Chenalho. Signed left turn for Batutula, 7k. Rough dirt road slowly gains in elevation.
15	Paraje Tzayaltetik. Refrescos.
17	Paraje Cruz Quemada. Start dropping elevation.
19	Left turn for San Andres Larrainzar, no sign.

DETOUR TO SAN ANDRES LARRAINZAR (7.5k)
0   Bear left, begin climbing. Road surface deteriorates.

.5	Road splits, veer right.
3.5	Three-way split. Right-hand turn becomes main street.
7.5	San Andres Larrainzar. Paved streets, cafes on the plaza. No accommodations. Weaving co-op open Sundays only.
21	Paraje Temtik. Drop 900 meters over next 10k.
24	Short .5k climb over ridge that blocks view of Chenalho valley.
31	Bottom of descent. Store with cold beer.
36	Chenalho.
	Casa de Don Alberto Aguilar, 2 blocks north, 1 block east of the plaza. Pink house with green pillars. Clean private rooms, meals available. 3,000p.
76	Pantelho. A day's ride beyond Chenalho.

SAN CRISTOBAL TO TENEJAPA

ROUTE: San Cristobal—Tenejapa.
DISTANCE: 26k.
RIDING TIME: Three hours.
DIFFICULTY: Difficult.
TERRAIN: Mountainous.
BEST TIME: Year-round. Be prepared for cool winter weather.
ATTRACTIONS: Terrific hiking, comfortable lodging, a textile coop and an interesting church.

Tenejapa, a gorgeous valley town in the Tzeltal-speaking region east of San Cristobal is another excellent overnight destination. Only 26k over good paved and dirt roads, a determined cyclist can easily roundtrip it in a long day. But the town is so appealing, it merits a longer stay.

Leaving Town

From the plaza, go one block north to Calle Ruiz. Turn right, and follow it all the way to the end. The altarlike blue and white Templo de Guadelupe marks where the street begins to meld into the *periferico*. Bear right. At the junction a sign indicates Tenejapa 27. The road continues to climb steeply but lessens after another kilometer. A signed detour (2k) for the Arcotete natural arch marks the top of the pass. There's an exhilarating but all too brief 2k drop to the Amarillo drainage which cuts through the valley. Climb up the opposite side to the village of Las Piedrecitas, and a sweeping view of the San Cristobal Valley. Relief on reaching this lofty vantage is tempered by the remaining 2k climb.

Deforestation and overgrazing are increasingly evident along the slopes. A series of uncharacteristically dishevelled communities appear. Among them, Romerillo is memorable for its awesome cemetery, a barren hillside with stark dirt mounds. No vegetation, no adornment, soften the image. Gullies twist like strangler vines across the naked field. The landscape seems in mourning. At the highest point a jumble of crucifixes, towering thirty feet high, are silhouetted against the sky. It's pure Mayan gothic.

Beyond Romerillo the gloom abates. The forest has been razed here, too, but more prudent managers have replaced it with orchards and terraced fields. The pavement disintegrates altogether, turning to gravel; pebbles crunch beneath your tires as the road winds between tilled fields. At Las Ollas there's a string of tiendas, the last of which sports a Carta Blanca sign. It's run by Jessica, a Tzoltzil woman of the Eighties.

Jessica spends the afternoon spinning and weaving, and caring for a crowd of children, several of whom are her own. She's barefoot. Her long braids, heavy black skirt, and dazzling blue shawl are by now a familiar visual refrain. "?Una cerveza bien fria?"— "How about a nice cold beer?"—she asks in the easy Spanish of a practiced barkeep. "How much does your bike cost? Why don't gringa women marry?" Such candor is startling and after a few minutes of conversation, Jessica's traditional costume seems part of an elaborate hoax. In a world where the limits of birthright are so unforgiving, her curiosity and candor are unusual.

The road drops quickly from Las Ollas but loose gravel limits your speed. The descent is broken by a 2k climb. At the top the dramatic twin peaks called Los Huacales come into view. They are named for the bowls in which *pozole,* a hominy soup, is served. The road angles left and pitches steeply downward, and the valley of Tenejapa opens up. This is the end of the road for touring bikes. Monstrous ruts and loose rubble will turn anything less durable than an 1.75-inch mountain bike rim into scrap metal.

Tenejapa

Tenejapa's weaving cooperative is on the right hand side as you come into town. A little further down the street is the plaza and a perfectly lovely Indian-style Catholic Church. Inside, often as not, a group of men play music and sing while women sit nearby, gossiping and weaving. Photography is not allowed in the church, and sometimes is not allowed outside.

There is a comfortable guest house (*casa de huespedes*) in a yellow building two blocks ahead on the left. Meals can be gotten here and at other private homes along the main street. Libation comes in the form of *posh,* a regional swill. During celebrations an impressive number of people are smashed on it, sprawled in the streets in their beautiful hand embroidered clothing. Curiously, Tenejapa's women have achieved a reputation as the region's most liberated *indigenas* in so much as it's considered proper for them to get plowed too.

If you're interested in a little tippling, *posh* can be had from any number of backdoor distilleries. Or, ask for a glass at dinner. Be sure to order a mixer, the stuff can knock the wind out of a windmill.

Nearby Hikes

There are a couple of wonderful nearby hikes from Tenejapa. Trails along the massive limestone cliffs that form the town's backdrop go to the village of Navil. Along the base another path leads to La Canada, a picturesque community set in a narrow canyon of the same name. Without even leaving town it is possible to visit the dramatic "sumidero," a yawning (and dangerous) abyss. The surest approach is to follow the creek behind the *casa de huespedes,* downstream. After slicing through a deep gully, the water volume begins to diminish, seeping into rock fissures and bedding planes. Finally, the stream tumbles into a frightening maw. Peering over the brink you can hear an echo as the waterfall dissipates into mist. It's impossible to see the bottom. Not many years ago a foreigner plummeted to her death attempting to photograph the chasm, and many locals now claim no knowledge of the cave's location. Others insist it can't be reached on foot—it's almost within shouting distance of the plaza. Please, use extreme caution when exploring the cave entrance.

Close Encounters of the Worst Kind

There is a hazard along this route whose unlikely potential for danger scarcely deserves mention. We'll mention it anyway.

Cultivation of honeybees is widespread in Mexico. Normally the docile insects pose a risk only when honey is being collected, so the likelihood of your blundering by at an inopportune moment is slim. Of course, the more time spent on various roads, the more the odds shift from unlikely to probable. It was on the road back from Tenejapa, after about 9,000 kilometers of riding in Mexico, that Eric's number came up.

Allergic individuals already know the grave danger bee stings pose. People who *haven't* been stung since childhood can't be sure whether they've become sensitive, a condition known as anaphylaxis. In such instances, bee stings, particularly if they occur in the face or neck, can be life threatening. Do carry an antihistamine in your first aid kit.

Near the *paraje* of Baluncanal, on the long return climb to Las Ollas, there is a large roadside apiary. Eric was grinding away in first gear as he approached. His ears were ringing from the elevation. Or was it the exertion? No, it wasn't a ringing at all, more of a buzzing sound, really. Yes, it was definitely a buzzing sound. Looking around, he saw bees. They seemed attracted to the bandanna on his head; bright yellow, like a sunflower. But now it wasn't the sound that was disturbing, it was the vibration, like a weak electric current. In fact, they weren't hovering around the bandanna at all! They weren't even *on* the bandanna. THEY WERE UNDER IT. And more, THEY WERE IN HIS GLOVES! THEY WERE EVERYWHERE!

Eric took this with something less than equanimity. Later, when he returned to retrieve his bicycle the bastards nailed him again. His first aid kit contained little more than a bottle of Kaopectate and a collection of antique condoms. He arrived at Las Ollas, face puffy, fearful he'd swell up like Mr. Potato Head and die. Laughing, Jessica twisted the cap off a Carta Blanca and assured him he would be okay.

ROADNOTES

WHAT'S AHEAD: A lovely and hospitable Indian town. Invigorating ride over good paved and dirt roads. Touring bikes can handle all but the last three kilometers.

Kilometer 0	From the plaza, go north one block to Calle Ruiz. Turn right and follow it to the *periferico*. Begin climbing.
2	*Periferico*. Follow signs for Tenejapa.
3	Gradient lessens.
4	Signed detour, 2k, for "Arcotete," a natural arch.
6	Las Piedrecitas. Collection of homes clinging to the ridge. Continue climbing.
7	False summit. Incline lessens. Deforestation.
8	Top. Begin long section of gently cresting S-turns through overgrazed country.
12	Romerillo, a brooding, unpleasant town with giant crucifixes.
13	Terrain flattens. Orchards and terraced farms.
14	Road drops.
15	Begin climbing again. Pavement turns to a well-graded dirt road.
17	Las Ollas, small settlement. Store with the Carta Blanca sign is run by a voluble Tzotzil woman named Jessica.
18	Pitch steepens.
21	Baluncanal. A paraje with no services. Apiary below village.
22	Begin 1k climb on a surface of burnished clay. The twin peaks to the right are the Cerro de Huacales. Road enters thick pine forest.
24	Cross ridge, lose sight of Huacales, gain view of Tenejapa's valley and the towering cliffs behind it. Road deteriorates to a sorry state. Rocky switchbacks hold your speed to 12–15 kilometers per hour.
25	Cerro de Santa Cruz on right. Turnoff has nice closeup view of town.
26	Tenejapa.

CYCLING FOR THE NON-PEDALER

ROUTE: San Cristobal—Chiapa de Corzo—Tuxtla.
DISTANCE: 83k.
RIDING TIME: One day.
DIFFICULTY: Easy to moderate.
TERRAIN: Mountainous but mostly downhill.
BEST TIME: Year-round.
ATTRACTIONS: A 47k downhill run, thought-provoking scenery, a wonderful boat ride into Sumidero Canyon, the "Zoomat."

Between San Cristobal and Tuxtla Guterriez, a distance of 83 kilometers, the altitude plummets a dramatic 4,500 feet. Forty-seven glorious kilometers of this are downhill. With hardly a turn of the pedal, there's plenty of time to enjoy this long paved descent.

Of course, there's no such thing as a free lunch. Heading west from San Cristobal on Mex 190, the Pan American Highway begins an immediate 6.5k ascent. Partway up, San Felipe Ecatepac, an unassuming town of pre-Columbian heritage offers great views of the San Cristobal valley. The surrounding hillsides reportedly hide numerous unexcavated ruins.

At the top of the climb is the Corfu furniture factory, unremarkable except for the armed guard at the facility entrance. Peasants, challenging the government's title to the property, briefly homesteaded here only to be run off. The presence of militia now prevent their return.

The Backroads of Chiapas

As you continue riding, a sign on the right indicates a backroad to Zinacantan, one of the many unmapped dirt roads which snake between Chiapas's plentiful backwoods settlements. For the truly intrepid, these back routes offer the greatest opportunity to observe the "other" Mexico in an undisturbed, and very ordinary, context. By utilizing such routes it is possible to extend

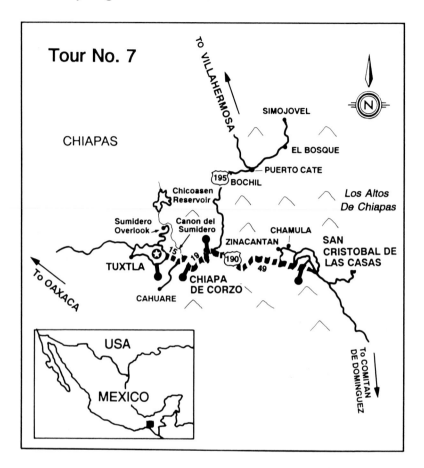

Tour No. 7

TO VILLAHERMOSA

CHIAPAS

SIMOJOVEL

EL BOSQUE

PUERTO CATE

195 BOCHIL

Chicoasen
Reservoir

Los Altos
De Chiapas

Sumidero
Overlook

Canon del
Sumidero

CHAMULA

ZINACANTAN

SAN
CRISTOBAL DE
LAS CASAS

15

19

190

49

TUXTLA

To OAXACA

CHIAPA
DE CORZO

CAHUARE

To COMITAN
DE DOMINGUEZ

USA

MEXICO

your ride to Tuxtla by several strenuous and, almost certainly, gratifying days.

But, back to the main road. Traffic is nominal. Descending into the town of Nachig, the highway is lined with stands selling a variety of fruit: peaches, plums, mangoes, watermelons and snot-fruit. Snotfruit? Well, if looks and texture are any clue, it's an apt name. It took us ten months to learn that snotfruit is a gelat-inous variety of pomegranate—pretty obvious once you know—and in more refined circles is called *granada China*. In Ricky's opinion snotfruit ranks right down there with menudo and okra, and she was long-suffering as Eric consumed them by the kilo.

From Nachig, another long climb cuts a 5k swath up the mountainside. At the crest the wide, gorgeous Grijalva River valley comes into view. This area is only beginning to experience an incursion of slash and burn to clear the land for cultivation. In spring the effects of the *quemazon,* or burning, are awesomely apparent. For miles into the distance patches of mountainside smolder and blaze.

Approaching the top, the road decreases in steepness. There's a series of false summits, it winds around a couple of huge turns and gradually shifts down. You know you're finally in the anticipated descent when the Zinacantecan *artesania* shop on the right comes into view. This is the last chance to buy something to drink until the road bottoms out at Chiapa de Corzo.

The road to Tuxtla is generally good but there are some patches which are positively ragged. Clusters of gravel make it difficult to slow down and easy to slide. Exercise a bit of caution and don't go as fast as you know you can. The road is curvy and what little traffic there is, mostly commercial, tends to be fast-moving trucks and busses. Let them pass, even if it means pulling off to the side to do so. Who needs a 10-ton truck on your tail?

The turnoff for Simojovel is marked by a sign for Chorreador (see Simojovel sidetrip at chapter end) but Mex 190 continues straight ahead. Alas, 49k into the ride, a climb appears. It seems the fun is over, but only a ¹/₂k to the top and another 2,000-foot drop sends you packing for Chiapa de Corzo and the Grijalva River.

Around Chiapa traffic picks up, and so do the epithets from passersby. It's curious. One person, riding in the back of a truck, heaved a grapefruit at Ricky, a potentially life-threatening gesture had it hit her. Yet, it didn't seem to be done maliciously— only out of stupidity. Turn on the ignition, turn off the brain. Another good reason to wear a helmet, right?

There's an abundance of great truckstop dining on the outskirts of Chiapa and the selection is far superior to anything you'll find in town. The **Columnos de Mendoza** doles out fabulous roast pork carnitas by the quarter-kilo and, across the street, a nameless little venue serves big, tasty plates of shrimp. It's a dirt floor affair, chickens running about picking up any dropped scraps of food. Zillions of shiny bottle caps are imbedded in the dirt entranceway and rickety card tables complete the picture.

Chiapa de Corzo, with a population of 33,000 and main departure point for tourists boating up Sumidero Canyon, has only one hotel. Not inexpensive, it is, unfortunately, run by one impressively unpleasant woman. Across the street, a rather enormous plaza is dominated by a unique 16th century fountain. Its delicately curved brick buttresses alledgedly found their inspiration in the curlicues of Queen Isabel's crown. Photos of the unusual monument adorn many a travel brochure. Those who value tranquility may want to spend the night in Chiapa, but for more diversion bike on to Tuxtla. If you're planning to explore Sumidero Canyon it's a simple matter to return to Chiapa by bus the following day. Regional busses depart from Tuxtla on Calle #3 Oriente between Calles #2 and #3 Sur. (That translates as Third Street East between Second and Third Streets South).

The Sumidero Canyon

Two dams have been built on the Rio Grijalva to harness its tremendous hydro-electric potential. Before the valley was flooded, the vertical walls of the narrow Sumidero Canyon towered 1,900 feet. What was formerly a thrilling flume known to white water aficionados is now a pacified basin of water almost 900 feet deep. Magnificent waterfowl nest along the meager shore. Groups of pelicans sail low, in formation, across the gently undulating water; stunning white egrets bob rhythmically on the protruding branches of a submerged tree. Overhead, in a startling flash of green, a flock of parrots swoosh by.

Along the canyon walls accumulations of minerals have created bizarre formations. The guide points out one, named the "Christmas Tree" which looks—hmmmph, just like a Christmas tree. He maneuvers the boat into a cave, slows down for photos, and rushes at perched birds, forcing them to flee. Presumably, this last is done for your pleasure and, at your behest need not be continued.

Boat rides into Sumidero Canyon cost about 50,000p for up to six passengers. It's a two-hour trip. The boat operators are syndicated and prices are only marginally negotiable.

It is also possible to hire a boat to go into the canyon from Cahuare, 5k past Chiapa on the way to Tuxtla. The embarcadero is down a long rocky road, and several restaurants line the shore. We think it more pleasant than Chiapa but unless you are planning to go on the weekend, when the canyon is very crowded with sightseers, you are less likely to find a group to share a boat in Cahuare than in town.

Tuxtla Gutierrez, Capital of Chiapas

Tuxtla Gutierrez is not the industrial hellhole most people expect it to be. In fact, it's quite an amenable town.

Tuxtla boomed with the discovery of nearby oil reserves in the 1970's and, despite a global collapse in petroleum prices, remains the thriving commercial center of Chiapas. Modern glass and steel structures border the enormous central plaza, and the streets are in a thrall of activity from early morning to late at night. There's an abundance of restaurants, fast food places and juice stands, numerous movie theaters, and an array of cultural events. Interspersed among the city's fashionably dressed, Indian women, barefoot, traditionally garbed, tend their children and sell handcrafts from blankets spread out on the sidewalk. Foreign tourists remain an infrequent sight.

Tourism, the nation's second leading source of income, receives short shrift in Tuxtla. The state tourist office is inconveniently located on Blvd. Dominguez #950, Plaza of the Instituciones (two flights up). The building is shared with two government-run shops, **Bazar Iscanal** and the **Instituto de la Artesania Chiapeneca,** which stock crafts from all over Chiapas. We found many items tagged with prices that did not account for recent devaluations of the peso and nearly came to blows with each other in the scuffle for bargains.

One of Latin America's Finest Zoos

While we are hardly zoo aficionados (Ricky had to be dragged there), we heard enough compelling things about Tuxtla's zoo, to warrant a visit. "**Zoomat**" (the Zoologico Miguel Alvarez del Toro, under the auspice of the Instituto de Historia Natural), is considered one of the finest zoos in Latin America. For forty years, under Sr. Alvarez's leadership, the IHN has been in the forefront of Mexico's conservation movement. Zoomat evolved out of his concern about the disappearing Chiapan forest.

The park is beautifully laid out so that you enter one end and follow a path around to virtually all of the exhibits. With the exception of birds and reptiles, the animals are in open cages.

The trip to Zoomat is worth the effort if for one animal only—the harpy eagle. This astounding creature is the biggest bird of prey in the world and is the only monkey-eating eagle in the western hemisphere. They are known to snack on tree sloths, crushing the skull of their victim with awesome talons. Zoomat's magnificent harpy is likely Mexico's last. One was reportedly sighted in 1976 in the Lake Catemaco area of Veracruz—possible, since that is the most northerly existing patch of rain forest. No subsequent sightings have occurred, however. The largest bird either of us had ever seen, the harpy eagle is housed next to the largest mango tree either of us had ever seen.

To get to Zoomat, take the bus for the prison marked "Cerro Hueco" which stops on #1 Oriente between Calles 6 and 7 Sur. Tell the driver where you want to get off. It's about a 20-minute ride.

A Wonderful Sidetrip

We know of only two reasons to go to Simojovel. One is to buy amber, the other is for the excitement and fun of getting there.

Amber is fossilized tree resin, a lustrous, translucent material which has value as a semi-precious jewel. Simojovel is one of the few areas in Mexico from which large quantities are mined. It's a seasonal business. In early spring, after the crops have been planted, men turn to the mines for a few months of work, returning to the fields when the fall harvest begins.

Inexpensive and maleable, amber is ideal for use in jewelry. The appealing combination has made amber very popular with foreigners trying to finance long-term travels. This, combined with nebulous governmental plans to submerge the Simojovel valley, have caused the price of the resin to increase and local craftsmen are being forced out of the competition. We went to Simojovel ourselves, intent on investing in amber to help finance the writing of this book. Indeed, we met quite a few other opportunists scurrying from shop to shop, but we never did become the amber barons of our dreams. We did discover that the trip makes a great bike ride, though.

From Tuxtla, backtrack on Mex. 190 to the Chorreador turnoff, 34k, and bear north on Mex 195. The road is paved as far as Pto. Cate, where the highway divides. Mex 195 continues north, but you bear northeast to El Bosque on a good gravel and irregularly paved road. Coming into Pto. Cate, a sign on the right indicates San Andres Larrainzar, one of the Indian towns northwest of San Cristobal. This is one of those zillions of unmapped backroads which make it possible to travel through much of Chiapas, never crossing a major highway.

The road between the Chorreador turnoff and Simojovel winds through the most extraordinary mountains we saw in Chiapas. Harsh and craggy, they jut abruptly up from the earth, seemingly unconnected to the surroundings. Their peaks reach into a cloak of mist, sides steep beyond cultivation by the most land-desperate peasants. In the lowlands, traversing these mammoth projections grow forests of banana and coffee trees, and, as ever, fields of corn. It's gorgeous, and the numerous towns along the way provide plenty of interesting diversion. Bochil is particularly notable; its women wear some of the finest embroidery in Chiapas.

It's possible to travel to Bochil by bus from Tuxtla. There, pickup trucks ferry passengers as far as El Bosque, where another truck goes on to Simojovel. It's a cheap and quite exciting way to travel.

ROADNOTES

WHAT'S AHEAD: Two tough climbs out of San Cristobal pay off with a 49k jackpot downhill. Bus service on Cristobal Colon from Tuxtla makes it simple to roundtrip in a single day.

Kilometer 0	San Cristobal. Take Calle Miguel Hidalgo to Mex 190 and turn right for Tuxtla.
4	Town outskirts; begin 6.25k climb.
5.5	San Felipe Ecatepec, oldest settlement in the San Cristobal valley.
10	Corfu furniture factory. Marks the top of the pass.
12	Unsigned dirt road; opportunity to detour for Zinacantan.
13	Cobbled road, another detour for Zinacantan.
14	Nachig, at bottom of 4k descent. Roadside vendors selling peaches, plums and snotfruit. Begin 5.5k climb.
17	Road becomes markedly less steep; climb continues.
20	Zinacantecan crafts shop on right marks the start of the grand downhill.
23	Yalentey. Indian village off highway and kids selling fruit along highway.
49	Chorreador turn-off, junction with Mex 195. Continue straight for Chiapa de Corzo and Tuxtla. Turn right for Villahermosa and Simojovel. 1/2k climb before resuming descent.
64	Descent ends.
68	Chiapa de Corzo. Moderate to heavy traffic from here on.
83	Tuxtla.

INTRODUCTION TO EAST CENTRAL MEXICO

Mountains, mountains, and more mountains! Three imposing ranges crisscross the states which make up the region we have gathered under the banner of East Central Mexico. The Trans-Mexican Volcanic Belt, as its name implies, slices through Mexico from San Blas on the west coast to Veracruz on the east. The Sierra Madre Oriental intersects from north to south, obliviously mushing into the Trans-Volcanic Belt, adding another demand to an already formidable challenge. Not to be outdone, the Sierra Madre del Sur rises up from the Pacific, bearing the State of Oaxaca aloft and making it one of the more mountainous regions in all of Mexico. From Zempoaltepec, Oaxaca's highest peak, both the Gulf of Mexico and the Pacific Ocean can be observed.

Mexico City, usually called "D.F." for Distrito Federal, or simply "Mexico," is the hub not only of the east central part of the country, but of the nation. Some twenty million people live within the metropolitan area, nearly a third of the entire country's population. Bus routes, railheads and plane connections converge here, making at least some interaction with the city difficult to avoid. Given the choice, many tourists would indeed write off this simmering amalgam of humanity, the largest such concentration in the world.

The city's detractions are legendary: intestinal amoebas which travel by air, birds that drop dead from a sky so polluted it's comparable to inhaling two packs of cigarettes a day, distressing poverty, and subway pickpockets so smooth *te roban la leche y te dejan el café,* they can steal the milk out of your coffee.

Despite its many drawbacks, D.F. is exhilarating, urbane, entertaining. Great international cuisine, up-to-date foreign films, street music, nightclubs and dancing, terrific shopping, gorgeous parks, and magnificent museums, compete for your attention. But it's no place for a bike.

Rather than stay in Mexico City, we suggest basing yourself in delightful nearby Cuernavaca. *Flecha Roja* provides the most regular bus service between the cities. Departures are continuous and cost only a dollar. Within an hour the bus arrives at the *Camionera del Sur,* the southernmost of four giant bus terminals which ring D.F. Outside is the *Taxqueña* stop of the D.F. metro system. It costs pennies to ride and is a model of intelligent, farsighted mass transit. It is quiet, efficient and, at any time other than rush hour, is a pleasure to ride. The metro is the secret to enjoyably including the nation's capital in your cycling vacation. Leave your bike in Cuernavaca. Take the metro—and remember to hang onto your wallet. Train service stops at midnight, something to keep in mind if catching a return bus to Cuernavaca for the night.

If He Can Do It, Your Bike Can Too

Cuernavaca's proximity to D.F. rules out nothing in the way of cycling potential. Distinct adventures lie in every direction: alpine, off-road and desert with a sprinkling of ruins for good measure. They're described in Tour #10, THE CUERNAVACA DAY TRIPS.

The mountains which entangle Oaxaca are young, folded, and arid, as yet untamed by time or erosion. They form a protective barrier around the state capital, also called Oaxaca, a pot of gold at pavement's end. Within day range of this tranquil, sophisticated city are the most magnificent ruins of the Zapotec and Mixtec civilizations. Nearby, too, communities of craftspeople produce fanciful woodcarvings, distinctive black pottery, embroidered textiles, and weavings which mimic the geometric patterns of the ruins at Mitla. It brings out the closet shopper in everyone, even cyclists without a cubic inch of pannier to spare. See Tour #9: THE OAXACA DAY TRIPS for specifics.

Tour #8: WHEELIN' IN OAXACA, is a long loop through a relentlessly mountainous state. The ride bores through range after range to Pto. Escondido and the sea. That's the easy part. Should you decide *not* to return by bus, a really challenging ride awaits. The closing leg, through the Sierra Madre del Sur, is a marathon in low gear. Between gasping breaths you can debate which are more beautiful, the tropical mountains or the magnificently garbed Trique Indian women. The region is both visually and cardiac arresting.

As in Chiapas, sociopolitical strife is endemic to East Central Mexico. By some estimates, Oaxaca is the poorest state in the country and, no surprise, the indigenous people have fared the worst. The state is home to seventeen distinct tribes of Indians, with more than half of the people non-Spanish speaking. Land disputes are common and harken back to the mid-1500's when the King of Spain issued the first land grants. The titles remained legally valid even after conflicting certificates were issued following the 1910 Revolution. Add a third set of documents, those issued by Presidential decree, and you have an intractable legal morass.

Disputes occur not only between *ejiditarios* (communal farmers) and landowners, but between tribes as well. Generally confined to the remote communities of the Sierra Madre del Sur, they are not infrequent, yet go largely unreported by the press. Literally

Sierra Madre Del Sur

dozens of towns throughout Oaxaca are involved in the bitter, chronic violence.

Conflicts, for the most part, occur far from tourist view. However, before pedalling a mountain bike into Oaxaca's more recondite corners, it behooves you to be aware of local turmoil.

Poor communication between natives and foreigners can result in misunderstandings and has sometimes led to open hostility. Near the village of Huatla de Jimenez there is a monstrous cave that speleologists suspect is among the world's deepest. Efforts to bottom *El Sotano de San Aqustin* have been hampered by local Mazatec Indians, who may regard the intrusion as a religious trespass. While the exact nature of their objection is unclear, registration of their disapproval has been intimidatingly frank. Climbing parties have returned to find stationary ropes cut behind them and, in one instance, a large boulder was dropped on a descending team of spelunkers.

Granted, these are dramatic and uncharacteristic events but knowing that such potential exists enables you to respond to situations as they arise. When in doubt, TALK TO PEOPLE and remember that *you* are the intruder, the one who must demonstrate benign intent.

One more thing: Drugs still draw a lot of people to Oaxaca. Marijuana grows in the mountains and towns like Huatla de Jimenez and San Jose del Pacifico are notorious among psylocybin buffs. If you do dabble with the time-honored stimuli, don't be foolish enough to carry them. Military checkpoints are familiar throughout Mexico and are particularly common on the road from Oaxaca to the coast. All travellers are subject to search.

Have we now dissuaded everyone? That is not our intent. Most of the problems mentioned are confined to the hinterlands of Oaxaca, backroad towns where few tourists ever go. Even then, gliding down from cool, rugged, mountainous heights to the sun ripened Pacific shore, it takes a willful effort to imagine that all is not right in this part of the world.

WHEELIN' IN OAXACA

ROUTE: Oaxaca–Puerto Angel–Pto. Escondido–Pinotepa Nacional Parque–Oaxaca.
DISTANCE: 853k.
RIDING TIME: One week to ten days.
DIFFICULTY: Very tough.
TERRAIN: Mostly mountains, some hot coastal plain.
BEST TIME: Year-round.
ATTRACTIONS: A real workout ride, interesting landscape, oceanside relaxation, nightlife and fun.

This long, often excruciating tour encompasses endless ascents, narrow, serpentine roads, and sweltering heat. But Tour #8 is not entirely hard work. Roiling Pacific waters, enthusiastically acclaimed by surfers, await the intrepid. Protected swimmable bays and delightful, sun-drenched beaches beckon. Huatulco Bays and Pto. Escondido are well known to tourists, but the coastline between them remains an overlooked and pleasing alternative to the high-rise glitz of big-buck resorts.

Malaria

A word of caution: Malaria is endemic along much of the Pacific Coast. Government health officials sometimes distribute chloroquine on the beaches of Pto. Escondido and Zipolite, but an effective regimen requires that weekly chloroquine pills be taken for two weeks prior to entering and six after leaving a malaria zone. Fill a prescription before leaving home.

Leaving Oaxaca

From Oaxaca's main plaza take Calle Miguel Cabrera to the *periferico*. Turn left and follow signs for Mex 175 south. At the Pemex station near the edge of town the road funnels into a two-lane highway and from here on the heavy traffic gets progressively lighter.

The Oaxaca loop was, for us, uh, memorable. For one thing, on his way to the post office to mail them home, Eric lost four rolls of

Tour No. 8 [190]

To PUEBLA
YANHUITLAN
TEPOSCOLULA   NOCHIXTLAN
43
YOLOMECATL   EL CORTIJO
[190]
To PUEBLA   49   73
[92]   30
TLAXIACO   CARBONERA
89   OAXACA
LAGUNA GUADELUPE
MONTE ALBAN   [190]   To TUXTLA
                                              GUTIERREZ
PUTLA
MESONES   OAXACA   62   OCOTLAN
87
SANTA MARIA ZACATEPEC   [131]
[125]
LOS LLANOS   EJUTLA
CACAHUATEPEC   SOLA DE VEGA
SAN SEBASTIAN IXCAPA   [125]   MIAHUATLAN
PINOTEPA   12
NACIONAL
To ACAPULCO   JAMILTEPEC   SAN JOSE   SAN MIGUEL
34   DEL PACIFICO   SUCHIXTEPEC
30
SAN JOSE DEL PROGRESO   CANDELARIA
43   RIO GRANDE   39   LOXICHA
[200]   35   CHACALAPA
Lagunas de Chacahua CACALOTEPEC   POCHUTLA
TOMATAL   ToHUATULCO
PUERTO ESCONDIDO   71   PUERTO ANGEL
CHACAHUA   ZIPOLITE

USA   Pacific Ocean

MEXICO

film. We placed newspaper ads, posted a reward, arranged for radio announcements, and did one live appeal on Radio Oaxaca. Then we left town to research the route and tried, as much as possible, to forget about the film.

We got only as far as the Pemex station before meeting Horst, a German man who was touring the United States and Mexico by bicycle. We're always glad to see other cycle tourists and go out of our way to meet them, and this was no exception. But soon after introductions it became clear that Horst didn't like the United States, or mountain bikes, or us. Still, for the next two days, he proved impossible to shake.

The Oaxaca valley is huge, arid and pretty. In the spring, when the rains have yet to begin, the plowed fields and neat orchards crackle with nascent fertility. The ride across the valley floor is mostly level, with only one 3k climb as far as Ejutla.

Los Caballeros

During a late lunch at the **Restaurant Mary** in Ejutla, Horst pulled in. On his third beer he told us we ought to slow down and get into the pace of Mexico. After eating, the three of us went to the bus station to determine the price, schedule, and probability of Ricky getting help putting her bicycle on the bus roof. No problem, we were told, *Hay muchos caballeros aqui,* "There are many gentlemen here." Eric and Horst biked off, leaving Ricky to the caballeros.

She sat on the fence, trying to read. A group of men drew close. "What country are you from?" "How much did your bike cost?" "What is your name?" The usual stuff. "How far did you bike?" one man asked. "Your legs must be *very* strong." His fingers twitched at the thought. The guy sitting next to her reached out and squeezed her thigh. Before she could figure out how to say "Get your damn hands off me!" the bus rolled in.

Five kilometers out of Ejutla, there is a rapid terrain change and the hills begin. Agriculture slackens, towns become less frequent, the ride increases in difficulty. The road clutches the hillside. Laboring uphill, the bus passed Horst and eventually caught up to Eric. Now into the pace of Mexico, he was cycling with a group of kids, not one over 13, sporting shirts that said, "Miahuatlan Junior Racing Club."

Miahuatlan is large and has no paved streets. There's a state prison in town, so guards in uniforms are all over the place, and maybe that's why it feels a little discomfitting. Eric stopped for a juice on the way in and the woman at the stand said, "You just rode here from Oaxaca." She turned to her friend. "Can you imagine riding here on a bike all the way from his country?" Eric asked her how she knew. "I heard you on the radio this morning. Did anyone return your film?"

We met in the plaza (our usual meeting place when arriving separately) and were surrounded by a swarm of kids. They, too, asked about the film and whether anyone had claimed the 50,000 pesos. Paranoia set in: How many thousands of people had heard about the reward these gringos were offering? Eric excused himself and went to the market for another juice. At the counter two women whispered, "Is this the cyclist who lost his film?" Stunned, he returned to the plaza. "Ricky, *everyone* listens to Radio Oaxaca." One of the kids asked the price of our bikes. He lied, "Our publisher gave them to us."

There are three mediocre hotels in Miahuatlan, and Horst managed to pick the same one we did.

Hard Riding Ahead

Leaving Miahuatlan the road begins an arduous 35k haul to San Jose del Pacifico. Of this, 16k are relentlessly steep. San Jose marks the highest elevation between the city of Oaxaca and the coast. Eric biked, Ricky bussed, and we met in one of San Jose's truck stop cafes, **El Crucero.** This place was right out of northern California—photographs of tractor-trailers on the walls, immaculate, lacquered-wood interior, and trucker-sized portions of steak and eggs.

There's a little cluster of foreigners who hang out in San Jose and rent the squalid cabanas behind El Crucero. Psychedelic mushrooms grow here but late in the dry season, they're impossible to find. An Austrian fellow offered to give us some powdered mushrooms, but we declined. Too risky. Three young hipsters gave us a collectively cold shoulder except for one in dark glasses and dreadlocks who asked, or rather demanded, "Hey, man, sell me your bike."

We paid our bill and, excitement building, headed for the coast. We'd repeatedly been assured the road from here on was "pura bajada," completely downhill. The slide ended abruptly 2k later and a 7k climb lay ahead. Then another of 3k, and another of 6k. Tiny villages, some with 24-hour trucker's cafes, appear sporadically. It is not until after the 1k climb out of Soledad, that the road begins to descend in earnest. The view towards the Pacific opens up and the foliage turns increasingly tropical.

Seven kilometers down we rolled to a stop at a military checkpoint. Young soldiers checked our bags and asked whether we liked to smoke marijuana. Our dreadlocked acquaintance, handcuffed to a tree, must not have answered so convincingly.

A couple of short climbs break the descent into Candalaria, where the Posada San Jose provides a chance to call it a day. Take it. Racing sunset and believing Pto. Angel to be only 20k away—our Oaxaca state map was incorrect—we streaked by. Twenty kilometers later in Chacalapa, enveloped in darkness, we learned that the coast was still another 25k.

There is a hotel in Chacalapa, but no rooms were available. We struck a deal with an enterprising merchant, who rented us an expensive empty room for the night. Empty, as in concrete floor. It was a sweltering echo chamber. All night long busses and trucks shifted into low gear and pushed up the hillside, a few yards from our open door. We ate supper at **El Morenito.** Halfway through heaping plates of shrimp, Horst rolled in. Joining us, Horst expounded on the aesthetic inferiority of mountain bikes and could not understand why we'd write a book when selling newspaper articles was so much more profitable. He declined our suggestion to split the rent, but spent the night on our floor anyway.

By now the ride south is a breeze, albeit a hot one. Get an early start and San Pedro Pochutla will be awake by the time you arrive for breakfast. Pochutla is the busy merchandising center of Huatulco Bays, the upcoming Cancun of the Pacific.

The Pacific Coast

At Pto. Angel Mex 175 intersects Mex 200, then ends. Mex 200, the Pacific Coast highway, goes all the way from Tepic to Guatemala. In Tour #15 we follow it east; here, we ride it west.

Pto. Angel is a no-nonsense fishing village and accommodations for tourists exist mostly as an afterthought. But there are enough restaurants and budget hotels to choose from, and the beach is good.

Zipolite

A far more primitive alternative to Pto. Angel, only 5k away, is Zipolite. Down a sandy, hummocky road, Zipolite is a spread-out collection of private homes and tourist cabanas; there is no town center. Rough cabins and open-air thatched roof ramadas are the rule here, as are bucket showers and outhouses. The more luxurious places (take that with a grain of salt) have electricity. Two funky, popular resorts, **Lo Cosmico** and **Shambala,** are near the western end of the cove. Both have good vegetarian restaurants, but the food is not inexpensive. Neither serve alcohol. If planning an extended stay, stock up on fruit, snacks and booze in Pto. Angel.

While not condoned locally, beach nudity is at least tolerated on the shores of Zipolite. Having lots of people around lends to the feeling of safety, but a woman alone or sunbathing with another woman may have to tolerate the irritating attentions of Mexican men. "Irritating" is a far cry from genuine danger. Women may have to make a choice based on individual comfort level; put on a bathing suit, perhaps, or join the company of other sunbathers.

And don't find some nice secluded place to strip down, either; it may not be as private as you think. A couple we met had spent a few days romping in supposed solitude. Then, while he was off buying food, she was attacked. Okay . . . it happens, and *it is devastating* (this was the only rape we heard about), but sometimes a little common sense can go a long way towards prevention.

Maps don't show it, but the dirt road to Zipolite continues west and, after an hour or so, rejoins Mex 200. Navigable on standard touring bikes, it twists and climbs steeply through the wooded bluffs. Glimpses of the ocean periodically come into view.

The Turtle Trade

The road passes by Silva's, well-known locally for custom made hammocks, and then comes upon a gruesome sight—the sea turtle slaughterhouse at Macinta. The stench is overwhelming. Green, Hawksbill and Ridley's sea turtles are all threatened species, yet harvests continue at a tragic pace. Business is not conducted with an eye to the future; behind the building an entire hillside is covered with untold thousands of eggs from females butchered before they could spawn.

Even in Mexico, where ecologic issues are often regarded simply as a concern of the wealthy, the plight of the sea turtle is recognized. In 1977, to allay environmentalist's concern and continue mass harvests, an appalling, elaborate ruse was staged by a private corporation. A sea turtle research station was established in Escobilla and during the breeding season the international press was invited to observe the new, enlightened approach to managing this precious resource. Once the press left, the facility was abandoned and indiscriminate hunting resumed. You can read more about this shocking ploy in Tim Cahill's "The Shame of Escobilla," from the book *Jaguars Ripped My Flesh.* It is illegal to bring turtle products into the United States and many other countries. Don't buy tortoise shell trinkets and jewelry, avoid body lotions in which turtle oil is an ingredient. Pass on the *tortuga* menu items.

People who want even more of a backwater environment than Zipolite, should consider camping at the pristine fishing settlement of San Augustin. Stay in an inexpensive beachfront ramada, with thatched-roof and without walls. There's drinking water and food available; it's pretty and very peaceful.

At the point where this dirt road intersects Mex 200, there are several *comedors* (eateries) and they appear sporadically hereafter. The highway is in great shape, rolling in nature, and traffic is light, but even with a breeze the heat is oppressive. Drink up whenever possible. At Sta. Elena, dirty, garbage-strewn and heaven-sent when you're on a bike, there are a couple of stores and a real restaurant. Between us, we washed breakfast down with nine bottles of soda and beer.

Pto. Escondido

Make no mistake, since its discovery by surfers several years ago, Pto. Escondido has evolved from a quiet fishing village. It's big time now, clearly demarcated into a tourist strip along the beach, and the rest of the town, across the highway. Don't bother with the residential districts for dining. For only a dollar or two more, truly terrific meals can be gotten at many of the high profile tourist restaurants, and the difference in quality is worth it. Bars stay open late and long into the night, music filters through the splendid palm groves which line the shore. There are two excellent, inexpensive campgrounds right on the beach. The cove stretches

Fresh Fish For Supper, Pto. Escondido

for two glorious miles, at the south end terminating in a rocky point where surfers congregate and sun worshippers bask nude.

Pto. Escondido is an exciting melange of vacationing Mexican families, international travellers, fishermen, gill nets, lounge chairs and children, food, music and fun. Get your fill of beach bumming, for it's the last to be found on this tour.

A Grueling Ride

From here the road gradually turns inland. A long, exhausting ride lies ahead in which the altitude increases from sea level to 4,600 ft. It's gratifying in challenge and visual appeal, but less than ardent cyclists and people on a schedule may want to consider returning to Oaxaca or continuing to their next stop by bus. To do as we did, read on.

Maps show a large national park, Lagunas de Chacahua, 65k west of Pto. Escondido. It's not all it's cracked up to be. Facilities are minimal. Bird watching is the chief activity but there is a high concentration of mosquitoes. Remember, this is a malaria zone. Tents are recommended, as well as slathering up with insect repellent.

It's tedious pedalling until Jamiltepec, a vibrant oasis in the foothills of the Sierra Madre del Sur, and 28k more to where a river slices through the mountains, providing a much-needed rest stop. Enjoy a swim and a cold beer while marshalling the energy for the upcoming haul to Pinotepa Nacional.

The largest city on the way back to Oaxaca, Pinotepa is otherwise nondescript. If it is still early enough in the day, refuel and push on. Six kilometers beyond Pinotepa the road splits and Mex 200 continues west. Bear right, north, on Mex 125. In another 41k, Cacahuatepec, a delightful mountain town, offers simple, inexpensive lodging. Overnight facilities are also available in Sta. Maria Zacatepec, an additional 35k through rolling hills. Water is abundant, vegetation is lush, fields are rich with produce, and opportunities to swim are frequent.

Just beyond Mesones a difficult 10k climb goes over a range of mountains and drops to the large, riverine community of Putla.

Now the Real Work Begins

On the far side of Putla there is a climb to a ridge and a descent into a dazzling green valley of sugar cane and corn, and at k 574, the real work begins. Ahead there are a couple of short drops, a couple of small towns, but overall this is a parched, brutal, endless 40k climb. Food is scarce for the next 90k. Carry snacks and replenish water whenever possible. At the hairpin turn at k 594, there is a stream, and again around k 607, where the road begins a brief drop, a spring gushes out of the hillside. As always, drinking water should be treated.

Trique Country

High in the Sierra Madre now, this is the homeland of the Trique Indians. The men are mostly dressed in western garb but the Trique women still wear traditional clothing, ankle-length orange and red embroidered dresses. The first village you encounter, San Isidro Chicahuaxtla, marks the end of the climb. Nice going, kid.

The road follows mountain contours to nearby La Laguna Guadalupe, a very poor town that has a *Conasupo* (supermarket). But even if you have money to shop, there's precious little to buy. The lake is stocked with fish destined to be fried at the **Comedor Trique.** This restaurant, not yet open when we were in La Laguna, should be by now. Filtered water can be gotten at the spigot near the basketball court. Reportedly, the overlooking cliffs contain petroglyphs.

Emergency Lodging

A good place to try to find lodging in a town without any is the *palacio municipal* on the plaza. If there's no room in a private home, it's a good bet someone may suggest an alternative. Eric arrived at the village of La Laguna Guadelupe at dusk and was invited to spend the night in a room awash with recently arrived government beans. The guard waded through the shiny, shifting mass and set up a cot. Home for the night. Before he could bed down, a contingent of school teachers materialized to provide a tour of the village. In the morning a group of young Trique girls, wearing handloomed dresses, assembled in the plaza to raise the flag and sing the national anthem in celebration of Cinco de Mayo.

Smaller Mountains, Bigger Towns

More typical accommodations can be found in Tlaxiaco, k 658. It is at a lower elevation but there are several climbs to break up the descent, one of which is 6k long. Beyond town the country opens up into wide plains and rolling tree-covered hills. At times the wind is pretty stiff but after the challenge of the last few days, the riding is a joyous breeze.

Yolomecatl is the first large town beyond Tlaxiaco and, after 35k of riding, it is tempting to stop here to eat, but don't. Only another 12k, Teposcolula is a far more interesting place. Pine trees and date palms shade the plaza and the most beautiful church on this trip. *Liquado* stands sell delicious, thirst-quenching fruit drinks. And, almost surely, your bike will draw the attention of some of the town's many bike racers. On the highway the active cycle club has painted finish lines at varying distances.

At k 721 the highway joins Mex 190, the main road to Oaxaca. Turn right. Soon, the character of the landscape changes. Deep roadcuts highlight vibrant layers of red sandstone. There is a commanding view of expansive plains, dominated by the ruins of the ex-convent of Sto. Domingo de Yanhuitlan.

This fascinating former convent is well worth a visit. Built by Dominican missionaries and completed around 1575, the church and convent have a curious history. Epidemics brought in by the monks caused the deaths of huge numbers of Mixtec Indians and forced the survivors to emigrate south. The buildings remained vacant until the mid-1800's, when Maximilian's forces ransacked and destroyed the church archives. Until 1928, the convent was intermittently used as a military barracks. Today, you can tour the buildings, but some of the most interesting sections are closed to the public. Often, however, a greased palm helps turn the locks.

There is a hotel next to the convent, but if there's still daylight, we recommend riding another 15k to Nochixtlan. It's a large town with a choice of hotels and plenty of places to eat. And from Nochixtlan, you can almost hear Oaxaca call your name.

The last day out is a long one, 103k through never ending hills. With a little effort, you'll reach the city in time for dinner. After days of hardly seeing an automobile, it's easy to get careless about traffic now. In your headstrong dash to complete this circuit, please be careful. The last 31k are crowded with vehicles.

P.S. We never did get our film back.

ROADNOTES

WHAT'S AHEAD: Oaxaca City to the Pacific Coast is no simple drop to the sea. The climb from Miahuatlan to San Jose del Pacifico is awesome and the "descent" from San Jose is interrupted by frequent climbs. Plan on a *long* two days.

Kilometer 0	Oaxaca. From the plaza take Calle Miguel Cabrera south to the *periferico*. Turn left, follow signs for Pto. Angel.
	Posada Arnel. Calle Aldama #404 and Hidalgo, three blocks east of Paseo Juarez Park. Worth the walk. Firm beds, immaculate rooms, shared and private toilets, lovely courtyard and charming hosts. Concha is a treasure trove of local knowledge. 12,000p/dbl.
3	Divided highway.
9	Road narrows to two lanes. Pemex station.
13	San Bartolo Coyotepec. Groceries.
17	Junction for Sola de Vega, alternate route to Pto. Escondido.
18	Begin 3k climb.
34	Ocotlan. Full service, big marketplace, bizarre church. **Hotel Diaz.** On the main street. Clean enough, soft beds. 5,000p/dbl. **Pedal de Oro** bike shop nearby.
63	Ejutla de Crespo. Full service.
68	2k climb signals start of hill country, few services.
103	Miahuatlan. Full service. Barely perceptible climb begins on leaving town. **Hotel Mansion Real.** Big rooms, hot water, long flight of steps, stinky toilets. 8,000p/dbl. **Restaurant Marisol.** One block from the prison, where all of the guards eat, good and cheap.
111	Start climbing in earnest, next 14.5k.
127	Popstand. Road weaves through the mountains.
134	Begin 3k climb.
138	San Jose del Pacifico. Delightful truckstop town. Numerous places to eat, mushrooms nearby. **Cabanas.** Behind El Crucero restaurant. Bare dirt floors, psychedelic artwork, very basic, outhouses. 2,000p per person.
140	Begin 2k climb.
147	El Manzanal. 24-hour restaurant. Begin 13k descent.
154	San Miguel. Such ugliness; major deforestation.

160	Begin 3k climb.
185	Sta. Maria Jalatango. Begin 6k climb among pine forests and waterfalls.
187	Soledad. *Refrescos.* Short climb beyond town begins 42k, mostly downhill, stretch.
201	La Gallena. Groceries.
208	El Trapiche. Junkfood.
215	Candalaria. Continue winding downhill through shady forest, brief climbs break up the descent.
	Posada San Jose. Next to the Pemex station.
235	Chacalapa. Restaurants.
248	Pochutla. Full service.
	Casa de Huespedes Gloria Estela. On the highway south of town. Clean rooms with ceiling fan. 6,000p/dbl. A deal.
250	Intersection with Mex 200. Brief climb through coastal mountains to the Pacific.
259	Pto. Angel. Full service. Follow main street past harbor to get to Zipolite.
264	Zipolite. Beach and palappas.
	Lo Cosmico. Appealing low-budget resort. Ingeniously designed bamboo palappas and good vegetarian cooking. 15,000p/dbl.
	Shambala (aka Gloria's). Just past Lo Cosmico. Similarly fabulous ocean views and fanciful accommodations. 2,000p to hang your own hammock, 2,500p for a trapeze style swinging bed, 3,000p for a tiny cabana.

WHAT'S AHEAD: Zipolite to Pinotepa Nacional. Return to the highway through Pto. Angel or continue west from Zipolite on the dirt road that parallels the coast. About an hour later it rejoins Mex 200. Either way, take precautions against the coastal heat. Start early and carry plenty of water. Towns appear regularly all the way to Pinotepa Nacional.

289	Pto. Escondido. Full service.
	Neptuno's Trailer Park. Camouflaged by shady palms, directly on the beach, cold showers. 2,000p per person. What more could you ask for?
	Trailer Park Camping. Across from Neptuno's. A bit more sedate. Cabanas with two platform beds rent for 10,000p/dbl.
	Perla Flamante. Adjacent Neptuno's. Fantastic seafood specialties served with saffron rice and salad, 8,000p, *mas o menos.*

BEYOND PTO. ESCONDIDO: Consider the bus. There's no more beach and the climb is brutal, for gung-ho cyclists only. Should you get stuck there are pickup trucks called *camionetas* which provide passenger service along Mex 200.

304	**Las Hamacas** restaurant.
315	Hidalgo. Swimmable river. *Refrescos* for sale.
328	Cacalotepec. Restaurants.
340	Rio Grande. Restaurants.
350	Signed detour for Lagunas de Chacahua National Park. Few services.
361	San Miguel. Small village, *refrescos.*
371	San Jose del Progresso. Restaurants.
382	Chaquito. Restaurants, *camioneta* stop.
391	3k climb signals end of the coastal plain. It's inland from here.
401	Jamiltepec. Signed .75k detour to plaza. Busy little mountain village, active market.
	Restaurant Dani. Next to building with "Juridico Despacho" sign. Good place.
	Hotel Diaz. Rooms are up two flights of stairs, firm beds. 15,000p/dbl.
416	Huaxpaltepec. Restaurants.
429	La Arena river, excellent place to swim. Restaurant.
435	Pinotepa Nacional. Large, noisy town. Full service.
	Hotel Marisa. Long flights of stairs, shabby but clean, private baths, firm beds. 30,000p/dbl.

WHAT'S AHEAD: Pinotepa to Oaxaca. Good roads, few services, continued hard riding. The climb from Putla to La Laguna Guadelupe is particularly brutal. Thereafter it is easier but never easy. Rolling hills and invigorating climbs accompany you all the way to Oaxaca.

453	La Catalina. *Refrescos.*
463	El Limon. *Refrescos.*
468	San Sebastian Ixcapa. Restaurants.
470	Begin 11k climb.
482	Cacahuatepec. Full service. Good town for the night.
	Casa de Huespedes, on Calle Zaragosa next to the *Conasupo.* Hot water intermittent.
495	San Pedro Amuzgos. Restaurant.
519	Santa Maria Zacatepec. Restaurants.
	Las Palmas Hotel.

533	**El Rosario** restaurant.
542	Mesones. Cafes, groceries.
569	Putla. Big town. Stock up on supplies, monster climb ahead.
574	Begin the climb.
584	2k drop ends in Concepcion de Progreso. *Refrescos.* Good place to break and study the nasty mountains.
594	Junction with paved road to Santiago Juxtlahuaca. Turn right, continue climbing.
614	San Isidro Chicahuaxtla, a small Trique village. Minimal supplies.
617	La Laguna Guadelupe. End of the torture! *Conasupo,* water available from spigot on plaza.
621	Begin 16k downhill.
637	Creek crossing, unpaved road goes to Sto. Tomas Ocotepec. Begin 6k climb.
643	Luquila. *Refrescos.* The next 50k is equal parts up and down.
658	Tlaxiaco. Big town, full service.
	Hotel Mexico. Hot water, private baths, beautiful courtyard. 10,000p/dbl.
670	San Jose de los Cedros. *Refrescos,* pretty cedar covered hills.
695	Yolomecatl. Restaurants, interesting plaza undergoing renovation. Terrain levels considerably.
707	Teposcolula. Great town. Lots of bike racers, beautiful plaza and the nicest church on the route. Several cheap hotels.
721	Junction with Mex 190. Begin 2k climb to bus stop and restaurant.
725	Gradual 7k climb begins among spectacular red sandstone formations.
732	Great view of Yanhuitlan on the plains below.
735	Yanhuitlan. *Refrescos.* The old cathedral bears looking into.
750	Nochixtlan. Big town, full service.
	Hotel Central. Pleasant open-air courtyard with high ceilings, rustic furniture and lumpy old mattresses. Management reluctantly provides soap and towels: "This isn't Acapulco." No kidding, Sherlock. 5,000p/dbl.
773	El Cortijo. Cafes, groceries.
782	Llano Verde. Restaurant, begin 4k climb into piney hills.

795   **La Herradura** restaurant.

803   Tejocote. *Refrescos.* Following 20k is largely downhill.

823   Junction with Mex 131 for Telixtlahuaca. Turn right for Oaxaca. Traffic gets heavy.

853   Oaxaca.

THE OAXACA DAY TRIPS

Oaxaca defines colonial grace, an aesthetic of stately architecture, breezy courtyards and verdant public spaces. Its hospitality, as casually affable to visitors as it is unimpressed by their presence, seems of another era, too. Oaxacans go about their business with barely any deference to tourism. The atmosphere is exceptionally relaxing for tourists weary of targeted marketing.

Nonetheless, Oaxaca is synonymous with great shopping and is the source of many of the finest crafts in Mexico. Agents for import shops worldwide come here to purchase weavings, sculptures and pottery which originate in nearby communities. A very large covered bazaar and separate covered crafts market serve the day-to-day needs of residents and abound with shopping surprises for tourists.

The city's diversions include movie houses which show first-run American films, nightclubs, and a calendar laden with theatre, music and dance festivals. And, of course, there's always schmoozing with a friend over beers in the *zocalo* or plaza, as pleasing a pastime here as anywhere.

Surrounded by porticoed cafes, Oaxaca's *zocalo* is surely one of the loveliest in Mexico. Tall trees whisper in the breeze, old men doze on benches under the sun-laced boughs, the shrill peal of children at play blends with bandstand music. In the evenings the square pulses with life, but the pace is never frenetic, is always genteel.

A constellation of day-rides fans out from Oaxaca, really terrific locations in each direction. Route 190, between Oaxaca and Mitla, a distance of only 50k, is so packed with ruins and side-trips it can take days to see them all. We cover some but suggest you study the map to discover others that suit your plans.

No tour of Oaxaca is complete without a visit to the ruins of Monte Alban, a great archaeological treasure. Their grandeur is enhanced by the site's mountaintop locale and lack of crowds.

Oaxaca

The modern visitor's center sells icy Dos Equis lagers and affords breathtaking views from the veranda, ample reward for the effort it takes to get there.

Day Trip 1

OAXACA TO MITLA

ROUTE: Oaxaca—Tule—Tlacochahuaya—Yagul—Mitla.
DISTANCE: 50k, one way.
RIDING TIME: 6 hours or more, depending on your pace.
DIFFICULTY: Easy.
TERRAIN: Almost flat.
BEST TIME: Year-round.
ATTRACTIONS: Ruins, churches and shopping.

The road to Mitla, Mex 190 east, is so chock full of sidetrips you may want to plan more than one day to see them. To get to the highway take Calle Vicente Guerrero from Oaxaca's central plaza, three blocks east to Calle Melchor Ocampo. Turn left and proceed 1k north to the main highway, called Calzada Ninos Heroes de Chepultepec. Turn right.

The Widest Tree in the World

There's hardly time to set a rolling pace before roadside stands and parked cars indicate the village of Tule. Tule was put on the map by the *ahuehuete* tree which grows in the church courtyard. A kind of cypress, this tree is of truly monumental proportions— 165 feet tall and 160 feet around. Estimated to be more than two thousand years old, the *ahuehuete* is younger than a California sequoia, and not so tall, but is believed to have the widest girth of any living tree. It's supposed to take a full minute to walk around it. A festival dedicated to the tree occurs each year on the second Monday in October.

Across the church, food stalls serve up outrageous *quesadillas* stuffed with squash blossoms and cheese or chicken, smothered in red mole sauce. They're inexpensive and delicious.

The turn-off for Tlacochahuaya is at k 18. The town is 2k further down a paved road, which you stay on until the 16th-century Dominican Church of Saint Jeronimo comes into view on the left. The adornments make this Catholic church most fascinating; both saints and humans display the grotesque distortions common in ancient indigenous art. The depictions are very non-Hispanic in character.

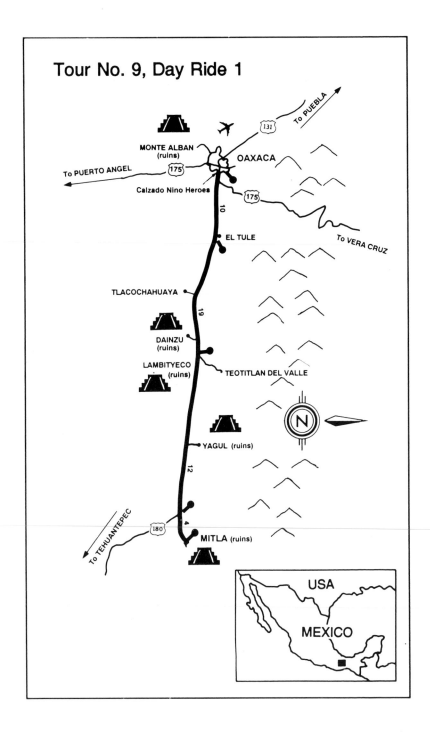

Tour No. 9, Day Ride 1

The church is now open only during mass and we have heard that theft is the reason why. It's so tranquil here "crime" seems most unlikely, but in point of fact, we met a woman whose purse had been slashed while she and two friends were in the parish courtyard. So be alert, but go anyway—the traveller's mantra.

Back on the main road, there are turn-offs for the ruins at Dainzu and Lambityeco. Ongoing reconstructions at both sites are dependent on an irregular flow of money.

Continuing east, you pass the turn-off for Teotitlan del Valle, production center for the finest wool rugs in Mexico.

At k 32, the Tlacalula intersection is bustling with several restaurants and beer joints. At least one of the beer halls, on the southwest corner of the intersection, serves *botana*, free food with drinks.

Tlacalula is an old town, dating from 1250. In the 16th century a chapel was constructed and decorated with finely detailed hand carvings. Today it remains one of the most ornate churches in the State of Oaxaca. There is a small museum next door. Tlacalula's brilliantly colorful Sunday market primarily serves the surrounding communities, but there are some items, pottery in particular, which many tourists find interesting.

Only a few kilometers from Tlacalula is the turn for Yagul, a Mixtec city that was contemporary with Mitla. There are several interesting structures, built on two levels, including three tombs and an enormous carved stone animal. Yagul was not a major settlement, yet the largest ball court to be found in the Oaxaca area is here. Its hilltop fortress provides unparalleled views of the surrounding valley.

Unique Artwork in Mitla

Mitla is 5k north of the main highway. On one side of the plaza is the excellent **Frissell Museum of Zapotecan Art,** regional archaeological center for the University of the Americas. In addition to art and culture, the museum's lovely patio is a welcoming place for refreshments either prior to or after the rigors of ruin-hopping. From the plaza it is a short but gizzard-shaking, cobble-stoned ride to the major excavations. Far better to walk and enjoy the crowded byways of touristy distractions.

Indian Market, Tlacolula

Mitla was an important Mixtec ceremonial center at the time of the Spanish conquest. The five groups of ruins, while not extensive, are renowned for their unique artwork, unlike any found at other major sites. There are no depictions of humans or animals at Mitla. Instead, the buildings are adorned with precise geometric patterns of carved and inlaid stone, designs still mimicked in contemporary weavings. One building, 125 feet long and 23 feet wide, contains more than one hundred thousand pieces of stone, so intricately cut, no mortar holds them in place. This is all the more astounding because metal cutting tools were not used. Equally impressive are the 15-ton lintels over door entryways. A sophisticated knowledge of engineering was necessary to incorporate the system of joists used to resist the region's frequent earthquakes—a design that has weathered the test of time.

A distinctively patterned wall partially surrounds the Catholic church. Erected, as was the conquistadors' custom, on the site of a former Mixtec palace, stones from other Mixtec buildings were also used for its construction. The remains of some can be seen behind the church.

Mescal, the stuff with the dead worm floating in it, is Mitla's other *raison d'etre*. There are two kinds of premium mescal—pechuga, which tastes like kerosene, and gusanito, which tastes like kerosene. It's sold in lovely, innocuous stoneware jugs. Try a few complimentary shots—and be especially careful riding home!

ROADNOTES

Kilometer 0	Oaxaca.
5	Three lanes shrink to one.
10	El Tule. Giant tree, giant mangos, giant quesadillas.
18	Turn for Tlacochahuaya, 2k detour. Wonderful sandstone bluffs and desert tapestries. Sixteenth-century church.
29	Lambityeco, small ruin and museum. Interesting place to take a breather.
31	Intersection. Pemex, several restaurants.
38	Yagul, 1.5k detour. Fortified ruins of small city. Magnificent views.
41.5	Signed turn for Mitla.
45	Mitla. Follow signs through town, past the t-shirt and mescal shops to the ruins.

OAXACA TO MONTE ALBAN

ROUTE: Oaxaca—Monte Alban.
DISTANCE: 14k round trip.
RIDING TIME: 1 or 2 hours.
DIFFICULTY: Difficult.
TERRAIN: Very steep, but on a good paved road.
BEST TIME: Year-round.
ATTRACTIONS: Marvelous ruins and views.

Cycling to Monte Alban is a most pleasing day ride. Don't be fooled by its proximity to Oaxaca; negotiating the steep curvy road to this archaeologic site is a brief but intense workout. The views are tremendous, the transition from city to country is swift, and the return to the city involves a thrilling, speedy descent. All this and great ruins, too, in the course of a few hours time.

Finding the right road from Oaxaca can be a little tricky and the easiest way is to start at the second class bus station on Calle Valerio Trujano. The city traffic is very heavy and getting across the four-lane street divided by railroad tracks can be intimidating. Need we say, do it on foot? Once across, it thins out and the real exertion begins.

Through a Pleasant Peasant Suburbia

The narrow road to Monte Alban weaves through what can best be described as "peasant suburbia." Single-lane dirt tracks and well-trod foot paths lead to ramshackle houses. Children and dogs play in the street, herds of goats graze along the roadside under the scrutiny of a young shepherd, women hang out the laundry and tend backyard gardens. As you gain elevation the population, too, thins out. Yet, for a nowhere little road, there are a fair number of vehicles. Rent-a-cars, small tour busses, and regular public transports lumber uphill, their pace moderated (as is yours) by the angle and kinks in the road.

After 5k, a government sponsored reforestation project, an intended showcase, appears on the barren rounded landscape. A few scattered forlorn trees, many dying, many already dead, cry out for a drink of water.

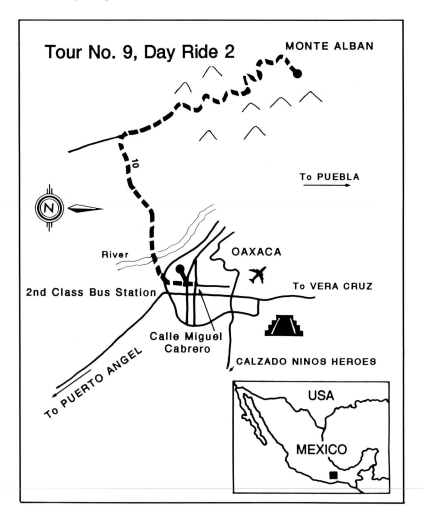

Tour No. 9, Day Ride 2

MONTE ALBAN

10

To PUEBLA

N

River

OAXACA

To VERA CRUZ

2nd Class Bus Station

Calle Miguel
Cabrero

CALZADO NINOS HEROES

To PUERTO ANGEL

USA

MEXICO

At last there is a point in the road where the angle of ascent
decreases for a few feet, and the modern Monte Alban visitors'
center looms on the hilltop. A go-for-broke effort is required to
reach it, for the remaining couple of hundred meters are a cork-
screw climb. Thankfully, the *aqua* ladies, eager to sell their cool
fruit drinks, are waiting in the parking lot. For more sophisticated fare there is a good, inexpensive restaurant in the visitors'
center. It has a wonderful open-air patio and dazzling views of

the Oaxaca Valley, 1,200 feet below. After this grunt, you've earned a beer—to hell with the ruins!

The Ruins of Monte Alban

Well, as a matter of fact, these are some pretty impressive ruins. Aerial photos reveal what is not so obvious up close: an entire mountain summit, 750m by 250m, has been levelled. Outcroppings of rock which could not be removed, were simply incorporated into buildings—hearts of stone, so to speak.

Home to several Oaxaca Valley civilizations including the Olmecs, Monte Alban flourished under the Zapotecs, and later, the Mixtecs. It was occupied by them between 800 B.C. and 1500 A.D. Huge, sprawling structures have been excavated but the restored area, large as it is, represents only a small part of the old city. At its peak, an estimated 25,000 people lived nearby and many buildings still lie under the protective earth of surrounding hills.

Monte Alban was an important ceremonial center, a point made evident by the elaborately designed and decorated structures which encircle the large, stately plaza. Many of the buildings are honeycombed with passageways and crawlspaces, some apparently intended for the high priests to move about unseen by those outside. If you intend to explore these tunnels, bring a flashlight and, if really serious about it, kneepads. At least one tunnel is barely two feet high and perhaps one hundred feet long.

We found these nooks and crannies to be notably free of used toilet paper, spent condoms and human-ex. Perhaps it's because anything that passes as a hiding place at Monte Alban also serves as an "office" for local antiquities dealers. These guys can be a real hoot. Clutching small figurines alledgedly found in nearby fields, the salesmen conspiratorially whisper to any tourist who wanders by. They furtively glance around, keeping a sharp lookout for authorities who, in reality, couldn't care less. Some of these artifacts may actually be genuine, but most are reproductions. We were approached by a blind man and young boy and, despite Ricky's admonitions, Eric took the bait. Bartering for a small statue began at 100,000p; the deal was clinched at 20,000p. A few minutes later, while passing through the visitors' center, we saw a shelf in the gift shop filled with identical statues, and they were selling for 12,000p each!

The return to Oaxaca is furious and fun. You may have to check your speed on some sharp turns, and remember that traffic will also be moving at a heightened clip.

ROADNOTES

Kilometer 0   Oaxaca. From the plaza take Calle Valerio Trujano west to the *periferico*. Cross the railroad tracks, past the second class bus station. Follow signs for Monte Alban.

7   Monte Alban.

THE CUERNAVACA DAY TRIPS

Since the era of Aztec rule, powerful and famous personages have made their second homes in Cuernavaca. Montezuma, Cortes . . . Helen Hayes? Yes, well, history is a funny thing. The Aztecs called it *Cuahnahuac,* the place surrounded by forest. The conquistadors reduced Montezuma's magnificent summer palace to rubble and, with their usual flair for Meso-American dialect, corrupted the city's name as well. *Cuahnahuac* became *Cuernavaca,* cow's horn. A more poetic sobriquet stuck, however, "the city of eternal spring," and it is upon that reputation that Cuernavaca has grown into a small, flourishing metropolis.

Mexico City is only one hour away by bus. If faced with making international travel arrangements, clearing up visa problems or simply wishing to avail yourself of the capital's urbane pleasures, Cuernavaca makes an excellent and pleasant base of operations.

One of the few tranquil havens in hectic downtown Cuernavaca is the **Borda Gardens,** an idyll built in 1716 by the silver baron Jose de la Borda. During the short Mexican reign of French Emperor Maximilian and his wife Carlotta it was a favored retreat. Located across from the cathedral on Calle Morelos, the loveliest time to visit is during late afternoon. Cobbled paths lead through a tangled jungle of splendorous decay, growth thick and impervious to the clamour of the street. It is an arboretum out of time, a vegetable equivalent of Lady Haversham's room where gardeners haven't trained a plant since Maximilian stepped in front of the firing squad.

Another wonderful place to visit is the **Palacio de Cortes,** once a military garrison, which dominates the southeast side of Cuernavaca's two adjacent plazas. Near the museum's entrance, a panel of glass covers a small tomb holding an Indian skeleton *in situ.* Inside, the stone foundations of Montezuma's summer court are exposed. The museum houses an excellent collection of Spanish armor and weaponry, and on the second floor balcony a wall is dominated by an enormous Diego Rivera mural.

The name for haute cuisine in Cuernavaca is **Las Mananitas,** considered one of the finest restaurants in the country and comparably expensive. That is to say $US 10–15. The food is stupendous, served on a patio open to flower-scented bushes and towering palms. A menagerie of exotic fowl strut about the manicured lawn. At the very least, go for a late afternoon beer before the animals have been rounded up for the night.

Eating in Cuernavaca doesn't necessarily mean a binge. Woven into the town's high-priced fabric are many economical restaurants. Small *fondas* on the streets off Calle Matamoros serve *comida corrida* for under two dollars. Two of the finest *botana* bars we know, **Tapatia** and **El Danubio** serve platters of fried

Diego Rivera Mural, Palacio De Cortes, Cuernavaca

perch, tacos and steaming *caldo,* a fiery seafood stew, all with the purchase of a few cold beers.

Foreign language students are the most recent to discover Cuernavaca's charms. A clutch of private Spanish academies, the "bouganvillea league," offer instruction in the way of the participle and the pluperfect subjunctive. Similar programs can be found in other cities but few are in such delightful surroundings and none is so close to Mexico City.

Cuernavaca lies midway up the range of mountains which ring the Valley of Mexico, poised between timberline peaks and dry desert ground. The chilly alpine lakes of Lagunas de Zempoala National Park and the sunbaked ruins of Xochicalco are both mere hours away. Tepoztlan, an artist's colony with a rich Indian heritage, and the exquisite village of Malinalco, with its monolithic ruins perched above town, merit visits. Tepoztlan is an afternoon jaunt, but Malinalco is a true backroad adventure requiring an overnight stay.

Day Trip 1

TEPOZTLAN

ROUTE: Cuernava—Ocotepec—Tepoztlan.
DISTANCE: 24k one way.
RIDING TIME: 1¹/₄ hours.
DIFFICULTY: Moderate.
BEST TIME: Year-round.
TERRAIN: Rolling hills.
ATTRACTIONS: Crafts, a museum and convent, unusual scenery and a memorable hike to the pyramid of Tepozteco. Bring a bike lock.

Fifteen kilometers east of Cuernavaca, lying at roughly the same elevation, is Tepoztlan. If ever a town's character was molded by geographic setting, Tepoztlan, with its dynamic, brooding spirit is it. Immense cliffs form a towering backdrop, layer upon layer of volcanic ash etched into a collection of bizarre spires, minarets and stacked terraces. They press, almost claustrophobically, upon the village. High above, concealed from view, the Aztec ceremonial center of Tepozteco keeps a quiet vigil over the town.

The surreal landscape has inspired many visions. Carlos Fuentes wrote *El Gringo Viego* in a friend's Tepoztlan home. The town is thinly disguised as "Tomalin" in Malcolm Lowry's *Under the Volcano* and John Huston filmed parts of the screen adaptation here. Oscar Lewis's epic study of rural Mexican life was conducted in Tepoztlan as well. Today Tepoztlan draws a bevy of new age enthusiasts, followers of such esoterica as crystal healing and aura balancing.

To get to Tepoztlan, take Calle Morelos north from Cuernavaca's plaza. A beleaguering 5k climb starts immediately; cars and busses lumbering uphill make the going unpleasant indeed. At the second *glorieta*, or traffic circle, vehicles swirl around a statue of Emiliano Zapata mounted on horseback. Turn right and proceed straight. The climb ends, traffic slackens. In Ocotepec there is a good roadside restaurant, the last place to eat before Tepoztlan.

From Ocotepec, the road traverses the flank of the massif encircling the Valley of Mexico. After a few more kilometers the first peculiar rocky spires come into view. There's a brief but steep

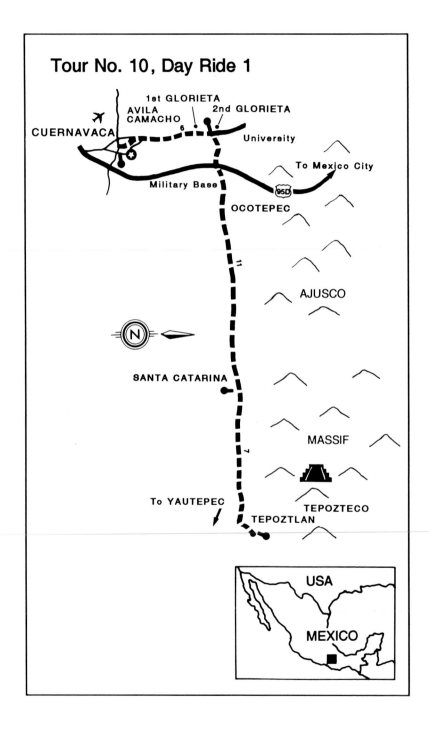

climb, a rapid descent, and at k 24 you roll—or rather, bump—over cobbled streets into town.

An Unusual Town

It is prudent to see Tepoztlan's attractions before making the long hike to Tepozteco. You may be too tired to investigate afterwards, and the beautiful ex-convent, with its hushed stone corridors, is a peaceful, touching experience. The small, informative museum of archaeology is also worth a look.

Adjacent to the convent courtyard, the daily market gathers. Most of the crafts are familiar; hand painted bark scrolls, ceramic masks, woodcarvings, unexceptional clothing and, of course, food. But one item, a musical instrument, does stand out. Called *ayacaxtli* in Nahuatl and *palo de lluvia* in Spanish, and made from a bamboo staff about four feet long, the "rainstick" resonates a marvelous tinkling cascade of tiny shells when inverted.

As Mexican towns go, Tepoztlan is one of the more unusual, of a style suggesting a lot of foreign involvement. Certainly a different aesthetic is in vogue. There are trendily lettered signs and galleries exhibiting contemporary art. In the cafes and restaurants, curtains grace sills normally bare, there is a higher standard of hygiene, and menu offerings such as whole grain breads, tofu and tempeh. At the local theatre Bergman has knocked Bronson off the marquee. Advertisements in Spanish tout services seldom heard of elsewhere in Mexico. One banner exhorts *Ven y Voler un Ultraligero,* Come and Fly an Ultralight.

Yet it is the nearby natural wonders which command the most interest. One of the most obvious stands on the southeast horizon, a rocky pinnacle in the shape of a stubby, erect . . . thumb. For a sure conversation starter, point it out and ask someone for the Spanish translation of "Devil's Schwanzschtucka."

The Tepozteco Ruins

The tiny pyramid and sacrificial altar of Tepozteco were built in 1502 during the reign of Ahuitzotl, Montezuma's predecessor and the last Aztec emperor to die a natural death. A comparatively new edifice, it is one of the few pyramids with an established date of construction. While the architecture is only moderately impressive, the buildings perch at the very edge of the cliff, and the view is awesome.

The hike takes about one and a half hours and you'll have to leave your bike in town. We suggest locking it in a highly visible public place or possibly at a restaurant where you intend to eat later. Making such intentions known is always a good way to bolster the insurance policy.

The trail begins at the east end of main street, Calle Cinco de Mayo. The well-trodden path is steep and some rather rickety ladders have been lashed together to ease the ascent. It's a lark for some, a feat for others, but there ought to be a medal for the snack concessionaire who climbs the route daily with a case of cola on his back. And, of course, our hats are always off to those valiant Mexican ladies who scale the heights in high heels.

If a visit to the ruins means a late return to Cuernavaca, take a bus. Regular departures leave from the tourist office on main street. Most don't have luggage bays, but virtually all have over-head racks.

ROADNOTES

Kilometer 0   Cuernavaca. Leave plaza on Av. Jose Maria Morelos. Start climbing.

5   First *glorieta*. Emiliano Zapata statue. Condos on left, 25th armored regiment on right. Continue straight.

6   Second *glorieta*. End climb. Turn right for Tepoztlan.

7   Ocotepec. Restaurant.

17   Santa Catarina. *Refrescos*. Begin gradual 3k descent.

21   Start serpentine descent to Tepoztlan.

24   Tepoztlan

Hotel Meson del Indio. Av. Revolucion #44. 20,000p/dbl.

Day Trip 2

LAGUNAS DE ZEMPOALA NATIONAL PARK

ROUTE: Cuernavaca—Huitzilac—Lagunas de Zempoala.
DISTANCE: 26k one way.
RIDING TIME: 3–4 hours.
DIFFICULTY: Very difficult; an unmitigated climb.
TERRAIN: Alpine.
BEST TIME: Year-round.
ATTRACTIONS: Icy trout-filled lakes in one of Mexico's most beautiful national parks. It's chilly up there; bring a sweater.

Better get in training for this one: no sex before, no energy after. In the morning you can carbo up at the plaza kiosk on such south-of-the-border smoothies as an *alfajor,* a blend of pineapple, lime and alfalfa, or a *bomba atomica.* Pay your money and take your chances. The *panaderia* **La Luz,** one block south on Calle Matamoros is usually open by 7:00 a.m. A few of their jumbo croissants will provide some much needed fuel for this 26k rampway to heaven.

The ride begins with the same vexing 5k climb to Emiliano Zapata's monument. "Las Lagunas" lie straight ahead. The gradient eases on entering the expensive suburb of Sta. Maria and immense eucalyptus trees grace both sides of the road. By k 9 the surroundings are rural. The road sweeps left, providing the first good view of Cuernavaca. Smog permitting, the graceful bulk of Popocatepetl soars up against the eastern horizon.

At k 12 the sign for Huitzilac appears; beyond it, the blacktop deteriorates and catapults directly up the mountainside, a stirring reminder that the shortest distance between two points is a straight line. The barbarous climb predisposes one to liking Huitzilac, a pleasant village, even if the climb didn't pause here. The old highway, Mex 95, passes through Huitzilac. Once Cuernavaca's main link to Mexico City, it is still the best route for cyclists going there. Picnic supplies are available at the open air market and, adjacent the church, a kiosk serves good, inexpensive *liquados.*

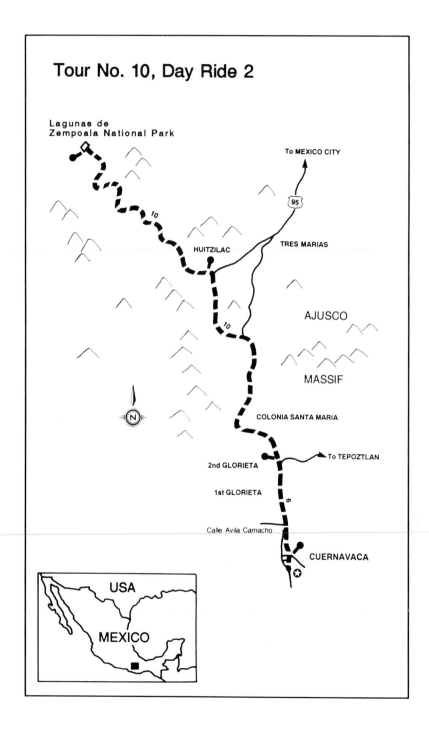

Tour No. 10, Day Ride 2

Lagunas de
Zempoala National Park

To MEXICO CITY

95

TRES MARIAS

10

HUITZILAC

10

AJUSCO

MASSIF

N

COLONIA SANTA MARIA

To TEPOZTLAN

2nd GLORIETA

1st GLORIETA

9

Calle Avila Camacho

CUERNAVACA

USA

MEXICO

Above Huitzilac, dense forest begins. A notch in the ridge indicates where the road passes from view. Take heart, friend, it's still uphill but you've vanquished the worst of it. Only 10k remain, a distance that seems shorter now that the pavement is again smooth. At k 24, the climb ends and the 2k which follow are sheer exhilaration, spelled a-c-c-e-l-e-r-a-t-i-o-n.

The Lagunas de Zempoala nearly are divine. The soaring crags, towering trees and cold trout-filled lakes are so unexpected they seem to belong in another country. Anyone accustomed to hiking above timberline or camping near a cold stony tarn will feel right at home.

The first of the pristine *lagunas* is a shimmering gem. Fishermen step gingerly between the rocks and shrubs along the lake shore. Sterling reflections of encircling peaks appear rippled on the water's surface, obscuring the fish which circulate in the clear green depths.

Camping has yet to really catch on in Mexico and only a few tents dot the shoreline. Facilities are nonexistent; bring anything you may need for the night. No directions are necessary for the return to Cuernavaca . . . brake pads, maybe, directions, no.

ROADNOTES

Kilometer 0	Plaza. Start by climbing Calle Jose Maria Morelos.
5	*Glorieta,* a traffic circle. Military base, Zapata statue.
7	Colonia Santa Maria, an expensive suburb.
11	Road briefly levels.
12	Signed left turn onto old road to Huitzilac. Start climbing steeply.
16	Huitzilac. Good village to rest in. Marketplace, *liquado* stand on the plaza.
17	Worst part of climb ends.
24	Top.
26	Entrance to Park. No services.

CUERNAVACA TO MALINALCO

ROUTE: Cuernavaca—Mexicapa—Ahuehuete—Malinalco.
DISTANCE: 63k (one way).
RIDING TIME: 6–8 hours.
DIFFICULTY: Difficult to very difficult. Mountainous, with 16k of unpaved road. Mountain bikes recommended.
BEST TIME: Year-round.
ATTRACTIONS: A challenging ride through gorgeous scenery. Aztec ruins.

Despite its difficulty, the ride to Malinalco rates high among our favorite overnight trips. A forgotten, dilapidated road, at times only a dirt track, transects several deep valleys in Morelos before emerging onto the mountainous slopes of Mexico State. The scenery is absolutely breathtaking, in every respect equal to the climb. But shifting vistas are only part of the pleasure. In Ahuehuete, the route crosses paths with devotees of the patron saint El Senor de Chalma. An uncommonly light-hearted pilgrimmage, everyone, including stray cyclists, is invited to dance. The day concludes in Malinalco, a lovely town shaded by ancient Aztec ruins.

Directions for this tour are trickier than most since this route is not on many maps. A good chunk of the riding is offroad where, admittedly, it can be unnerving to roam. With neither street signs nor people for guidance, even language skills become irrelevant. But don't sweat it, there's almost no place to go astray between Cuernavaca and Chalma.

The toughest part is getting out of Cuernavaca. From the main plaza head north on Av. Morelos. Go 2k, and turn left at the second Pemex station onto Calle Avila Camacho. There is a "Y" in the road at 2.8k. Bear left, downhill. Cross a creek, turn right and begin following signs for Col. del Bosque and Campamento Lomas Pinar. (At this same crossing a left turn leads to Salto de San Anton, an impressive waterfall. It's worth a visit, but not this day. There's plenty on the agenda already).

Now the climbing starts. The exclusive suburb of Col. del Bosque marks the top of the grade. Sterile, modern ranch-style homes

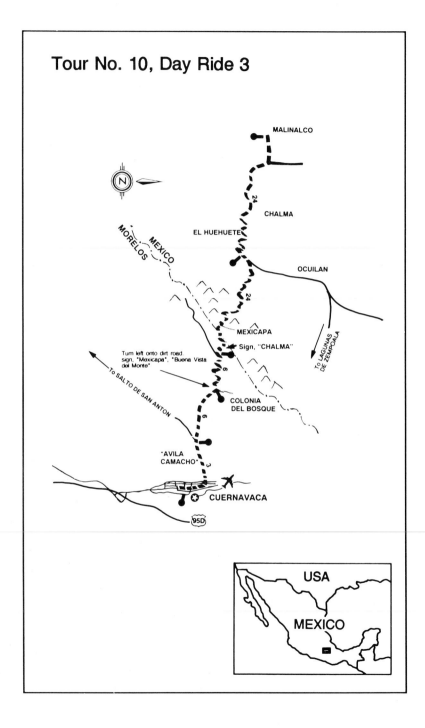

Tour No. 10, Day Ride 3

MALINALCO

24

CHALMA

EL HUEHUETE

MORELOS

MEXICO

OCUILAN

24

To LAGUNAS DE ZEMPOALA

MEXICAPA

Sign, "CHALMA"

Turn left onto dirt road.
sign, "Mexicapa", "Buena Vista
del Monte"

6

To SALTO DE SAN ANTON

COLONIA
DEL BOSQUE

6

"AVILA
CAMACHO"

3

CUERNAVACA

95D

USA

MEXICO

are conspicuous newcomers to the plateau. On the lawn of the tennis club an old *campesino* scurries, machete dangling from his belt, as he repositions a lawn sprinkler. Better homes and gardens, Mexican style.

The road splits at k 9. No signs indicate what lies in any direction. Go left, following the pavement down, into a deep ravine. One hundred feet away, carefully concealed from the intersection where it might do some good, a sign indicates the way to Mexicapa and Buena Vista del Monte.

In case you're wondering, this is only the warm-up—where the tough get going. Several ravines lie ahead, with a little gain in altitude each time you top the far side. The pavement deteriorates, the shoulder becomes ratty, the centerline disappears. Velvety green moss clings to shady walls. Water drips through the pungent vegetation, and the rush of a stream mingles with breezes scudding through the pines. The pavement continues to dwindle, terminates altogether at k 14, and is replaced by a dirt track which extends to the top of the grade. It's so smooth the pavement is hardly missed at first. At k 15 a sign for Chalma miraculously appears in the middle of nowhere. The road veers right, penetrates a huge roadcut and begins a long rough descent into the small, nondescript village of Mexicapa. A tiny cabin next to the school sells warm sodas. Yum yum.

On the climb out of Mexicapa a bed of melon-sized cobbles is all that suggests a road. Thankfully, the execrable surface doesn't last long and soon turns to well-maintained gravel, presumably for the benefit of logging trucks. The buzz of chainsaws echoes in the distance. At the climb's apex a solitary refreshment stand beckons. Time to guzzle up.

Now the road is sinuous but remains level. Time and kilometers fly by and, when the pavement resumes at k 30, the going becomes still easier. The nearly flat terrain is a relief but the sight of a government tree nursery at the forest's edge is even more welcome. Acres of shiny seedlings bristle in the sun, offering hope that enlightened self-interest will save this forest from a Chiapas-style fate.

The level land results in a quick transition from forest to farm. Abundant rain and rich volcanic soil have blessed Mexico State, making it one of the nation's great agricultural producers. The road slices between cultivated fields. Volcanic craters rise like atolls from the undulating waves of grain.

At k 39 the pavement merges with a two-lane road. Vehicles stage a comeback but the gradient is steep and cyclists easily keep pace. Watch for speed bumps in Sta. Clara. With nary a turn of the crank the sweeping descent continues into a valley rimmed by the same strange lava cliffs that make Tepoztlan (Day Ride #1) so unusual.

Ahuehuete

Still heading downhill, the road swings through Ahuehuete, k 45, where a group of food stalls operate in the shade of the town's namesake—an enormous ahuehuete tree. Sizzling *comals,* metal griddles, turn out *empanadas* and a vegetarian hash to beat the band. Well, sort of. The band, across the street and up a flight of stairs, is playing an old fashioned country waltz. People dance the "Ahuehuete Shuffle" to the accompaniment of fiddle and guitar while Polaroid photographers capture the moment.

Weekends, Ahuehuete explodes with festivity when the followers of the saint called El Senor de Chalma gather to make the 10k trek to the saint's sanctuary. As people arrive in town, old women with armloads of brilliant flowers swarm to greet them, urging the purchase of bouquets and the woven floral tiaras stacked like bracelets on their skinny arms.

Straggling groups of pilgrims escort your exit from Ahuehuete. The long descent continues all the way to Chalma, set in a steep-sided valley surrounded by high peaks. This once-beautiful village has become cluttered and dirty. There are several funky *casas de huespedes* or guesthouses, but we don't recommend them. Stay only if darkness overtakes you.

In Chalma, a sign indicates a left turn for Malinalco. Ignore it and continue on the road you are on, downhill all the way. At k 54 the road bellies out onto the valley floor, and at k 60 there is a signed left turn for Malinalco.

Near the entrance to the town of Malinalco a road sign depicts a fish chasing a hook, the international trout farm insignia. But at **Las Truchas** they do the fishing for you. Trout costs 10,000p per kilo, and you can get the catch cooked to suit for an additional 2,000p.

A dining alternative is the wonderful **Los Arcos** restaurant, in town, one block from the plaza. Lodging is almost as uncompli-cated, with a *posada familiar* next to the open air market. It's clean and pleasant. The only other budget hotel is the **Santa Monica,** an unknown quantity to us.

There is one other lodging choice in the neighborhood, **El Pa-raiso** campground. On the approach to town look for a sign which depicts a pyramid. El Paraiso is located at the foot of the trail to the Malinalco ruins. It's a good place to leave your gear while making the climb to the site, and a good place to spend the night. It's clean and they even have a swimming pool.

Malinalco and Tepoztlan

Both Malinalco and Tepoztlan are modern towns surrounded by remarkable cliffs which harbor ancient cities. But there the simi-larity ends. Tepoztlan's cliffs are higher, rougher and almost op-pressive in their proximity, while Malinalco's mountains do not intimidate. The ruins themselves are capitivating and the site, accessible. This Aztec city is probably best known for the Temple of Initiation, one of the largest monolithic structures in the world. The phenomenal building, including decorative details, was carved from a gargantuan slab of rock. Spread a picnic lunch across the temple steps, lean back against a ceremonial altar and stare into the past.

If returning to Cuernavaca by bus, the schedule from Malinalco is irregular and indirect. Connections are easier in Chalma, where a collection of rickety busses, known locally as the *ranas verdes,* the green frogs, depart throughout the afternoon. Direct service stops at 6:00 p.m. which gets into transfer woes at Sta. Marta. Try to time it so you catch the ride from Chalma.

ROADNOTES

Kilometer 0	Main plaza. Begin by climbing Av. Morelos.
2	At the second Pemex on Av. Morelos turn left onto Calle Avila Camacho.
2.8	Bear left at the "Y," downhill.
3	Cross a narrow creek and turn right. Begin a 5k climb. A left at the bridge leads to **El Salto de San Anton,** an impressive waterfall.
8	Col. del Bosque, an exclusive suburb.
8.8	Turn left onto an old paved road that enters a deep ravine.
9.5	Begin 1k climb.
10.5	Briefly emerge at the ravine edge only to descend again. Pavement deteriorates.
14	Pavement terminates. Dirt for the next 16k.
15	A roadsign says "Chalma." Turn right and begin long ragged drop to Mexicapa.
17.5	Mexicapa. Warm *refrescos* sold at shack adjacent the school. Begin 11k climb.
28.5	Hilltop.
30.5	Pavement resumes.
39	Junction with a busier road. Start down.
45	Ahuehuete, gathering place for the light-hearted pilgrimage to the sanctuary of El Senor de Chalma. Good stall food.
50	Chalma. Full service. Go straight at the left turn sign for Malinalco.
54	End downhill.
60	Signed left turn for Malinalco.
63	Malinalco.
	Posada familiar next to the market. Clean, comfortable rooms, 8,000p/single.
	Las Truchas trout farm and restaurant.
	Los Arcos, on Calle Guerrero, serves a good, inexpensive *comida corrida.*

INTRODUCTION
TO WEST
CENTRAL MEXICO

For our purposes, West Central Mexico is defined as the region from Pto. Vallarta to Acapulco, inland to Tasco, and north to Barranca del Cobre. It is characterized by wide geographic and climatic diversity, modern cities and preserved colonial architecture, dense population centers and boondocks. Indeed, more than anywhere else in Mexico, the tours included in this section present a smorgasbord of what the country has to offer.

And just what is that? One word can be used to describe what awaits you: mountains. No matter what direction you head in, they are never far away. Yet the characteristics of these mountains vary, at times plunging straight into the Pacific's waters, elsewhere pocked by volcanoes and snowcapped peaks, sometimes spreading into vast high altitude plateaus. Huge lakes, manmade reservoirs, hot springs, geysers, caves, and the migratory havens of the monarch butterfly create a diversity of natural phenomena that is tough to match.

For those who enjoy riding waves or basking on the seashore, Mex 200, a taxing and solitudinous road, connects the resorts and hidden beaches of Tour #15, the Costa Grande. But your efforts are rewarded with incomparable views from spectacular headlands, with great seafood, internationally famous vacation spots, and a terrific sense of accomplishment.

Tour #14, The Bahio, is a treat for history buffs. A moderate to difficult ride, the route traces the earliest battles of the War of Independence from its birth in Dolores Hidalgo to the site of the first great victory, in Guanajuato. Guadalajara, Morelia, and Tasco, colonial cities whose architectural heritage has been painstakingly saved, enjoy the temperate effects of higher elevations. They offer amenities and urban excitement which help to round out and balance the rigor and, perhaps, loneliness of the miles covered in Tours #12 and #13.

As elsewhere in Mexico, the countryside is dotted with small towns and villages for whom modernization and cultural integration have come slowly. The duality with city life is fascinating. While most people are friendly, if not downright cordial, machismo can sometimes present a problem. Women are advised to dress conservatively beyond the limits of popular beach resorts, and may have some trouble anyway.

Your own bravado will be met by the tough climbs which await you. These rides have been selected not just for their exciting cities and natural wonders, but for the extremely challenging terrain that connects them. For those who like to play hard and to ride even harder, West Central Mexico offers a lot of both.

THE PLEASURE OF THE SIERRA MADRE

ROUTE: Guadalajara/Lake Chapala—Mazamitla—Zamora—Zacapu—Uruapan—Patzcuaro—Morelia.
DISTANCE: 470 k.
RIDING TIME: 6 days.
DIFFICULTY: Moderately difficult.
TERRAIN: About 60% mountains, high plateaus and lakeside rides.
BEST TIME: Year-round.
ATTRACTIONS: Cycling in central Mexico offers rewards commensurate with the challenge. Purepecha Indian towns, ruins, and Paricutin volcano add variety to the beauty of the lake country.

The route from Lake Chapala to Morelia, in continuation with Tour #13 from Morelia to Tasco, creates one of the most satisfying grand tours in Mexico. The countryside you pass through, long on solitude and short on human habitation, is extraordinary in its barren beauty and ruggedness. At the point where you've had all you can stand of the bucolic serenity, a large, busy town appears to fortify you once again.

Wonderful Guadalajara, Mexico's second largest city, is the obvious starting point for this tour. It is a huge, modern, sprawling megalopolis which, despite urban renewal, has managed to retain much of the architectural heritage of its colonial past. The enormous and lovely Plaza de la Liberacion is dominated by the cathedral, built between 1558 and 1616.

Guadalajara is the traditional home of mariachi music. By late afternoon musicians in tight fitting sequined outfits take to the streets, the sound of their lively music playing against the din of urban life. Nearby, one of the country's largest covered bazaars sells an accumulation of items you will be hard-pressed to find elsewhere in Mexico. Now is the time to buy the cycle supplies you forgot to bring, or restock if you've been on the road awhile.

Guadalajara, however, does not lend itself to cycling. The traffic congestion is too intense and life-threatening. Once you have ne-

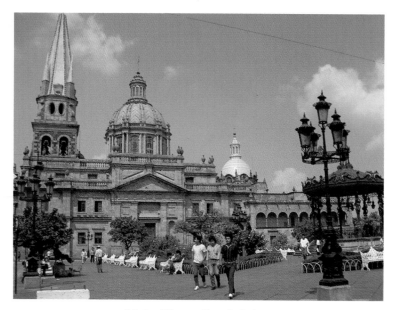

Main Plaza, Guadalajara

gotiated your way to the centro from either the airport or the
large bus terminal located at the city's outskirts, stash your bike
in a hotel room until you are ready to leave this exciting place.
Then, a second-class bus from the old Camionera Central on
Calle 5 Febrero can take you to the town of Chapala, where your
riding begins.

Lake Chapala, the largest natural lake in Mexico, measures approximately 65 miles by 20. The waters of its life support system,
the Lerma River, have been diverted to answer the needs of Guadalajara. Environmental irresponsibility has been exacerbated
by drought and the shrinking lake now suffers a troubled and
threatened ecology. Wide expanses of the lakebed lie exposed,
cracked and drying. Hyacinths clog the murky receding shoreline.

The road which circles Lake Chapala is flat, but as you head west
large mountains draw near. Tucked into the foothills are expensive homes, the brick and bougainvillaea fortresses of the expa-
triate community. Summer homes and weekend retreats are
visible in all of the towns and way stations along the lake's
northern edge.

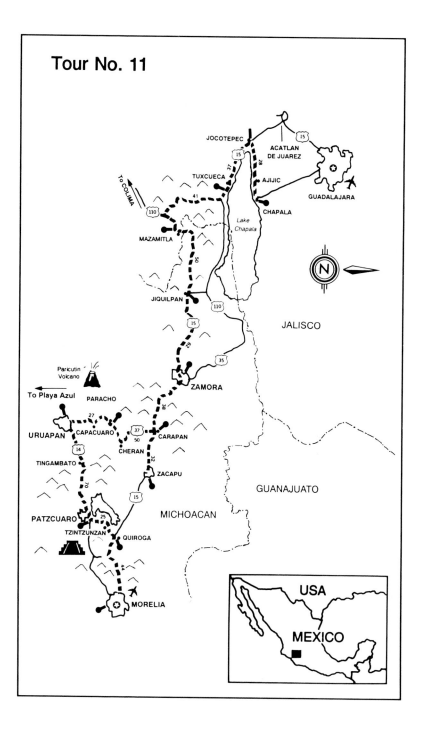

Tour No. 11

JOCOTEPEC
ACATLAN DE JUAREZ
15
15
37
TUXCUECA
AJIJIC
28
GUADALAJARA
CHAPALA
To COLIMA
110
41
Lake Chapala
MAZAMITLA
50
JIQUILPAN
110
15
JALISCO
35
ZAMORA
Paricutín Volcano
To Playa Azul
PARACHO
38
27
URUAPAN
CAPACUARO
37
CARAPAN
50
TINGAMBATO
14
CHERAN
32
70
ZACAPU
15
PATZCUARO
25
MICHOACAN
GUANAJUATO
TZINTZUNZAN
QUIROGA
44
MORELIA

USA
MEXICO

Unless you're a fitness fascist, determined to make Mazamitla in one haul, we recommend that you opt for an easy first day. By going no further than Jocotepec (28k) you will be able to soak at the hot springs, enjoy the lake shore, and visit two of its most interesting communities.

You've barely started when you roll into the first of these, Ajijic, a pretty town with a reputation as an artists' retreat. There are few tourists here and most of the foreigners one sees are residents. It is a town of white-washed buildings and cobblestoned streets, a movie theatre, and a couple of galleries. At the Posada Ajijic, down a long bumpy street leading to the lake and a worthy stop if your schedule permits it, you can watch the sun set and linger over good, cheap drinks.

A few more kilometers up the road are some restaurants, all bunched together and all serving the same thing: whitefish. If you've been waiting to try Lake Chapala's most famous resident this is a good chance to order up.

After lunch you can digest your meal at the hot springs of San Juan Cosala. The area is developed with everything from private condominiums overlooking private pools to a clean, well-kept public facility. Five different pools with water of varying temperatures are available at the public resort, as well as the services of a masseuse. Adjacent to the hottest pool a sign boldly proclaims the ailments the medicinal water will heal. We don't guarantee it will cure your rheumatism, but you are assured several hours of soothing bathing.

Jocotepec is the westernmost town on Lake Chapala and, as you approach, there are progressively fewer vacation homes stashed in the bushes. Amazingly, given its proximity, Jocotepec is almost unaffected by the north shore's tourist boom. The plaza faces a busy market and is an excellent place to try some regional cuisine. One side is lined with stalls which sell *biria*, a tasty goat stew. In another corner a group of women skillfully shuck *pitume*, a thorny cactus fruit. Fist-sized, they ripen into deeply saturated colors of purple and rose. When ripe they pop out of their shells like lichee nuts. They're mildly sweet, refreshingly juicy, and gorgeous.

There are a few hotels and restaurants in Jocotepec but, unless you're spending the night, there's no time to tarry. Mazamitla is still a long way off and there is some tough riding ahead. Be sure to fill your water bottles before leaving town.

As you leave Jocotepec, you'll round the lake and double-back east. Whatever situation you faced with the wind will now reverse itself. Towns and services are few and far between. At k 65 you reach Tuxcueca, a village that marks the turn for Mazamitla. Sodas and junk food are available but if your strength is ebbing or it's late in the day, the junction is a good place to catch one of the frequent busses to Mazamitla.

At this point you head south and Lake Chapala recedes in the distance. The views become more notable and as you labor to the top of a difficult 6k climb the waters of El Refugio lake beckon invitingly. The summit presents a dramatic but demoralizing view of the mountains ahead. The road dips and climbs as you traverse the mountainside, bypassing the village of Concepcion de Buenos Aires. The Pemex station marks the end of the ascent and now it's rock and roll for the remaining 20k to Mazamitla. Long shadows penetrate the vibrant golden light. The cedar hillsides are utterly stunning in their sad, soft beauty.

Mazamitla

We counted five hotels in and around Mazamitla, and, at 16,000p (US$7.50) their prices were among the highest in the region. They were also a bit classier than usual. The town appears to be well-known to a Mexican clientele and virtually unknown to the foreign trade, leaving us pleasantly surprised to find the crisp atmosphere of this mountain retreat, only a few short hours from Guadalajara, so unaffected.

Erratic dirt streets, the color of fading vermillion, lead to the half-paved town center. The plaza is dominated by a most bizarre structure of puzzling heritage. Close examination reveals it to be a church, a fine example in fact of the Country Austrian/Chinese Pagoda school of architecture. Late classic we believe. At dusk young lovers sit on park benches, wrapped in its protective shadows, kissing and holding hands.

Dining in Mexico presents an ongoing challenge for vegetarians, particularly after you've tired of eggs, beans, and tortillas. Mazamitla is no exception. While long on rustic charm the town is hurting for decent restaurants. What does exist, while of the stand-up variety, is fantastic. One block from the plaza, on a corner open to the street, exuding the frenetic ambiance of only the most crowded bus terminals—yet not a bus in sight—is a building crammed with food concessions. Heeding the call of sizzling carnitas, Eric was drawn inside. The aroma of fried chicken diverted his attention when suddenly a bubbling cauldron of *menudo* overtook him. No one intervened. He paused from the grease stained feeding frenzy long enough to demonstrate his customary concern for Ricky. "Find any beans, yet?"

Mazamitla nights are undeniably chilly and offer a rare chance to snuggle under heavy blankets before returning to the warmth of lower altitudes. There's no point in rising early for a culinary adventure. Breakfast in Mazamitla is a lost cause. Instead, power up with a *liquado* from the outdoor juice stand near the plaza. It's only 10k, largely downhill, to San Jose de Gracia, a sweet town just over the Michoacan state line. At any of its several cafes you can enjoy a meal and great parting views of the Jalisco piedmont.

After San Jose, 40k of rangeland and volcanic mountains stretch into the distance. Traffic is very light but refreshment stops are few so be sure to carry plenty of water.

There is a steep 5k drop into Jiquilpan and the altitude change, about 1900 feet, is immediately felt. It's a hot little town. The Jiquilpan library is the little known repository of one of Orozco's masterworks, an allegorical mural depicting the history of the Republic. Despite the indication of hot springs on the Pemex map, there are only *balnearios* in town, swimming pools which are open to the public. If you're hungry, a bustling market operates in the shade of makeshift awnings and, if you are inclined to spend the night, there are several acceptable hotels. Otherwise, push on the remaining 63k to Zamora.

Michoacan is one of the agriculturally richest states in the Republic and around Jiquilpan there is a shift from rangeland to irrigated fields. Yet the towns along this route don't seem to have profited from the encircling productivity. At Emiliano Zapata a tall chimney rises out of the ruins of a mill at the entrance to town and a decrepit Palacio Municipal marks the center of this once thriving settlement. Via Mar would be almost totally nondescript, were it not for a beautiful church steeple towering over the disarrayed hovels, in stark contrast to the verdant, orderly fields.

Estacion Moreno is hardly more than a grain depot. It marks the end of a shallow valley and here, a good shade tree provides a resting place before you begin the sun-baked 3k climb to the top of the divide. At the pass it is an easy 28k to Zamora, nearly half downhill. On the way there are some good restaurants in Santiago Tanga Mandapio. Jacona, a large town 5k before Zamora, may provide better lodging than Zamora itself.

Zamora

Despite Zamora's urban advantages, such as restaurants, first-run movie theatres, and, reportedly, the best bike shop in the state (**Casa Moreno** on Calle Madero), it qualifies as a huge, noisy country town. It's an odd mix of neon-signed boutiques and dilapidated buildings, and retains precious little colonial charm. There is an exception, however, and it is a notable one.

The **Catedral Inconclusa,** begun sometime in the 1500's and never completed, is an arresting sight. Huge carved columns, unrestricted by a ceiling, reach heavenward and seemingly support the sky. Alcoves and reliquaries stand naked of adornment. Birds swoop overhead. The floor is littered with the remains of nestlings too young to fly. Outside, the church is surrounded by a spacious but quite barren yard. An old fountain projects from a stagnant pool of water. Yet the church is well-loved, and you will be one of many who come to visit.

Before continuing east you may want to make a detour to a noteworthy attraction 35k northwest of Zamora, the geyser **Ixtlan de los Hervores.** Situated in the middle of a pasture, the 94 ° C jet of water blasts nonstop about 60 feet into the air, then cools as it dramatically plunges into a tepid creek which transects the field. You can splash around in the muddy water, and probably there will be kids around who are doing just that, but frankly the swimming is less than inviting. Horses meander nearby, a goatherd directs his flock past you. It *is* quite visually impressive. Bring a picnic lunch. If you are not motivated to cycle the 70k round trip, the area is easily reached by busses bound for Guadalajara.

On leaving Zamora you merge with the main road between Guadalajara and Morelia. Traffic is moderately heavy, especially compared to what you have become used to, but the shoulder is wide and this is one of the best roads in Michoacan.

For the next 20 to 30k you roll up and down through shallow dish-shaped volcanic valleys. Neat basalt rock fences demarcate fields and line the road. At k 239 there is a restaurant and the Cabanas Manolo, with its inexpensive swimming pool. The road stretches into a beautiful lush valley and passes through pleasantly unmemorable towns whose major industry is the roadside sale of horrendously ugly pottery. Big stuff, like sequined garden planters. Hang onto your handlebars, the sight could knock you off your bike.

Back Into the Mountains

At k 254 you begin climbing and soon reach Carapan, a well-marked, busy, triangular intersection where busses and other traffic pass by in six directions. At this point you must decide whether to head south to Uruapan, or detour east to Zacapu, for the night. If you have elected to take the more direct northern route to Morelia, bypassing Uruapan and Patzcuaro altogether, Zacapu is the logical place to spend the night. There are numerous food stalls at the Carapan crossroad (and even a motel). If you are bound directly for Uruapan this is your last chance to chow down for the next tough 27k. Refreshments, too, will be limited.

At Carapan, the road to Zacapu turns into a long, staggered climb. You leave the irrigated fields behind and get back into rangeland and forested volcanic slopes. Fifteen and a half kilometers later an eagerly awaited road sign indicates the start of a mostly downhill run. Zacapu is an appealing town which offers such ammenities as inexpensive lodging, good food, and *real* coffee, a draw if ever there was one. Most of Mexico's coffee is exported and most of what is kept for domestic use is transformed and bottled as "instant."

Back at the Carapan intersection and heading for Uruapan, the road deteriorates markedly. You begin with a $3^{1}/_{2}$k climb, the first kilometer of which is particularly steep. Fields give way to forest. At the top, you can cool out with drinks at the tiny settlement of Morelos.

It's 17k from Carapan to Cheran over an incredibly lousy road which may necessitate letting a few pounds of pressure out of your tires to cushion the jarring shocks.

Purépecha Country

A modern green highway sign directs you to Cheran, the first of several Purépecha communities. Cheran offers a two-step crash course in social economics. Its populace is overwhelmingly Indian, and they are utterly poor. One still seems to equal the other in twentieth century Mexico. Even on market day, Sunday, when traffic clogs the streets and the town hops with activity, its poverty is evident.

On the far side of Cheran the road miraculously improves, just in time to enjoy the hellacious 5k plummet onto the plain, a real rip. You steam across the flats into Paracho, the guitar manufacturing capital of Mexico. Guitars are for sale in the candy store, the liquor store, the Pemex station. There are places to eat in Paracho, and a couple of hotels if you choose to spend the night, but the remaining 37k to Uruapan is mostly downhill.

Leaving Paracho you cruise the last of the high plain and descend 5k into another Purepecha town, Capacuaro. Colorfully-garbed Indian women prepare food in stands along the highway. The town is best known for good quality carved wood furniture. Headboards and dining room sets line both sides of the highway ready to be loaded onto trucks.

The 15k-long final descent into Uruapan begins a few kilometers outside of Capacuaro.

Uruapan

It is no coincidence that the country's most popular chain of refreshment stands chose to be called "La Michoacana." Throughout Mexico the name is synonymous with fruit and Uruapan is the distribution center for much of it. The highway at the edge of town appears to be one long loading dock. Traffic jams behind long-haul trucks as they take on loads of mango, melon and avocado for distant markets.

Sidestreets, overflowing with activity, tumble downhill beneath a fabric ceiling of jiffy-rigged bedsheets. A tangled web of guy lines and tent poles reach maliciously for your pedals. You weave carefully between shoppers and tables piled high with bluejeans and bootleg cassette tapes before arriving at a boisterous and cosmopolitan city center.

Within Uruapan's city limits is the **Parque Nacional Barranca del Cupatitzio.** Here, the headwaters of the Rio Cupatitzio burst from beneath the earth's mantel in a multi-pronged gush, flowing out along both natural and manmade channels. Paved pathways, waterfalls, swimming holes, and picnic areas intertwine beneath a canopy of trees and flowering bushes. It is an extraordinarily lovely riverine retreat from the surrounding urban chaos.

It is fortunate, indeed, that Uruapan is such a hospitable city. We highly recommend the sidetrip to the volcano Paricutin which will require spending an extra night.

The Birth of a Volcano

One of the world's youngest volcanoes, Paricutin sprang up suddenly in a farmer's cornfield in 1943. It erupted in February of that year, destroying the village of its namesake. Over the next nine years its lava flows engulfed the town of San Juan but, because of its slow incremental growth, both towns were evacuated without any loss of human life. Only one building remains standing and partially intact as a result of the molten encroachment: San Juan's church. In the back, a reliquary still exists and townspeople make pilgrimages to leave flowers and offerings of thanks that their lives were spared.

A visit to the volcano begins in the village of Anguahan, served by busses from Uruapan which continue on to Las Reyes. As you debark in Anguahan, shaken from bouncing down a long dirt road, you will be met by a group of village men who offer their services as guides to the volcano. A guide really is necessary. Prices are subject to barter. Typically, they begin at 20,000p. per horse including the guide and his steed, for the day. You can bargain from there. No matter how you slice it, it's a great deal.

The journey is about six hours and includes a stop, on the way back, at the devastated village of San Juan. Be sure to bring plenty of water and some juicy kinds of fruit. Long pants will help prevent chafing.

Expect your guide to accompany you no further than the cinder cone's base. After corralling the horses he'll point out some geologic features, such as fumaroles hot enough to heat a can of soup, and the shifting trail that leads to the crater's rim. The climb up is two steps forward, one step back. Irregular chunks of

Paricutin

black lava clink sharply as they slide beneath your steps. Finally reaching the volcano's lip, you feel a bit like the bear who went over the mountain; the inside is as barren and hardened as the shell. You are well advised not to climb down into the bowl. Paricutin is dormant, not extinct, and evidence of its vitality is all around you in the form of hot rocks and rising steam. Returning to the horses, down a cascading slope of fine volcanic sand, is some of the best fun ever, a slide ride through an igneous playland.

If you decide to go only as far as the village of San Juan, the trip can be made on foot and without the service of a guide. Finding your way through the maze of trails will not be easy but a good starting point is the *albergue,* the town's lone hotel, from whose balcony you can survey the volcano and surrounding countryside. Of course, you can also spend the night there but accommodations are dormitory style, expensive and pretty basic. An alternative is to rent a room in a private home, which your guide can help find. In either case, if you may want to spend the night, plan ahead and bring a sleeping bag. The last bus back to Uruapan comes by at *approximately* 7 p.m.

Leaving for Patzcuaro you again transit the fruit salad paradise that is Uruapan's perimeter. Thick wedges of watermelon and pineapple chill on cakes of ice. Stall after stall is heaped with a tropical rainbow of papaya, mango, and banana. Pannier capacity is the only constraint as you stock up and head for the hills.

Resume Climbing

As you leave town, much of the traffic veers south for Playa Azul, but you continue east on Mex 14. The road begins to climb . . . and climb . . . and climb, with a short respite coming after 12 long kilometers. There's a fast drop and then the work begins all over again with a more gradual climb to Tingambato. It's a little deceptive because when you reach town you think you've reached the peak and are tempted to scarf down a big meal at one of the truckstop cafes. But the toughest part of the ride is still ahead.

Well into an exhausting day you top a short rise and Lake Patzcuaro comes into view, dominated by the cone-shaped volcanic island of Janitzio. The island itself is overshadowed by an enormous statue of Jose Maria Morelos, one of the heroes of the War of Independence from Spain.

Patzcuaro—Almost

You coast down to the lake expecting to greet Patzcuaro and instead discover that the town proper is another 2.5k away—uphill. Oy! The climb is lined with cedars, each one systematically marred with political graffiti, and a clutter of tourist shops. It's pretty disheartening until you reach the inner city and then, what a gem it is! Patzcuaro has all of the colonial majesty of large cities such as Oaxaca and Morelia, but without the attendant sprawl. The beautiful plazas and stone boulevards have not been swallowed up by urban development and its market hums with vitality. Household items and farm tools, crafts, local produce, and food stalls all compete for space and shoppers. The entrance is blockaded with *comal* stands, the air heavy with the scent of crackling chicken and vegetables frying in these upside-down-sombrero-style metal cooking plates. Fresh *liquado* stalls elbow sitdown restaurants, which serve the region's unique and now familiar delicacy: whitefish.

Tarascan Indian communities ring the lake, each known for its respective craft. A wide variety of copper utensils, cookware and jewelry are available at the market in Patzcuaro. The island of Janitzio, the most frequented of the lake's several islands, makes no pretense, however, of being anything other than a tourist trap. A broad spiral cobblestone staircase extends from the island's base to the monument of Morelos, leading through a gauntlet of knicknack shops and restaurants. Inside the huge statue another staircase spirals to the head, the walls lined with murals depicting the hero's life.

The island of Janitizio is accessible by water taxis, called *lanchas,* from Patzcuaro's embarcadero. The 20-minute boat ride, walk to the statue, and lakeside lunch, while not exactly a must-see attraction, do make for a decidedly pleasant afternoon.

There are two routes between Patzcuaro and Morelia. The southern route through Tiripetio is direct, reasonably flat, and largely uninteresting. The longer route allows a visit to the ruins of Tzintzunzan and the town of Quiroga.

Recite Tzintzunzan's sibilant name and you can visualize its translation, "Flight of the Hummingbird." With a little luck you may see one hover near the flagstone fences which hold back the terraces of the ruined city. The massive retaining wall gives the site a fortress-like air, and commanding views from atop its ramparts encompass Lake Patzcuaro and the domain of the ancient Purepecha. The buildings at Tzintzunzan have been reconstructed and are well maintained, but there are no facilities nearby.

Only a few miles away on the northeastern tip of Lake Patzcuaro, Quiroga provides an abundance of restaurants and food stalls to feed the happy shoppers who flock there. Mass produced crockery, laquerware salad bowls, copper jewelry and miniature guitars which will never carry a tune, glut its thoroughfares. After lunch and a stroll it is time to press on to Morelia.

The road from Quiroga involves one long but very gradual climb to a mountain pass and takes you through consistently pretty countryside. The serenity ends, unfortunately, when you come to an extinct volcano whose slopes are being quarried for road construction aggregate. For the remaining 19k you will be accompanied by an endless stream of dump trucks. They seem fitting preparation for a return to urban life.

Morelia, Michoacan's Stately Capital

The exquisite colonial city of Morelia retains the dignified pace, civility, and European cafe society approach to life one associates with a bygone era. Tourists congregate within a few blocks of the main plaza but there are modern districts and shopping malls to visit too. Its markets, movie houses, theatres, museums, cultural events and nightlife may tempt you to settle in for a while. In addition, there are good language schools, inexpensive lodging, and terrific riding nearby.

Morelia is a wonderful place to recover from a demanding journey. For outstanding *botana* pedal over to Calle Garcia de Leon, to El Ultimo Tren and, one block away, El Club. Both places provide heaps of food for the price of a drink.

But best of all, for those of you who want something more than just beans, there are two excellent vegetarian restaurants!

ROADNOTES

WHAT'S AHEAD: We recommend taking a bus from Guadalajara's second class terminal to Chapala. Once you escape the traffic of the greater metropolitan area the countryside is uniformly accommodating. Roads are good, the terrain is challenging and services are reliable.

Kilometer 0	Chapala. Hotels, restaurants and one of the largest communities of American expatriates in Mexico.
9	Ajijic. Hotels and restaurants. Posada Ajijic serves cocktails nightly by the lake.
	Hotel Villa Flores, Colon #43—Double, 30,000p (w/ breakfast). A splurge. Beautiful estate converted to hotel by American owners.
15	Lakeside restaurants.
28	Jocotepec. Most active and pleasant of the Lake Chapala communities.
49	San Luis. Restaurants, store.
65	Tuxcueca. Junction for Mazamitla. Busses stop regularly. Store on corner.
73	False summit. Toughest 3k yet to come.
80	Concepcion de Buenos Aires. Few services.
86	Pemex station. Refrescos. Hills get easier.
96	La Tienda Nueva. Tiny town, refrescos. Begin climb to Mazamitla.
106	Mazamitla. Hotels, restaurants, chilly nights. Begin long climb.
	Posada Alpina, 1 block north of plaza. Double 16,000p. Very clean, firm beds, private baths in a beautiful and rustic lodge.
114	Cross Jalisco/Michoacan border.
116	Puerta de Michoacan restaurant. Pemex station.
116	San Jose de Gracia. Picturesque town with great views, restaurants. Turn left for Morelia at sign one block beyond plaza.
139	Andiamo. Refrescos.
145	Fresno. Refrescos.
156	Jiquilpan. Big bustling town. Large market, hotels, restaurants, *balnearios* (bathing spas).
	Hotel Palmira, Av. Lazaro Cardenas Sur #200. Single 14,400, double 18,000p. Clean rooms, firm mattresses, private baths.
158	At the "Liconsa" factory turn right for Zamora; there is no other sign.

160	"T" intersection. Left at sign for Zamora.
173	Emiliano Zapata. At end of long downhill. Few services.
177	Villamar. Pemex station, restaurant, store.
186	Estacion Moreno. Grain depot. Begin 3k climb.
199	Santiago Tangamandapio. Good restaurants.
205	Begin fast 5k downhill. The pavement is very oily; be careful.
215	Jacona. A small city. Possibly a better bet than Zamora for lodging. It couldn't be any worse.
218	Zamora. Very big, noisy city. Follow signs for Guadalajara and Morelia to get to *glorieta* and Mex 35.
	Posada Moreno, Hidalgo Sur #325. Double 15,000p. Clean but awful soft beds, common bath, supply your own lock.
220	Mex 35. Right turn.
226	Begin a gentle 3k climb.
233	Tanganzicuaro. Pemex station, restaurants, hotel. Shoulder disappears, traffic decreases.
239	Restaurant and Cabanas Manolo. Swimming pool.
242	**Restaurants Mendoza** and **Mi Ranchito.** Next 10k features string of small agricultural towns in a well-irrigated valley.
256	Carapan. After long gradual climb, road splits for Uruapan and Zacapu. Restaurants and hotel.
	La Hacienda Motel, at the intersection. Single 12,000p, double 15,000p. Clean, good mattresses, private baths.

DETOUR FOR ZACAPU ON MEX 35 (32.5k)

0	Carapan. Begin gradual climb of 1k.
14.5	Indian village. No services.
15.5	Begin downhill.
20.5	La Yesca. Refrescos. Road descends gradually.
31.5	Pemex station. Left turn for central district, 1k further.

257	End of steep 1k climb from Carapan intersection. Road continues up for another 9k.
266	Morelos. Refrescos. Road turns down through forest.
271	Descent ends. Road turns to rubble. Pavement in terrible condition through Cheran. Begin series of long climbs.
284	Cheran. Big Indian town. Busy market, lots of services.

	Farmacia San Jose rents rooms upstairs for the truly desperate—3,000p per person.
306	Paracho. Guitar making capital of Mexico. Restaurants and hotels.
	Hotel Hermelinda, Calle 20 de Noviembre #239. Single 15,000p, double 18,000p. Adequately clean, soft beds, private baths.
324	Capacuaro. Stores and cafes, handmade furniture.
328	Signed turn for Anguahan. Detour here for Paricutin volcano.
333	Uruapan. Any of the market-filled streets spilling downhill from the highway go to the central district. To exit town it's uphill to the highway, about 1k.
334	Mex 314. Produce stands line road for 1k.
338	Junction with Mex 37. Turn left for Patzcuaro. Begin 3k climb.
349	Begin 24k climb. Not as bad as it sounds.
363.5	False summit. Truckstop dining. Tasty roast pork *carnitas* at Amkaty. Not the best fuel for another 10k of climbing.
373	Begin 5k downhill.
378	Begin series of 2k climbs and descents.
393	Hilltop view yields first sight of Lake Patzcuaro.
400.5	Right turn for Patzcuaro's centro. Begin 2.5k climb. Wharf with boats to island of Janitzio is on your left.
403	Patzcuaro. Exit by returning to wharf, 2.5k descent.
	El Pozo Trailer Park, camping, km marker 20 en route to Morelia—5,000p per person.
	Hotel Patzcuaro, Ramos #9 one block west of the plaza. Singles w/o bath 8,000p. Marginally clean, beds vary, lock bike in lobby. The cheapest place in town.
405.5	Wharf area. Right turn for Morelia, the sign says Quiroga.
409	Road splits. The short way saves 8k, skips the mountains and is generally quicker, though less scenic than the long way. Instructions which follow are for the long route.
409	The route bears left for Quiroga and Tzintzunzan. Follows the Patzcuaro lake shore for next 8k.
418	Ruins of Tzintzunzan.
428	Quiroga. Bustling tourist town. Lots of facilities and crafts. Begin 7k climb.
438	Pto. El Tigre, atop long hill. *Carne asada* (barbecue) stand. Begin 10k downhill.

439	Detour for Capula, 1k. Cafe and stores. Lots of ceramics for sale.
453	Asphalt quarry. Lots of dumptrucks roundtrip from here to Morelia. Traffic is annoying.
469	*Glorieta.* Follow signs for "centro."
471	Morelia.

Hotel Central, Abasolo #282. Single 8,000p, double 10,000p. Very clean, fair beds, common baths. The best deal in the city center.

La Fuente restaurant, #493B Madero Ote., 1 block west of post office. Has a very filling 4,800p vegetarian *comida* daily.

Covinda Vegetariano Hindu, on the west side of the plaza. Watch for their sidewalk sign to appear at 1:15, mas o menos. Vegetarian *comida corrida* in a soothing environment for 3,500p.

¿QUIEN ES MAS MACHO?

ROUTE: Morelia—Los Azufres—Ciudad Hidalgo—Angangueo—San Jose Perua—Valle de Bravo—Ixtapan del Oro—Temascaltepec—Ixtapan de la Sal—Grutas de Cacahuamilpa—Tasco.
DISTANCE: 445 k.
RIDING TIME: 6 to 9 days.
DIFFICULTY: The most difficult. Best done on a mountain bike, but the critical section can be circumvented.
TERRAIN: 85% mountains, 15% hills.
BEST TIME: Year-round.
ATTRACTIONS: Hot springs, mineral baths and geysers, butterfly sanctuary, astounding caves, huge forests, challenging riding, cool summer weather, and shopping.

The rugged mountains of central Mexico and the sheer abundance of natural wonders on this route defy your ability to see them all. Awesome caves, hot springs which bubble and steam with geothermal activity, magnificent forests and one of nature's most spectacular faunal displays—the winter sanctuaries of the monarch butterfly—all compete for your time. In addition the region is replete with beautiful colonial towns and twentieth century recreational facilities. Good lodging at intermediary stops allows you to design a route which caters to your particular interests.

A good map of the state of Michoacan can be found at one of the concession stands around Morelia's main plaza (a city map is on the other side). It's worth the investment. There's some pretty obscure riding ahead and none of the other maps we reviewed had adequate area detail.

A Quick Transition to Rural Mexico

Morelia lies near the eastern edge of Michoacan's characteristic volcanic topography. Heading east on Mex 15, the southernmost of the three eastern exits from town, the road climbs easily to the rim of a wide shallow valley. Fields neatly delineated by fences of stacked igneous rock soon replace urban development and by the

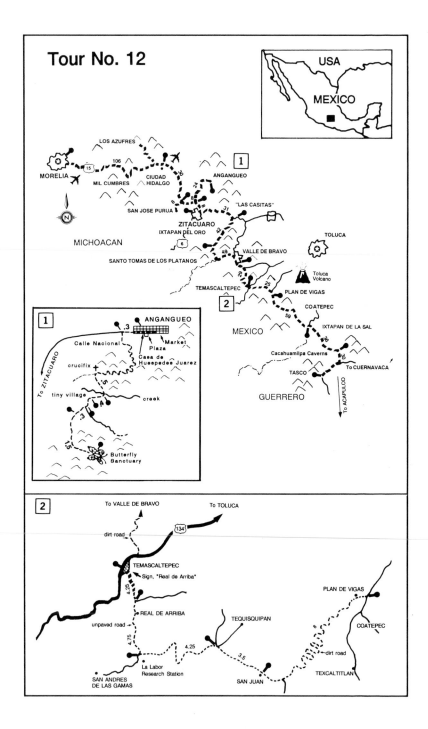

time you begin the down side of the climb all signs of Morelia have been replaced by rural Mexico. A major metropolitan center so nearby is already difficult to imagine.

Ahead, jagged mountains come into focus, their serrated profiles intimidating. But they are not terribly high and the serpentine route through them involves more endurance than arduous effort. The lovely tree-shaded road is extremely sinuous and most bus and automobile traffic choose an alternative northern route.

Refreshments can be found in two hamlets and, finally, at k 52 San Jose del Cumbre provides a welcome break from what seems an endless ascent. The road ahead is ample with commanding views but short on amenities so either eat lunch here or buy picnic supplies. After leaving San Jose you hardly have time to burn some calories before the start of a glorious surrender to gravity.

Judging by the map, Mil Cumbres—Thousand Peaks—suggests a fearsome haul so it is with considerable delight that you glide into it at the end of an 18k descent. This once busy way station has fallen into disuse with the completion of less torturous thoroughfares. A decaying concrete lookout hangs cliffside but the real attention grabber is the gutted shell of the old tourist hotel. A small cafe is all that remains now to serve the diminished flow of customers. From here the descent into Ciudad Hidalgo resembles the stepped passage of a ship through the locks of a canal.

Camping aficionados who started early enough in the day and have remaining stamina may choose a detour to Los Azufres. The turnoff is at k 100, a few kilometers before you reach Cd. Hidalgo. Los Azufres is an area of exceptional geothermal activity. Steam from at least fifty taps has been harnessed to drive turbines which generate electricity for Morelia. Huge clouds of snow white vapor billow upwards and the roar of escaping steam is deafening. But there are hundreds of untapped vents sprinkled across the hillsides, the fissures belching heated mist. It's quite a sight. Pools of water literally boil, splashing three and four feet high. At one large pond sulpherous muck churns under convective force. A peculiar sign warns that bathing is dangerous, implies that it is done, and states that no one should have to pay for it. Frankly, you'd have to be out of your mind to immerse yourself in the stinking, cloying, hot sludge, yet a group of shoreline crucifixes indicate that more than one person has done just that.

But if your body aches for restoration, don't despair. A thoroughly delightful bathing and overnight camping facility is available down the road. In fact, you will have passed it on your way to the seething mudhole.

The **Campamento Turistico Los Azufres,** built into the slope of a wide, shady ravine, is particularly beautiful. Warm thermal water cascades from one manmade pool to another, the sound almost musical in its multi-leveled descent. Small rustic cabins are tucked into the folds of the hillside and the vegetation, very lush, and kempt, creates one of the most pastoral hideaways in Mexico. There is a restaurant on the premises or you can cook out if you want to picnic, but plan to bring supplies with you as few are available.

The swimming facility next door to the Campamento Turistico has a sparsely stocked store or *tienda,* and even that may be an overstatement. Again, if you hope to eat, bring food. The swimming is no great shakes, at least compared to what's available on the other side of the fence, but it's very cheap to camp and you may have the whole place to yourself.

Cd. Hidalgo

Development of Los Azufre's geothermal resources and extensive logging have spurred the growth of nearby Cd. Hidalgo. Although it still appears as a dot on most maps, the city is surprisingly large. The main thoroughfare is choked with traffic but the rest of town remains slow-paced and unexceptional. Except on Sundays. Then the central plaza in this model of provinciality becomes crowded with families, food and curio concessions, and reverberates with the sound of music. Surrounding the park, vying for space with the more traditional, are two discos, a fancy upstairs soda fountain, and a bicycle repair shop with a video games section. It's quite eclectic, and due to, or maybe in spite of it all, this town seems to really like itself.

But spend only one night in Cd. Hidalgo and don't tarry. You've some decisions to make, for between here and Zitacuaro there are two wonderful detours.

Mil Cumbres, Michoacan

The Balneario in San Jose Perua

The turnoff for the first of these, the mineral pools at San Jose Perua, comes at k 136. The town is near the bottom of a long, steep hill. On the way you will pass a not-inexpensive restaurant, presumably the only one around, and on the far side of town you will pass the quite reasonable **Hotel La Mansion de Perua,** which may serve meals. The *balneario* is even further downhill and besides five mineral baths, there is a luxury hotel and restaurant. The entire complex is perched beneath towering stone cliffs on one side and overlooks a deep river gorge on the other. The grounds are beautifully tended but some of the shower facilities don't work and we disagreed about the cleanliness of the pools. Even so, it is an undeniably lovely place to wander, or sunbathe, and cool off with cold drinks.

If you are inclined to camp, permission is readily granted to spend the night at the litter-strewn gateway to the resort. Although aesthetically unappealing, it is free and safe. A guard is on duty 24 hours a day—and so is an annoying naked light bulb.

The Monarch Butterfly Preserve

If you like the 8k grunt from San Jose Perua back to the highway, you'll *love* the push to Angangueo. Located 24k from the San Felipe turnoff (which is the best opportunity to eat for a goodly distance), the detour begins with an intense 9k climb. The terrain opens into heavily ranched land and you cross a ridge which separates two towns, San Cristobal and Melchor Ocampo. Melchor Ocampo offers more in the way of food.

A dirt road which begins in Melchor Ocampo's plaza provides the easiest route to the monarch butterfly sanctuary in the mountains behind town. The road is bikeable and the route rather obvious. But if you so much as look perplexed someone in a nearby field will wave to indicate the proper direction.

It is also possible to visit the preserve from Angangueo by way of a fantastically steep and rutted dirt road. We biked it and it is nuts to do so. Remember to carry water. If choosing to walk, start early and allow about three hours. The directions are compli-

Monarch Butterfly Preserve, Angangueo

cated and confusing. On weekends during butterfly season, late October to mid-April, trucks ferry tourists to the preserve.

The roads from both Angangueo and Melchor Ocampo meet at the entrance to the *Sanctuario Rosario*. A small parking area and a row of rough wooden booths are at its base. Lock your bike here. Souvenirs are on sale and the open air *comedors* serve lunch, weekends only.

To insure protection of the butterfly habitat, tourists are required to hire a guide who will lead the way up the 2k trail to the largest concentration of monarchs. The groves shift periodically and the ground cover is scored by a maze of freshly cut paths. The guide points out the *asclepia* plants on which the females lay their eggs. The air grows increasingly thick with butterflies. Many are on the ground, not dead, but merely resting. At the grove's nucleus, tens of thousands of the golden-black insects weigh down the trees. Their sheer mass is staggering. In shafts of warm sunlight the beautiful creatures stretch their wings and fly aloft.

From Melchor Ocampo it is 7k to a road fork and the signed turn for Angangueo. You cross a single-lane bridge and railroad tracks which lead to an active sulfate mine. A herd of boxcars wait impatiently to be loaded with the semi-processed ore. The din of heavy equipment is partially drowned out by torrents of discolored, rusty water, a byproduct of the refinement process. The water overflows the open concrete gutters and the whole thing is a little disorienting. For a place you've come to in anticipation of extraordinary beauty this is an interesting but unappetizing welcome.

But lo! Perseverance pays. Behind Angangueo's industrial evil is a beautiful settlement. You'll need gumption to see it though. The last three kilometers of the climb rise straight through this one-street town. And it will also take a sense of humor, for your painstaking progress will be monitored from every doorstep.

Dining choices in Angangueo are limited and reasonable. Lodging is limited and unreasonable. The town's cheapest bed is 15,000p.

The solution to Angangueo's housing shortage is in nearby Zitacuaro, so you might consider making the trip to the sanctuary a dayride from there. Zitacuaro is one of the region's largest cities but it remains hard to categorize. It's big and busy, yet rural and small townish. It would not surprise you to see cowboys herding cattle down main street, odd only because main street resembles the LA Freeway more than the Cimmarron Trail. Although we found not a single tourist attraction, it is a fine place for aimless meandering, and there are a lot of good, everyday-type restaurants. The **Neveria Flores,** across the plaza from the Palacio Jardin Central, is a genuine soda fountain and ice cream parlor, and they serve real coffee.

On leaving Zitacuaro you may be pedaling for half an hour, suspecting yourself of having iron-poor blood, before realizing that you have indeed been going uphill. Wide valleys and distant forested peaks disguise the 12k grade, while nearer the curvy road winds through stands of selectively timbered pine. Small groups of Indian children appear randomly by the roadside, selling buckets of raspberries. Two towns, Macho de Agua (Tough Water?!) and Lengua de Vaca (Cow's Tongue), offer meager supplies and there is a restaurant in Lengua de Vaca which is closed on Sundays. What DO you suppose they serve?

The turnoff for Ixtapan del Oro does not appear on most maps but is clearly marked. A fast 4k beyond Lengua de Vaca, the signed turn comes mid-descent at a spot known to bus drivers as "Las Casitas." After a 1k climb over a protecting ridge, you begin alternations of descent and level pedaling, passing through pretty towns which are secondary to glorious countryside. The dense wooded land of Bosencheve Nacional Parque extends to Ixtapan del Oro.

Ixtapan del Oro is named for an abandoned gold mine but we found it to be a diamond in the rough (!). Nestled cozily into an appealing valley, its two billboards aggressively promote the local mineral springs, but few tourists heed the call. Clean, inexpensive rooms are often vacant in any of several *posada familiares.* There's not much in the way of restaurants in Ixtapan del Oro, but you can picnic and possibly camp at the lovely "El Salto" waterfall, which feeds the town's water supply. Nearby San Juan Xoconusco, is another monarch butterfly preserve.

The ride between Ixtapan del Oro and Valle de Bravo is not just scenically spectacular, it's exciting and tinged with the adventure of the unknown. Ahead of you lie 30k of one-lane mountain road, most of it above the tree line. The climbs are gentle and the riding is utterly peaceful. There are a few hamlets but no towns.

Forget cars. The road, seldom used since the closing of the mine, shows signs of decay, evidence of its adversarial relationship with nature.

San Nicholas, a good-sized town which is not on any map we saw, marks the end of the wilderness stretch and is a good place to stock up if you need groceries. There is a captivating view of a fertile green valley and Santo Tomas de los Platanos, perched on a cliff overlooking a large reservoir. It's high on our list of future detours.

Beyond San Nicholas the road widens to two lanes. Signs of civilization become frequent. You cross a deep ravine and more reservoirs become visible, a concrete culvert appears irregularly through the foliage, and miles of pipeline snake across the terrain, all part of an extensive system of aqueducts which connect the Nevado de Toluca watershed to Mexico City, nearly 100 miles away. The El Durazno pumping station and a jade green algae-choked body of water at the entrance to Colorines are further examples of man's determined effort to alter the beauty of this region.

The mountain town of Colorines is more busy than charming, and supplies are readily available. It's a good place to have an *agua de limon* before starting the last climb of the day, a gentle one, to the shores of another huge manmade lake.

Your ride culminates with a 13k lakeshore circuit into Valle de Bravo. This wonderful lakeshore resort, a hideaway for Mexico City's elite, has earned a reputation for good restaurants, hotels, summer homes, *balnearios* and aquatic sports. No menus in English here.

When you are satiated with R & R, a long hard climb greets your departure from the valley. The road is excellent and lightly trafficked. Eleven kilometers from Valle de Bravo, a sign marks the right turnoff for Temascaltepec. The road is dirt but don't be dissuaded; with the exception of a few rocky kilometers it is in excellent condition. Busses travel the road hourly. The last descent into "Temas" is punishing, however, and a touring bike is not recommended.

The beautiful whitewashed town of Temas is very much like Valle de Bravo but without any of the tourists. The plaza is meticulously manicured, and a light breeze rustles breathlessly through the long fronds of date palms. Streams rush down the narrow incline valley. The University of Mexico's Agricultural School is located in Temas, and students constitute a visible portion of the town's population. You'll frequently see them on the road flagging down rides back to the main campus in Toluca.

As you progress from Temas it feels as though you are removing layers of civilization. Parts of this road appear on at least three different maps, but nowhere is it shown in its entirety. The information of locals is suspect as well since sections of the road have been virtually forgotten and in a whole lifetime many people never travel more than a few miles from home. Perhaps your best source of information is one of the numerous missionaries out plying the backroads—but, like policemen, they're seldom around when you need them.

If you are not yet accustomed to cycling in Mexico, this route may seem intimidating. Besides the physical challenge of a long mountainous climb, there's the existential dread of unmarked roads, isolation, and lack of assurance that you're on the right trail. But it's a fair price to pay, for this is exactly the sort of adventure mountain bikes make possible.

Real de Arriba is a gorgeous yet oddly quiet town located in a secluded valley. Beyond it, you're in the boonies. You ascend through thick forests and there's no opportunity for a wrong turn until La Labor, an experimental agricultural research station run by the University. Here, the road you've been riding leads straight to the tiny settlement of San Andres de las Gamas, but you bear left and scramble up an eroded, rocky trail. Heavy rainfall and lack of conservation measures have left the road in a condition which can only be described as execrable. "La labor" really begins here.

It is this stretch that is largely responsible for the fact that this route is seldom used. Although sufficiently obvious, when Eric attempted to confirm directions with one of the station's scientists, he received a blank look—what road? And they were both standing on it!

After three torturous kilometers you reach a pass and the road splits in three directions. The temptation, of course, is to barrel ahead to the village of Tequisquipan, but don't do it. Rather, take the road less travelled, the one on your right, the one that goes . . . up. Soon you break out onto an inclined plateau that's been cleared for pasture. A few scattered homes and a primary school constitute the rancho of San Juan. By now you are close to the main highway and if you need directions, they'll be dependable. Your ascent continues in a series of switchbacks until you reach the highway and Plan de Vigas. A shack dispenses Victoria beer and freshbaked bread, good staples to celebrate your emergence from the hinterlands.

At this point, bike touring will have never seemed so easy. You're back on the pavement, positive of your direction, it's largely downhill, and groceries are easily had. It's 35k to Coatepec, orchard country, and center for the country's floriculture. Miles of cultivated flowers spread before you. Coatepec is a perfectly reasonable place to spend the night, but if you're not too wiped out, Ixtapan de la Sal is a mellow 23k further.

Ixtapan de la Sal is a low key bathing resort and there are numerous, inexpensive hotels available. An abundance of restaurant stalls in the market make it a good lunchtime stopover or supper spot. Nearby are some of the country's most magnificent and least heralded attractions, the caves of south central Mexico.

Cave Country

The gaping entrance to Grutas de Estrella greets you at the bottom of a bottomless flight of stairs. The tours are guided, but unfortunately the guide's shopworn monologue is calculated to rush you through the cloistered marvel in about half an hour. You'll want more time to appreciate this phenomenon of geologic secrecy, and you'll surely be in no hurry to mount the stairs of death which await you outside. At the top a refreshment stand serves the only drinks for miles around. The owner safeguarded our bikes while we were in the cave.

It's another 25k to Cacahuamilpa, in the course of which you cross the Guerrero-Morelos state line. This is arid country. The road balances on a ridge between two spectacular, deep canyons and distant mountains portend a difficult ride ahead. Most of this can be forestalled until the next day. The exception is a tough 1k climb that is followed by a screaming descent into Cacahuamilpa. The town, tenaciously clinging to the hillside, goes by in a blur. You screech to a halt at its base, the Grutas parking lot.

Unless you arrive very early in the day, the two hours required to see the caves of Cacahuamilpa will necessitate your spending the night. There are no accommodations and you'll have to do some asking around to find possible camping. But *this* cave is worth the inconvenience, for it turns out that the wonders of Estrella are only a prelude to the grandeur of the Grutas de Caca- huamilpa. Enormous, high-ceilinged chambers stagger one's comprehension, the rooms a subterranean labyrinth of curiosity and utter beauty. The 4k walk reveals only a part of the cave. An underground river, the Amacuzac, which appears above ground outside, has claimed the lives of numerous daredevil tubers who have found the passage blocked and themselves trapped by unex- pected rising water.

Not far from the cave's entrance a grave marks the remains of its first European explorer. According to legend, the man became lost and weak from hunger. His dog found the way out and barked, trying to get attention, but when no one came to help the canine returned to die with his master.

The last leg of the journey to Tasco involves a very tough climb. If you are coming from Coatepec and sightseeing along the way, it will make for an awfully long day. From the Cacahuamilpa cave entrance the road goes pretty much straight up a barren, sun- exposed mountain. At the top you maintain elevation while cut- ting through rolling hills, as the mountains you will soon have to enter draw closer. There's a busy cafe at the Highway 95 intersec- tion, a comforting respite before the final onslaught. Ahead of you is a punishing 10k climb and another 12k of tough ups and downs. About halfway up the long stretch there is a place to get beer, soda and junk food, and the last gasp is punctuated with villages, leaving no shortage of refreshment.

Tasco

When Tasco comes into view, it is on the the far side of the valley. The town spills across the mountainside, little houses clinging precariously to the slope. It's all very pretty and prosaic until it dawns on you that you're going to have to climb to reach it. Your approach is hailed by an ever-increasing glut of tourist shops, hawkers out on the road waving for you to come into their shops. Some lure you with complimentary drinks. Relax. This is what Tasco is all about, except in town you'll get the high pressure pitch without the drinks.

And a good stiff drink may be just what you need when you reach Tasco. The final 100 meters is a cardiac-arresting wheely-popper.

Tasco lies on the main road between Acapulco and Mexico City. It's a convenient stopover for the droves who make the drive and, unfortunately most of them do. Hardcore shoppers will find Tasco irresistible, a year-round pre-Christmas sale. Those with silver fever will discover everything from inexpensive trinkets to one-of-a-kind designer jewelry. Its commercial blitz can be hard to take, but even non-shoppers will find the city appealing. Twisting, narrow streets lead from the crowded center to painstakingly kept colonial homes. Before leaving Tasco, you owe yourself a walk through its backstreets. The town is so unique and beautiful it deserves to be appreciated beyond the tourist onslaught. There's a noticeable absence of neon and modern structures. In fact, the city fathers have done all they can, short of erecting a barricade, to preserve a semblance of Tasco's old world character.

There are lots of hotels and restaurants in Tasco, but staying within budget requires a bit of effort. We've stayed at the hotel

Tasco

Casa Grande, the least expensive place near the town center. We recommend that you ask for a room on the roof. A movie theater occupies the hotel's first floor, and the ticket window is in the Casa Grande's courtyard. In addition to the great views, you won't feel as though your trips to the toilet are being applauded.

At night, food vendors set up their carts along the Plazuela de San Juan, in front of the Casa Grande. While a hungry throng waits impatiently, *sope* ladies cook mouth-watering open-faced meat and cheese tortillas on charcoal heated stoves. Old women sell hefty fruit tarts wrapped in corn husks, a substantial and cheap confection. *Pozole* (hominy soup) restaurants confined to side streets and second floor walk-ups serve the residential trade. A number of less expensive places can be found on Calle Miguel Hidalgo.

Whether or not your panniers load up with silver like the coffers of a Spanish galleon, consider taking a bus out of Tasco. If you're heading on to Acapulco the road is mountainous and heavily trafficked. Likewise, if you're going to Cuernavaca and Mexico City. Bus service from either of Tasco's bus stations is virtually continuous.

ROADNOTES

WHAT'S AHEAD: In a word, mountains. Long climbs of moderate to steep gradient are the rule. Roadside refreshments are generally available every 10 to 12k. Traffic, outside of population centers, is light. Large tracts of national forest are the only places not utilized for farming and are often too steep for camping. Ask permission from local landowners before pitching a tent. Lodging is available in numerous towns along the way.

Kilometer 0	Morelia's plaza.
1	Monument to the Tarascan women. Pass aqueduct, follow signs for Mex 15 and "Mexico," which means Mexico City.
5	4-lane intersection. No lights or stop signs.
7	Top rim of Morelia's wide, bowl-shaped valley.
24	Las Peras. Bus stop, refrescos. Road becomes very sinuous, ascends gradually.
34	Las Trojes. Bus stop, refrescos. Climb becomes more pronounced.
52	San Jose de la Cumbre.
55	Top. Begin downhill.
72	Mil Cumbres. Restaurant, tienda at scenic overlook.
75	Town. Taco stands and corn fields.
81	Climb. 1.5k ascent breaks up your downhill glide.
90	The valley floor.
100	Signed turn for Los Azufres, 21k uphill. Thermal springs, camping. Bring food. **Campamento Turistico Los Azufres,** on main road. Bungalows and camping, day use, picnic grounds and swimming pools. Inexpensive.
106	Cd. Hidalgo, a moderate-sized city. Full range of services. Lots of traffic. Leaving city resume drop in elevation. **Hotel La Morenita,** Av. Juarez #10. Double 15,000p. Immaculately clean, soft mattress, private bathroom, hot water. Lock bikes downstairs.
114	Valley floor. End series of stepwise descents through progressively lower valleys. Las Grutas caves not yet open to the public.
119	Begin 2k climb. Foliage thins as you reach top of divide. Broad, green Tuxpan valley appears.
125	Tuxpan. Pleasant uncluttered town, surrounded by spectacular scenery. Restaurants, hotels and a Pemex station.

127   Begin 6k climb up cultivated hillside.
136   Signed turn for San Jose Perua.

DETOUR TO SAN JOSE PERUA (8k)
Completely downhill. Thermal springs, balneario facilities close at 6:00 p.m. Camping is possible in cluttered field near resort gate. Lodging in town is moderate to expensive. Restaurants at edge of town.
Hotel La Mansion de Perua, main street down the hill. Single 20,000p, double 22,000p. Very clean, firm mattress, private bath, hot water.

139   Pop stand. Ride through gentle hills cleared for ranching and farming.
144   Signed turn for Angangueo. Terrain becomes variable, more hills and timber.

DETOUR TO ANGANGUEO (24k)
0   Begin 9k grunt.
11.5 San Cristobal. Good sized town with a dearth of services.
14.5 Melchor Ocampo. More in the way of food and drink. The easiest route to the butterfly sanctuary begins here. Everyone knows the way. Begin gradual 6.5k climb to Angangueo.
21   Right turn for Angangueo. Begin steep 3k climb up town's main street.
Casa de Huespedes Juarez, main street two blocks before the plaza. During the week and off-season prices are negotiable. Probably the cheapest place around; adequately clean.
Hotel Albergue Don Bruno, Morelos #92. Single 32,000p, double 36,000p, suite for 2 w/fireplace 46,000p. Spic and span, great beds, private bath, hot water, fireplaces in suites. This might be the time to break down and splurge.

152   Begin 2k climb to Zitacuaro's center.
154   Zitacuaro. Large, busy city. Full range of services. Lots of facilities.
Hotel Mary, Av. Revoluccion. Single 9,000p, double 11,000p. Adequately clean, mushy beds, private bath, hot water.
155   Signed turn for Huetamo.

156	Join main highway, Mex 15.
159	Climb mellows. Broad slopes disguise fact that you are still climbing. Continue to do so for 18k.
166	Enter Bosencheve National Park. Road becomes more sinuous, shaded by pines, children sell berries along the roadside.
172	Macho de Agua. Refrescos, tienda. Road levels, follows mountain's contours through the forest.
180	Lengua de Vaca. Finally some towns with imaginative names. Restaurant (closed on Sundays) and store. Begin fast descent.
185	Las Casitas. Signed turn for Ixtapan del Oro. Cafes and stores at intersection. Bus stop.
186	Top a twisty little climb, road starts back down into farmland.
189	Signed turn for Sta. Teresa, and military firing range.
189	Signed turn for Ixtapan del Oro, right. Villa de Allende, left. Supplies in Villa de Allende and good ice cream parlor on plaza but no restaurants.
199	Begin 10k, largely downhill.
204	"T" intersection. Right for Ixtapan del Oro.
209	El Chirrimollo. Refrescos. Forest gives way to farmland. Resume descent. To reach San Juan Xoconusco, lesser known monarch butterfly preserve, follow signs.
211	Begin 2k freefall.
217	Ixtapan del Oro. Small and undisturbed retreat. *Turisoro* thermal springs, inexpensive cabanas, peace and quiet. Camping possible near waterfall. **Posada Familiar Portal Madero,** Libertad #47 next to Jardin. 5,000p per bed. Very clean, mattress okay, private bath, hot water.

WHAT'S AHEAD: Ixtapan del Oro to Ixtapan del Sal. This 161k stretch serves up big portions of unimproved mountain road. Much of it is not to be found on road maps. The two Ixtapans and Valle de Bravo all have loyal tourist followings, but only crazed cyclists arrive via *this* route. There are virtually no facilities. Those with an explorer's bent will discover some of the most challenging and enjoyable terrain we know of. If you're not on a mountain bike you should detour from Temascaltepec through Toluca.

217	Leave Ixtapan del Oro's plaza. Pass Turisoro thermal springs.

218	"T" intersection, turn left, no signs. Cross bridge and follow pavement downstream.
219	Las Minas. Abandoned mine.
222	Village. Refrescos. Begin 18k of winding road that clings to the ridge tops. Lots of up and down in equal parts. Pavement is a narrow ribbon of macadam probably built when the mine functioned, now only used by aqueduct maintenance workers.
234	San Nicholas. Road from Sto. Tomas de los Platanos comes in from below and merges with your uphill trajectory to Colorines. Restaurants and supplies.
253	Climb ends. Emerge onto retaining dam for Valle de Bravo reservoir.
261	Junction with main road to Toluca.
266	Valle de Bravo's plaza. Busy tourist town and weekend retreat for Mexico City's well-to-do. 0.1k past plaza are signs for Temascaltepec and Avandero. Follow them down steep cobbled hill to waterfront.
	Hotel Carracole, west side of plaza. There's no sign, you'll have to ask. A few doors from Hotel Mary and Hotel Blanquita. Double 15,000 p. Fairly clean, good mattress, private bath, hot water.
267	Church. A little bit further is Mex 15. Turn right and begin climbing. Steep.
273	Pemex station. End climb.
277	Right turn for Temascaltepec, signed. Good restaurant at intersection. Unpaved road to "Temas" is excellent quality and regularly transitted by busses from Valle de Bravo. There is one rocky section but otherwise it is manageable on all species of bike.
287	Start downhill. Surface gets rough.
291	Backwoods interchange. Refrescos on sale.
294	Emerge on main road, Mex 130.
	Bungalows Regiltepec, on highway 200 meters before town. Bungalows with kitchenettes, single 14,000p, double 19,000p. Very clean, firm mattresses, private bath, hot water, also pool and jacuzzi.
295	Temascaltepec. Gorgeous mountain town. All of Valle de Bravo's beauty without the weekenders. Two hotels, several restaurants. Beyond Temas *you will need a mountain bike.* Otherwise cycle Mex 130 to Toluca and Mex 55 to Ixtapan de la Sal. Because directions are critical between Temas and where the pavement re-

sumes in Plan de Viga, distances which follow represent kilometers from Temas as well as cumulative distance.

295.3 (.3k from Temas) Turn at southern edge of town, signed, for Real de Arriba. Cobbled surface turns to dirt as it climbs through a wet canyon.

299 (4.25k) Right turn for Real de Arriba, signed. Follow main street uphill through town where road again turns to dirt.

302 (7.25k) Climb lessens, road surface improves.

304 (9k) La Labor research station. Road turns left and deteriorates to stream bed quality, no sign. San Andres de las Gamas to the right. Some supplies are available.

307 (12k) Lookout over San Andres and valley. Climb lessens, road surface improves.

308 (13.25k) Intersection of rarely used dirt roads. Tequisquipan is visible below (straight) *but is not the way!* Turn right, no sign, and continue climbing. Traverse open pasture for 3.5k.

311.5 (16.75k) San Juan primary school. Unsigned intersection just beyond it; continue on main "road," no sign.

312 (17k) Climb steepens as you leave corn fields for pine forest.

319 (24k) Top of the long, sinuous, evergreen-scented climb.

320 Plan de Viga. Pavement begins!! Fresh bread and Victoria beer for sale at wooden huts. Hey, go wild. The ride to Ixtapan de la Sal is a breeze from here.

326 Turn left for Ixtapan de la Sal, signed. Begin 11k of rolling farm country.

332 Begin fast 7k descent.

339 Chiltepec. Orchard country. Deep canyon below town.

356 Coatepec. A great little town. Full service. Local center of floriculture (Estado de Mexico leads the Republic in flower production).

Posada del Tio Pablo, on plaza. 7,000p per person. Very clean, good mattresses, private bath, hot water in morning. Simple, folksy and very nice.

372 Top of 3k climb. Ixtapan de la Sal visible ahead.

379 Ixtapan de la Sal's plaza. Big town with lots of affordable lodging. Thermal springs and aquatic park on outskirts.

Casa de Huespedes Yuyi, Morelos #8. 7,000p per person. Clean, good beds, private baths. A deal.

Casa Guille, Calle Jose Maria Morelos. Double

	15,000p. Very clean, firm mattresses, private bath, hot water. Nice homey place.
380	Left turn at intersection with Mex 55, no sign. Downhill.
384	Balneario Tonatico. Continue downhill.
384.5	Tonatico village. Hard left at sign in the center. Another sign indicates where to turn for El Salto waterfall, camping. Road drops steeply beyond Tonatico, then begins climbing again.
388.5	El Terrero. Refrescos, stores (tiendas).
391	Grutas de Estrella, 2k detour. No services at intersection. Cafe at cave.
396	Estado de Mexico/Guerrero state line.
399	Piedras Negras. Road levels. Huge canyon system, Barranca Grande, on right. Sierra Grande del Sur dead ahead. Tasco is nestled in them.
407.5	Begin steep 1.5k climb.
409	Begin high-speed drop to Cacahuamilpa.
415	Junction with Tasco-Cuernavaca highway. Signs left for Grutas, then right for cave entrance. Parking fee applies to bikes. No lodging. Ask around for permission to camp.

DETOUR TO GRUTAS DE CACAHUAMILPA (.75k)
A must, no matter how it screws up your itinerary and leaves you scurrying for a place to camp. Tour requires two hours.

	Begin tough unshaded 2k climb into big hill country.
423	Signed intersection. Right for Tasco on Mex 95. Cafe at intersection. Start backbreaking 6k climb.
429	Ancuitlan. Cafes, interesting church but steep rocky streets make detour less than appealing. Roadside cafes.
433	Top. Start down.
436	Road follows mountain's contours for 4k passing through numerous small villages. Supplies plentiful.
440	Tasco comes into view across valley. Road starts down, leaving you with a 3k climb to finish. Tourist shops begin.
445	Tasco. Gas station marks right turn for center, no sign. Follow the street's flower petal mosaic as it leads you to the plaza, ending with a cardiac-stopping final 50 meters. **Hotel Casa Grande,** Plazuela de San Juan #7. Double

18,000p. Clean, firm mattresses, private bath, hot water. Movie theater shares building, ask for a room on the roof, up narrow spiral stairs. Leave bike in office.

THE BAHIO

ROUTE: San Miguel de Allende—Guanajuato—Dolores Hidalgo.
DISTANCE: 201k.
RIDING TIME: 2 or 3 days.
DIFFICULTY: Moderate, with one estimable climb.
TERRAIN: Rolling plateaus and 25% mountains.
BEST TIME: Year-round.
ATTRACTIONS: A route that commemorates the birth of the Mexican Republic and includes two stunning colonial cities, a bizarre museum, vineyards and hot springs.

The Bahio, a wide depression in Mexico's high central plateau, sits at an elevation perfect for year-round riding. It is an agriculturally fertile region of former mineral wealth, whose present-day riches lie in its tumultuous and meticulously preserved past. Once the cornerstone of Spain's New World mining empire, the Bahio became the birthplace of Mexico's War of Independence.

In 1810, Father Miguel Hidalgo's impassioned plea, the "Grito de Dolores," summoned the peasants to arms. They began a 13-day march from Dolores Hidalgo to Guanajuato which today, on chromemoly touring bikes, you can retrace in two. No fortified Spanish garrisons will slow your progress, but gorgeous mountains, vineyards, mineral springs and two marvelous colonial cities, may induce you to stretch your travels to three days.

Spanish oppression in Mexico continued well into the 1800's. It was a legislated, thorough and brutal process which permitted privileges to the Spanish that no *criollos,* full-blooded Spaniards *born in Mexico,* could ever aspire to. People of mixed blood had fewer rights still, and the Indians had none at all. When the collective needs of Mexico's native-born constituents finally boiled over, they did so with explosive force. Reforms went beyond simple independence from Spain; they abolished slavery and established universal suffrage as well.

Regular bus service makes it possible to begin this tour from any of the three major cities on the route, but San Miguel de Allende's proximity to Mexico City makes it our preferred starting point.

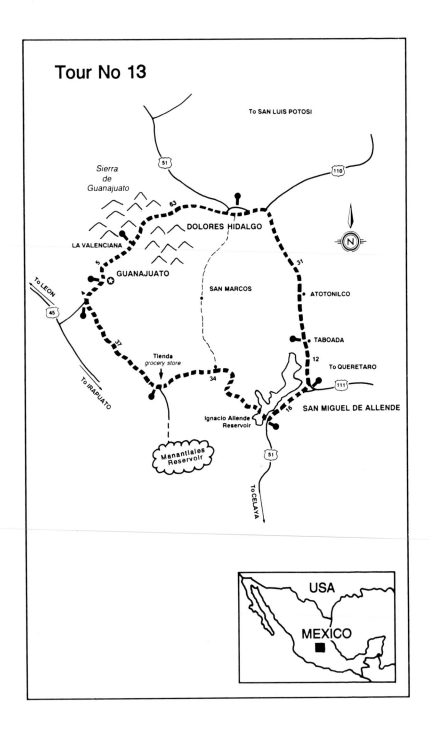

Tour No 13

To SAN LUIS POTOSI

Sierra
de
Guanajuato

DOLORES HIDALGO

LA VALENCIANA

GUANAJUATO

To LEON

SAN MARCOS

ATOTONILCO

TABOADA

To QUERETARO

Tienda
grocery store

To IRAPUATO

Manantiales
Reservoir

Ignacio Allende
Reservoir

SAN MIGUEL DE ALLENDE

To CELAYA

USA

MEXICO

San Miguel de Allende

There is enough happening in San Miguel to keep you side-tracked for several days, particularly if you're hard up for the sound of English. Because of its architectural beauty and in recognition of its role in history, San Miguel is considered a national treasure and tight laws have been enacted to restrict its growth. Beneath this facade of preservation, however, an unchecked foreign influx has brought wholesale cultural renovation. Several language schools, a small fine arts academy and a relatively low cost of living have induced many Americans to settle here. The community's reputation is mushrooming still and in the evenings, in the town's exquisite garden, you can hear foreigners carp about the rising prices of real estate which they themselves have driven up.

Straddle a bicycle and San Miguel ceases to be quaint. Picturesque designs of slate inlaid between the cobblestones create a cyclist's hell that can bounce you clear out of your toeclips. It's best to park your bike in a hotel and roam the town on foot.

San Miguel De Allende

Following the trail of the insurgents you leave for Guanajuato on what is now Mex 51. Ahead are small rolling hills and land so dry it seems to belie the region's reputation for agricultural fecundity. A low range of mountains appears on the approach to Comonfort but rather than crossing them the road curves at their base and bears west. They parallel your ride most of the way to Guanajuato.

There's a gradual loss of elevation as you drop to the Ignacio Allende Reservoir. On the far side of the dam a long gradual climb leads back to the previous elevation, a give and take typical of the next 30k. The countryside is sparsely populated and facilities are nonexistent until the road for another reservoir, Presa de Manantiales. At the intersection a tiny bunker-like store sells beer and junk food through barred windows, a somber note that suggests something inappropriately sinister out on these high, beautiful, windswept plains.

The mountains are closer now but despite this the riding becomes easier. Creeks spill down hillsides and the land is planted and irrigated. Two settlements appear. At La Sauceda there is a cafe with sit-down meals but the first bona fide restaurant doesn't appear until the outskirts of Yerba Buena, a town too close to your day's destination to warrant stopping. Low sandstone cliffs overhang the stream channel as it twists its way to Guanajuato. Glimpses of the city tantalize but should not command your attention: Traffic is fairly heavy and caution should be observed these last 7k.

The "Subterraneos"

Guanajuato, like Venice, Italy, is a city whose character is inextricably bound up in its thoroughfares. A maze of underground roadways, called *subterraneos,* burrows into the city's innards. The neatly tiled boulevard of your approach leads first under graceful stone arches, then between high walls, until at last you are totally enclosed by centuries-old masonry. You enter Guanajuato from the bottom up.

After the bone-rattling alleys of San Miguel, you'll appreciate riding on the finely fit stone parquet of Guanajuato's streets. But these *subterraneos* do more than relieve surface traffic and drain the rainfalls which periodically inundate the city. They create an aura of mystery that gives rise to legend and myth.

Signed stairwells lead to the city streets above. At "Jardin de la Paz," carry your bike up two short flights to Guanajuato's most popular plaza. A thick swatch of laurel trees fill the scimitar-shaped park which is bounded by cafes and the ornate Teatro Juarez.

Finding a room in Guanajuato can be a definite problem and the inexpensive ones fill up fast. Since the city's steep, narrow streets are an obstacle to bicycle exploration anyhow, it's best to locate a room and ditch your belongings ASAP. Even if your Spanish is lousy, consider making phone reservations from San Miguel. If you plan to be in Guanajuato during any of its festivals, you *must* have hotel reservations.

The most famous of Guanajuato's festivals is the "Cervantino," when visiting theatrical companies fill the town's two theatres and perform in the streets. At other times the city hosts international festivals which run the gamut from classical music, to film and puppetry.

By the time Father Hidalgo and Ignacio Allende marched into Guanajuato, the peasant army was more than 20,000 strong. With clergymen for military strategists and armed with little more than farming implements, the peasant army was badly outgunned by the Spanish. Even so, the Spaniards were forced to hole up in the "Alhondiga de las Granitas," a huge, fortress-like grainery. On a hillside overlooking the city's central plaza a massive red sandstone statue commemorates Pipila, the hero of the siege of the Alhondiga. Fastening a stone tablet to his back as protection from bullets, the Indian miner Pipila managed to torch the garrison doors, but not before an estimated 12,000 peasants died. The battle was an early high water mark for the revolutionary forces. Following this victory the neophyte army moved south to eventual defeat, a temporary delay in Mexico's long fight for independence.

No visit to the city is complete without a visit to the Alhondiga, now an excellent regional museum. On weekends, Sr. Rafael Canchola leads a spirited twenty-minute tour. His entertaining commentary ranges from a contemporary interpretation of the Alhondiga's original purpose ("sort of a pre-liberation supermarket") to an evocative retelling of the drama that occurred there. Eventually, each of the Insurrection's chief strategists, Hidalgo and Allende, Aldama and Jimenez, were captured and executed.

Their severed heads were hung from the four corners of the Al-hondiga's walls and remained there for the duration of the war, a shocking reminder of the penalty for treason.

But Guanajuato's propensity for ghoulish exhibitionism lives on. **El Museo de las Momias,** next to the cemetery, is one of those must-see attractions for connoisseurs of the macabre. Here, bodies exhumed when their descendants defaulted on burial payments, are displayed. The hideous collection of remains is a bizarre and entertaining diversion. Unfortunately, the museum's small size and poor design limits your necrovoyeuristic enjoyment. Loud reactions from the crowds both ahead and behind you rebound against the chamber walls, rendering your guide's commentary incomprehensible, although the mummified grimaces do speak for themselves. You'll love the Reagan lookalike and the woman who was buried alive. On crowded days any urge you may have to escape is thwarted by the stream of bodies—live ones—that block the pipeline corridor.

Outside, predictably, there's a lineup of souvenir stalls, but despite the potential for morbid creativity, there is a dearth of innovation. And tact. Ribbon candy replicas of someone's shriveled granny are cute but many of the curios are downright odious, key chains with epitaphs, "Died of AIDS," and swastika-emblazoned steel helmets.

It is best to postpone a visit to **La Valenciana Church** until you are cycling away from town. Built with profits from the adjacent La Valenciana silver mine, it perches dramatically above the city and affords grandiose views of Guanajuato. As well, it provides a badly needed break after a torturous five kilometer climb. You can refill water bottles from a spigot below the church steps and visit the grounds of the still active mine a short walk away.

The climb resumes and Guanajuato recedes into the distance. A false summit at k 99 yields a parting view of "Christo Rey," a distant mountaintop statue that purportedly marks the geographic center of Mexico. The road dips briefly into Sta. Rosa, a good breakfast stop if it's still early, before finally topping the pass.

You are really in the mountains now and human habitations are few among a landscape of scrub oak and cliffy grey rock outcroppings. Zooming downhill you swoop past abandoned mining excavations and littered tailings. Crumbly roadcuts expose the blue-green hue of sulfate bearing minerals. Halfway down the mountainside two restaurants present the only opportunities for sitdown meals before Dolores Hidalgo. The switchbacks straighten and the flight ends with a high-speed landing onto the piedmont.

What appeared to be expansive plains from above turn out to be not so planar after all. Erosion and millenia have deeply wrinkled the terrain and you'll be thankful for a wide range of gears while wending across the puckered surface. Numerous roadcuts offer glimpses into the geologic past. Sand and gravel from shifting deltas and smooth, fist-sized cobbles from abandoned stream beds testify to a period when the emergent mountains shed their overload of sedimentary debris.

There are no services in Ojo de Agua but a 3k hill that follows makes it something of a landmark anyway. Then the road settles back down and only 16k of level riding remain.

Dolores Hidalgo

A small hill is enough to block Dolores Hidalgo's single-spire skyline from sight. Known as "La Cuna," or "the cradle" of independence, Dolores Hidalgo remains a blessedly simple town. Whereas San Miguel is overrun by Americans and Guanajuato brims with everyone else, Dolores Hidalgo has made few concessions to outsiders of any kind.

Not that the place has completely dodged modern commerce. It is one of the Republic's leading producers of pottery. Those privy to the secret who have come directly to the source to buy may be disappointed; instead of finding assiduous craftsmen working near backyard kilns, they encounter wholesale warehouses specializing in pottery by the bushel. Loading docks are piled high with terra cotta throwaways which, while okay for what they are, certainly don't qualify as fine crafts.

This knicknack industry is largely confined to town's outskirts and Dolores Hidalgo's central plaza remains unsullied. No tacky t-shirts to commemorate Independence here. In fact, tourists are few and not many seem to spend the night. Those who do can find good, clean lodging and a number of simple restaurants at prices which have not inflated from demand. Most of them are located around the *zocalo* or main plaza.

The plaza is dwarfed by the portentious bulk of the Parroquia, the immense cathedral from which Father Hidalgo issued his famous "grito." Even now, with music by the Bee Gees drifting over the outdoor speaker system, it's easy to conjure a hundred and fifty year old image of unrest and rebellion, of an enraged peasantry ignited by the padre's catalyzing speech.

Three main highways converge on Dolores Hidalgo but a triple bypass saves its tranquil heart. Only five blocks from the peaceful central district you begin riding on the busiest of those thoroughfares, Mex 51/111, leading to San Miguel de Allende.

High traffic volume, the lack of a shoulder, and view-obscuring blind spots make riding this stretch a drag. On the plus side, it's only 43k, and there are opportunities to slake your thirst at the two vineyards en route. Wine enjoys a brief fall season around here and at other times of the year quarts of grape juice are on sale. Hot springs in Taboada and Atotonilco offer a choice of soothing soaks before ending this ride where you began, in San Miguel.

La Valenciana Church, Near Guanajuato

Whether you've biked directly from Guanajuato or tarry at the hot springs after a night in Dolores Hidalgo, try to arrive in San Miguel before 6:00 p.m. for one last history lesson.

Hidalgo's was no spontaneous cry to arms. Plans for the war of liberation had been discussed for months prior to any action. To avoid drawing attention to the church, covert meetings were held in the *fragua*, a local smithy's shop. Today gatherings continue in the "Fragua" bar, THE place to be from 6:00 to 8:00. "Twofers" (two drinks for the price of one) are served to the tune of live music. After that, head on down to the plaza to watch the promenade and complain about the rising price of real estate.

ROADNOTES

WHAT'S AHEAD: San Miguel de Allende to Guanajuato. Pleasurable cycling through open countryside, but with few services. Buy your day's supplies before leaving San Miguel.

Kilometer 0	San Miguel's plaza. Head 2 blocks west (downhill), left on Zacateros, go straight (signs indicate Presa de Allende, Guanajuato and Celaya). Turn for Zacateros is *before* the stone archway.
	La Huerta. Follow Mesones to Aparicio, continue uphill alongside the drainage ditch and under the archway. Single 8,000p, double 10,000p. Clean, so-so mattresses, private bath. Set in a peaceful vegetation-choked ravine. Not as hard to get to as it sounds; cheapest place in town.
	El Meson, Mesones #58—US $10 per person. Beautiful rooms in renovated home of mountain biking enthusiast, price includes all-u-can-eat breakfast.
1	Pemex station. Stone surface turns to pavement.
2	Mex 111 intersection. Continue straight, following signs for Celaya. Begin rolling hills.
10	Signed right turn for Guanajuato.
16	Ignacio Allende reservoir. Hills get bigger.
34	Private ranch, no services.
42	Small village, no services.
43	Begin 2.5k hill. Longest climb in the area.
46	Terrain levels out, great views.
50	"T" intersection for Presa de Manantiales reservoir. Turn right for Guanajuato. Store sells beer and refrescos. Pedalling continues to get easier.
71	La Sauceda. Small village, store, cafe.
81	Good restaurant.
83	Yerbabuena, an industrial satellite of Guanajuato. Few services.
87	Intersection. Right for Guanajuato. Traffic increases, road traces stream channel uphill into town. Enter via *subterraneo*.
91	Guanajuato's central district.
	Cheapest hotels in Guanajuato are clustered on Calle Juarez between the Cine Juarez and the market.
	Casa de Huespedes Kloster, Calle de Alonso #32 at the base of Callejon de la Estrella—8,000p per person. Clean, good mattresses, decent communal bathroom,

hot water. Nice family-style place, international crowd. Worth calling ahead, phone 2–00–88.

To exit: follow Calle Juarez downhill, away from the plaza and towards the marketplace.

91   Central market. Right turn after Cine Reforma, under archway, follow signs for Dolores Hidalgo.

92   The Alhondiga, now a regional museum. Begin 17k climb.

WHAT'S AHEAD: From Guanajuato to San Miguel de Allende. One tough climb. Lots of beautiful views with little in the way of services beyond Sta. Rosa and before Dolores Hidalgo. Beyond Dolores Hidalgo traffic is heavy and the road narrow. Use caution.

95.5	La Valenciana. Church and mine of the same name. Restaurants.
99	False summit, parting view of "Christo Rey."
114	Second false summit.
116	Sta. Rosa. Hotels and restaurants.
119	Summit. You're there when you see the picnic tables. No services.
122	Restaurants.
124	Restaurant.
130.5	Bottom of descent. Begin long gradual hills.
132	Pulloff for Calvillo. Stores, cafes in town below.
135	Ojo de Agua. No services.
138	Terrain begins to settle down.
148	Los Hernandez. No services.
154	Dolores Hidalgo comes into view.
157	*Glorieta.* Continue straight. Bear left on Calle Jalisco.
158	Dolores Hidalgo.
	Posada Cocomacan, Plaza Principal #4. Single 13,500p, double 16,000p. Spotless, good mattresses, private bath, hot water until noon.
	To exit: From plaza Calle Jalisco becomes Calle Queretaro. Follow it to reach the main road to San Miguel.
159	Intersection. Calle Queretaro joins highway, right turn.
160	Intersection. Right on Mex 51/110.
161	Monument to the Insurgentes.
162	Signed left turn.
164	Mex 51/110 split. Right for San Miguel.
171	La Capilla. Vineyard and produce stand.
174	Another vineyard/produce stand.
180	Galvanes. Store.

189   La Gruta, subterranean hot springs, currently closed. Signs for Escondido Place and Taboada, hot springs. Taboada is the one that most deserves a visit. Both can be reached by dirt roads from San Miguel. For more information see Phil Watson at El Meson, San Miguel de Allende.

199   Pavement ends and San Miguel's bruising cobbles begin.

201   San Miguel's plaza.

TOUR 14

THE COSTA GRANDE

ROUTE: The Pacific Coast from Puerto Vallarta to Acapulco.
DISTANCE: 1,037k.
RIDING TIME: 12 to 15 days.
DIFFICULTY: Moderate to very hard.
TERRAIN: About 30% very difficult, but mostly rolling hills and some flatlands.
BEST TIME: Winter.
ATTRACTIONS: The route includes some of Mexico's most famous resorts—exciting day and night life—as well as great beaches, challenging riding, solitude, and gorgeous scenery.

This one is a real tease. On the map, Mex. 15 looks like a classic ride. Playing hide-n-seek with the blue Pacific it calls to mind images of dazzling sands, shady palm groves and skinny dipping in undiscovered coves. This route appears to be perfect for the beach-loving biker, and is—but it's not for the weak of knee. In fact, if your idea of vacation fun involves more paddling than pedalling, consider the Caribbean.

This tour passes through some of the most rugged and least settled country in all of Mexico. Sheer cliffs limit beach accessibility; the most tempting coves are often unreachable. Steep mountains, long distances between towns and the likelihood that you'll camp more than once make this rewarding trip a demanding one, too. It's a ride that many are glad to have done, but few would do again.

Along the mostly underdeveloped coastline, neatly contained megaresorts and industrial ports spring up every few hundred kilometers. Their occurence adds welcome variety to the spartan regime of Pacific Coast cycling. While your journey may be christened in a Pto. Vallarta bar, may conclude the same way in Acapulco, and allow for a backsliding debauch in each resort along the way, the ride's predominant theme is one of rigor and solitude. Even Manzanillo's busy channel traffic and the no-nonsense industrial port of Lazaro Cardenas are welcome sights after the isolation of the coastal hinterlands.

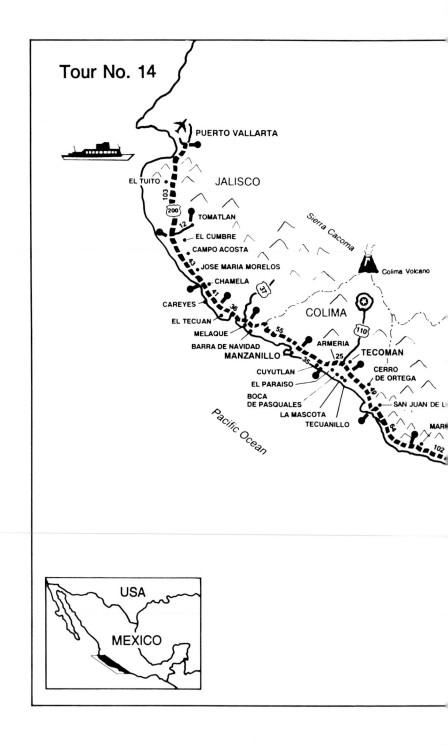

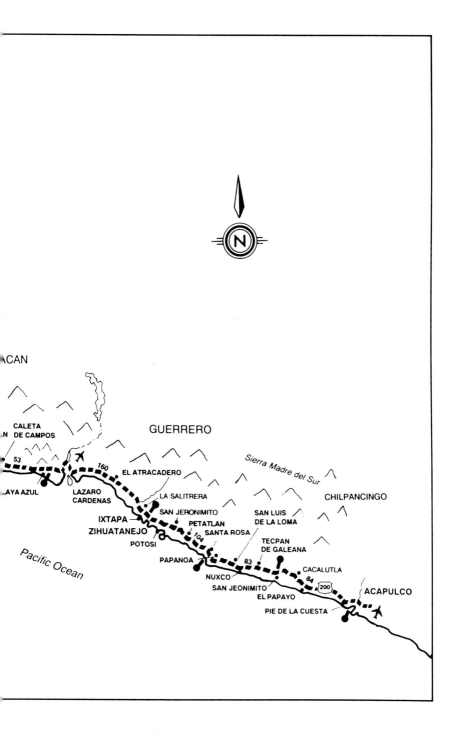

On this trip, we found several map inaccuracies which can cost you dearly. Indeed, cartographers seem eager to see the region settled. Both the AAA and Pemex maps indicate towns where none exist. Your discovery of one of these Mexican Brigadoons can be highly disconcerting if you've planned on buying groceries or spending the night there, but you can prevent the sort of memorably unpleasant evening that might ensue by studying our roadnotes and carrying sufficient supplies.

Many people tour the Costa Grande, the Pacific Coast north of Acapulco, as an extension of a trans-Baja tour. Throughout Baja and along the Costa Grande, extremes of temperature and humidity mandate carrying lots of fresh water. In addition, between May and August, the rainy season, a tent or bivvy sack will protect you from mosquitoes.

The Costa Grande South from Pto. Vallarta

Pto. Vallarta is only one of four places to ferry to the mainland from Baja, but we think it far and away the best option. Guaymas, Topolobampo, and Mazatlan are too far north. The road between them cuts deeply inland, bypassing most of the beaches. Most important, it is the major north/south traffic corridor. Above Tepic, where the Guadalajara traffic converges, it is simply suicidal. It isn't until just north of Pto. Vallarta that the road establishes even a tentative relationship with the sea anyway. Even if arriving by train, consider beginning your exploration of the Pacific Coast from here.

Pto. Vallarta comes unusually close to living up to tourist brochure hype: good nightlife, shopping, daytrips and recreation, and great beaches. Most of the large hotels are restricted to the outskirts of town leaving the central district a hint of its fishing village roots.

The inner city is divided by the Rio Ameca. To the north it is unabashedly commercial; yet, the south side remains a fairly typical Mexican town. You'll be able to eat and find lodging here with only moderate damage to your budget. The 18,000p you'll pay for a room is put in perspective by a short walk across the bridge, where drinks are easily 5,000p, rooms begin at 50,000p. Glitzy, nicely designed Tex-Mex restaurants and souvenir shops line one side of the seawall. From balconies, diners gaze out at a stirring palm-fringed beachfront.

The covered market in Pto. Vallarta is particularly notable. Downstairs is the usual profusion of handicrafts, but the second floor is crammed with budget eateries. These small *fondas* are so numerous, the stalls go by number as well as by name. We got hooked on Dona Cata (#10), whose seafood *comida* goes for 4,000p. Meals at this market are sometimes outstanding and the level of hygiene is among the highest we've found in Mexico. If you have been hesitant to try typical food in typical surroundings, this is your opportunity to go for it.

South from Pto. Vallarta the road skirts coastline cliffs. The water gets clearer and the beaches get cleaner. There's good beach camping at Mismaloya, 13k from town if you don't want to stay at a hotel. Mismaloya is famous as the one-time movie set for *Night of the Iguana*, and there is little chance of your completing a visit to Pto. Vallarta without being informed of this priceless bit of trivia about thirty times.

The road turns inland and you enter a narrow river valley, initiating a protracted and often steep climb. The landscape is breathtaking. Valley walls rise up on either side of the road, streams cascade over dark, sparkling diorite cliffs. High overhead the rock protrudes through the jungly growth and below, in the gorge, comes the angry roar of water.

Thirteen kilometers into the climb you reach a marvelous place to break, **Chico's Paradise,** a luxurious *palappa* or thatched-hut-style restaurant. Open to the air, it is surrounded by deep pools and natural waterfalls. The menu is rather expensive but lounging is well worth the price of a beer. The friendly staff recommends camping at the defunct "Frankie's Joy" next door. They also advise that during the rainy season swimming be completed early. Afternoon storms sweep the narrow ravine with dangerous torrents of water.

Although it makes for an abbreviated day you might want to spend the night at Chico's. Tomatlan, the next place with lodging, is a grueling 90k away.

From Chico's the road resumes a stepwise ascent. Two soda stands occur in the course of the 17k hump to the top, a distribution density that is only a bit higher than average. Along the entire coast, unless otherwise noted, you can expect to find soda, beer and a paltry selection of groceries approximately every 10 to 15k.

At k 42 you begin a disappointing downhill. Yep. For this you spent the morning in first gear. The views are modest and the descent is tame. 75k later, you near sea level. A Pemex station and several restaurants mark the intersection, called El Cumbre, but for overnight facilities you'll have to turn inland to Tomatlan. An excellent guest house and better restaurants make the level 12k detour worthwhile.

The 56k from Tomatlan to Chamela traverses small and medium sized hills marked by nondescript villages and cafes. At Chamela, the **Villa Polinesia** provides good moderately priced camping and luxury *palappas.* An excellent beach, decent food and free hot showers make this a great overnight stop. South of here camping opportunities are limited and no formal lodging is available for another 65k. A large supermarket in Chamela is the best place to restock before pushing on.

Careyes, prominently marked on most maps, is the turnoff to a Club Med facility and *nothing* else. Late in the day, the discovery that it is not a town comes as a frustrating disappointment. Even

Horse And Boy Swimming In The Pacific

worse, 26k further down the road, signs for "Los Angeles Locos Fiesta Americana" lead up a painfully cobbled road to an expensive resort on a secluded bay. Our intrepid researcher was driven off by a horrific swarm of mosquitoes. Camping is not feasible. Months later we returned by car. Gate guards refused us entry because we did not have reservations.

Eighteen kilometers of monstrous hills now await you. At the end of the grunt, so do two popular beach towns, Melaque and Barra de Navidad, only a few kilometers apart. The sands of Melaque are reputed to be less crowded, but Barra de Navidad has more exciting surf. Moderately priced lodging and inexpensive seafood *palappas* are abundant at both places, so it is no secret why Guadalajarans flock here on busy Mex 80. Traffic is heavy but localized.

At the Colima state border the landscape undergoes a relieving change. The beaches are typically of black volcanic sand and, with few exceptions, the terrain flattens for the next 160k.

Manzanillo

Manzanillo is a curious blend of industry and tourism. From its beautiful beaches north of town you pedal deep into its grungy urban heart. Commerce reluctantly shares space with vacationers, a potpourri of souvenir shops and boxcar switching yards. Band music in the plaza is punctuated by unsyncopated blasts from a freighter's horn. Across the channel, lights from a generating station burn brightly. Budget hotels on the plaza have a front seat view of the colliding imagery.

South of the city, development terminates abruptly.

An eerily deserted two-lane highway transits the barrier beach to Cuyutlan, a tranquil alternative to Manzanillo with good beaches and budget hotels.

The road turns inland to Tecoman, a prosperous, agriculturally based city. For the next 42k shoreline access is limited and prominently marked turnoffs for beaches such as Tequanillo, Pascuales and El Paraiso are all about 10k from water. Bathing is often a secondary attraction at these places. Most people come to eat fresh seafood and drink beer at the numerous *ramadas* which dot the strand. These palm-thatched pavilions spring up wherever a road meets the beach. In the event of foul weather they make good emergency shelters, but too often boisterous revelers make camping imprudent. If you must spend the night, ask one of the *palappa* owners if it's okay to camp on his turf.

South of Tecoman, you enter the state of Michoacan and the free sailing is over. Ahead lie 140k of arduous climbing. Supplies and lodging diminish in frequency. In many places the highway has only recently been completed and communities have yet to appear. Monitor your water supply continuously and take advantage of cafes and villages when they occur. These cautionary notes should not dissuade you, however, for the beauty of Michoacan's savage coast is worthy of the travail.

Ojo de Agua is situated beyond Michocan's first tough ridge. There's not much in town but there are several good seafood restaurants on the beach, 1k away. If you're thinking of spending the night, though, nicer places lie further south. The road continues in corrugated fashion and a fast descent brings you to Rancho San Juan, where the **Hotel Miramar** sits on the beachfront. Camping is free to all restaurant customers.

At La Placita, the **Hotel Martinez,** a real backyard affair, is the closest thing to lodging you'll see for the next 154k. Don't fail to stock up on essentials before leaving town. Beyond La Placita, groceries are exceptionally limited. The ride to Caleta de Campo is equally difficult, at least as beautiful, and even more deserted than the miles you have already cycled.

Few people reside hereabouts and those you meet will likely be divided between campesino families and adventure travelers. Surfers, those vanguard explorers of virgin coast, seem particularly drawn to the region. Dirt roads lead to secluded beaches which enjoy quiet fame among a small but avid group of international wave hounds. When conditions are favorable many set up housekeeping at beaches like El Faro and Rio Nexpa. You may want to join them but, as always when camping on a deserted stretch of coast, exercise discretion.

A landing strip and an abandoned highway construction camp greet you at Maruata. Not a pretty picture. But hidden from view is one of the loveliest coves anywhere. Maruata's beach is protected by a row of offshore rocks which absorb the brunt of the ocean's force. Choppy waves pound against them, but only diminished swells gently surge their last up a steep, sandy shore. Five seafood *palappas* are secreted into the crowded tropical canopy. You can practically hear the oysters shout from the rocks offshore and the fish are so fresh you'll want to wash their mouths with soap. Niconor, the owner of the centermost restaurant has a standing invitation for bike tourists to spend the night. For the price of a meal we imagine you'll find similar hospitality in vogue at the other *palappas* too. Get a good night's sleep, the road ahead is still a grind.

The next 50k come at you in kickass 3k ascents but around Tizupan the terrain relents—only single kilometer climbs follow. As the hills settle down, villages appear and services become more common. You're out of the woods, so to speak.

There's some last-gasp climbing to reach Caleta de Campos, situated atop high bluffs overlooking the ocean. Town welcomes you with a choice of hotels and restaurants and is a logical place to spend the night before continuing on to Playa Azul.

Playa Azul Means Relax and Recuperate

Playa Azul is a great town to relax and recuperate from the rigors of riding. Off-season, May to September, empty beach chairs stand sentinel-like facing the open sea. Sheltered by *palappas,* all in a row, they form a barricade that stretches for miles. While moderately-priced lodging is available, many people choose to camp here. A public showerhead at **Maracaibo's,** a popular restaurant at the beach's northwestern end, .makes camping in the salty air more pleasant than usual. At the other end of the scale, the cushy **Hotel Playa Azul** invites bar and restaurant patrons to swim in their pool and relax on their shady grounds.

It is a long 130k day to Ixtapa and Zihuatanejo. Poor towns en route afford convenient refreshment but little else to warrant tarrying. This is good country to count cadence and practice ankling.

A four-lane entrance to an airport alerts you to the presence of conspicuous wealth. You are approaching Ixtapa, one of Mexico's most glamorous, and possibly its most beautiful beach resort. A high mountain ridge stands between it and Zihuatanejo. Separated by only seven kilometers, proximity would suggest they were twin cities from a beach blanket mold. In fact, their characters could hardly be less similar.

Like mushrooms in the sand, Ixtapa's high-rise profile appeared overnight. Luxury development swept the cove before anything more plain could take root. Nightclubs, air conditioned restaurants and swank hotels share a rough and beautiful beach. Not a fisherman's shack is in sight. A trailer park is Ixtapa's only concession to budget-minded tourists.

Most of the army of employees who service Ixtapa's clientele commute from Zihuatanejo, a boomtown in its own right. The difference is that Ixtapa is a slick and polished international host. But Zihuatanejo seems positively enthusiastic about the foreign invasion. Perhaps it's that Zihuatanejo's identity existed before the tourist onslaught. Now, fishermen drop anchors under the gaze of early morning bathers and trek home past a barrage of t-shirt and souvenir shops. A good market and many moderately priced hotels make Zihuatanejo a haven for budget travelers.

Beach, Zihuatanejo

The terrain regains a variable character as you cycle south. The highway gently rolls through arid land dissected by streams and arroyos. Supplies are never far away. Numerous detours lead to seldom frequented beaches. Playa Potosi offers particularly idylic camping. Hotels, while spartan, exist in Petatlan, La Barrita, Coyaquilla and Papanoa and permit lots of flexibility in choosing where to lodge. The following night, most likely your last on the road, is best spent in either Tecpan or San Jeronimo. Both are large full-service towns. San Jeronimo has better beach access, with busses leaving often from the plaza.

Acapulco Beckons

By now your eagerness to reach Acapulco is hard to contain. But, not to worry, the mountainous approach from Pie de la Cuesta will curtail your haste. The cliffs are beautiful and the heavily trafficked serpentine road affords magnificent views. However, the satellite sprawl of Acapulco is increasingly apparent.

Acapulco's long history as a trading center preceded its transformation into Mexico's first world-class resort. Upstart resorts such as Ixtapa improved on the formula and mimicked its early success, while Acapulco began to turn rather dowdy. That trend has now been reversed by new construction and efforts to upgrade the area. The beachfront stands completely renovated and competes favorably with the jetset likes of Cancun and Mazatlan. The impoverished living conditions of its residents, while hardly unusual, are striking in the shadow of such opulence.

Between these two extremes middle class and budget-minded vacationers find lots to attract them. Acapulco has an especially lively plaza, and nearby is one of the country's largest and most colorful bazaars. There's great evening entertainment, daytime recreation and, of course, there's beach blanket Babylon.

The city is extraordinarily popular among middle class Mexicans and a bumper crop of inexpensive lodging exists to serve them. An entire street, Calle La Quebrada, is dominated by inexpensive, clean guest houses. Between the rock-bottom price of lodging and cut rate drinks on the hotel strip, you can affordably spend a long enjoyable time formulating your next vacation plans.

ROADNOTES

WHAT'S AHEAD: The Jalisco Coast, from Pto. Vallarta to Barra de Navidad. This tour's most challenging climb comes up front, a 24k grind that separates resort development from rural heartland. Tiny settlements or lone stores selling a modicum of supplies appear on average every 10 to 15k. No hotels appear before Tomatlan, a rigorous 115k away. A range of coastal hills separates the highway, Mex 200, from the Pacific. Consequently, most beach detours involve climbing. All water taken from streams requires treatment. Campers will want an ample supply of bug repellent and may want to carry a tent.

Kilometer 0	Pto. Vallarta. Brutal cobblestone streets extend to city's edge. Highway begins by paralleling beach south. **Budget hotels** are located south of the bridge on the 300 and 400 blocks of Calle Madero.
13	Mismaloya. Popular beach area with good camping and restaurants.
17	**Chee-Chee's** restaurant. At the mouth of the Tomatlan river the road turns inland, leaves coast, the climb begins.
18	Boca Tomatlan. Town with grocery.
22	Foot trail leads to gorge and water falls; bathe at your own risk.
24	**Chico's Paradise.** Swimming, beer and food in lavish *palappa* surroundings. Free camping on abandoned grounds of "Frankie's Joy".
26	First false summit.
28	**Coco's.** Cafe, beer and sodas.
30	Second false summit. Gotcha again!
31	**La Cabana.** Nice cafe, fresh spring water in back. Suck it up, you'll need it for the next 6k.
35	The crux move, 1.25k, the steepest section of the climb.
47	El Tuito. A few cafes, no overnight services. Begin a deserted 22k stretch of highway.
69	El Tigre. *Refrescos,* little else.
76	Junction for San Rafael. Two cafes at turnoff.
80	Tequesquite. Cafes.
94	Jose Maria Pino Suarez. Well-stocked market here is best bet for cyclists who intend to camp short of Tomatlan.
103	El Cumbre. Detour for Tomatlan. Services at junction include cafes, groceries and a Pemex station.

DETOUR TO TOMATLAN, 12k
An excellent choice. Worth the added distance.
Posada Carmelita, on the right as you head for the center. Single 8,000p, double 12,000p. Immaculately clean, firm mattresses, private bath. A wonderful family establishment.

104	Begin 8k of gentle hills.
120	Campo Acosta. Small, hot town scattered across a dry river plain. Groceries, little else.
130	Jose Maria Morelos. Stores, cafes, and on leaving town, a "Michoacana" popsicle shop. Big hills start here.
136	Restaurant. .5k further is an overlook of the Pacific, rare in these parts.
146	Chamela. Big supermarket on highway. Detour 1k to **Villa Polinesia** for lodging, beach camping and expensive dining.
154	**Chamela** restaurant. Cold beer and excellent seafood.
158	More big hills.
166	Signed turn for **Plaza Hotel Careyes,** a Club Med facility. Awful cobbled road. No groceries.
168	Beach access. Possible camping between beach and lagoon. Repellant handy?
179	Emiliano Zapata. Big rancho, cafes and a store.
187	Signed detour for **Rancho El Tecuan** resort, 10k. Expensive rooms, medium-priced restaurant, good and inexpensive camping.
192	Turn for **Los Angeles Locos Fiesta Americana,** very exclusive resort.
193	Signed detour for Tenacatita. Unpaved road leads to bay.
218	Melaque. Beach resort. Junction with Mex 80 from Guadalajara. Full range of services. Traffic increases dramatically.
223	Barra de Navidad. Low key beach resort, full range of services. Camping possible.
	Budget hotels don't really exist, though there are many in the 20,000p range up and down both beaches.

WHAT'S AHEAD: The Coast of Colima, Barra de Navidad to Coahuayana. Inland for most of its length, this is one of the easiest sections of the tour. Towns are frequent and offer as dense a selection of lodging as one ever finds on Mex 200.

241   Cihuatlan. Small city. One hotel, two theatres. Jalisco/
Colima border is 1k beyond town.
Hotel JJMS, near the plaza, next to the popsicle shop
"Janitzio". Double 15,000, grungy, OK mattresses, pri-
vate bath. Lock your bike in your room. Hey, any port
in a storm.

252   La Cienega. Fruit stands, stores. Last range of hills
before Manzanillo.

267   University of Colima Marine Science Center. First
signs of Manzanillo urban sprawl. Good beaches parallel the road.

272   Santiago, an expensive Manzanillo suburb. Lots of
beach paraphernalia shops. Turnoff for **Hotel Anita.**

279   *Glorieta* (traffic circle). Left for Manzanillo's center.

282   *Glorieta.* Right for Manzanillo's center.

286   "Y" intersection. Turn right and cross railroad tracks
for central district.

288   Manzanillo's plaza. Lots of facilities. Streets are poorly
marked.
Guest houses. For those determined to save there are
several of dubious quality near the bus station on
town's southern end. Rooms for 7,000p, mas o menos.
Hotel Emperador. Balbino Pavalos #69. Best deal in
town's center; double 16,000p, single 14,000p. Very
clean, firm beds, private bath. Many stairs, lock your
bike down in the restaurant.
To exit: Leave from plaza corner nearest Hotel Emperador. Bicycle away from harbor (toward rocky hillside).
Pavement turns to cobbles and bears left. After 1k this
unnamed street joins a harborside road. Turn right.

289   Pass the generating station, continue straight. Cycling
with the bay on your left side is discomforting after the
past few days but ignore it, you're not lost. This 32k of
deserted barrier beach road leads to Cuyutlan. No
signs, services nor habitations en route.

323   Cuyutlan. Quiet town and forgotten beach resort. Full
service.
Posada San Miguel. Calle Miguel Hidalgo #198—
10,000 per person. Clean, good beds, private baths,
breezy rooms and a nice porch for lounging.

326   Signed right turn for Armeria and El Paraiso.

332   "T" intersection. Right for El Paraiso. Hotels and restaurants, swimming pool, beach.

348	Tecoman. Small city with full range of services. **Casa de huespedes/guest house;** adjacent plaza next to variety store, **La Pulguita**—3,000p per person, adequate cleanliness, OK mattresses, no fans. Lock your bike. *To exit:* Follow Calle Revolucion away from plaza between church and Hotel Alba.
351	Signed detour for Tequillo beach, 10k.
373	Cerro de Ortega, a large town. Cafes, stores and a Bancomer Bank branch.
375	First Boca de Piza detour, 5k. Poor fishing village. Huts serving seafood on a littered beach.
378	Coahuayana River, marks the Michoacan border.
384	Second Boca de Piza detour, 3k. BEGIN TOUGHEST 100k.

WHAT'S AHEAD: The Michoacan Coast, Coahuayana to Lazaro Cardenas. The Michoacan Coast is, without question, the most demanding section of Mex 200. Mountains plunge to the water's edge for much of it and in many sections the road has only recently been completed. Settlements are infrequent. *Take advantage of them when they occur and carry lots of water.* The rigor and solitude is not without reward, for this is the most beautiful seacoast west of the Caribbean.

391	Ojo de Agua. Few supplies in town but several seafood ramadas huts on beach, 1k.
397	San Juan. Stores, beach access, lodging. .5k further lodging and camping at hotel Miramar.
411	La Placita. The Hotel Martinez is your last opportunity to rent a room before Caleta de Campos, another 152k. Good dining at restaurant **Anahuac**. **Hotel Martinez;** on the right as you enter town—a real backyard affair. Double 15,000p. Clean rooms, good beds, private baths, surprisingly.
426	Signed detour to La Ticla beach, 3k. Good surf.
432	**Restaurant Nahuatl.**
436	Signed detour for Faro de Belcias beach and light house, 3k.
442	Motin del Oro. Small town, beautiful cove, few services.
452	Colola. Store, refrescos.
461	Maruata. Restaurant on highway, better dining at thatched huts on cove. Entrance to town at end of airstrip. Free camping at Niconor's ramada.

477	Rio Cachan. Big river, good place to wash up. Following 22k is most recently completed section of highway, lots of loose rubble, huge hills, great views.
497	End of the nastiest long hills. Subsequent ones are merely nasty, still steep but only 1k in length.
506	Tizupan. Cafes.
508	Beach access. Unusual hereabouts.
516	Pichilinguillo. Cafes.
526	Huahua. Stores, cafes. Terrain becomes markedly more gentle.
558	Rio Nexpa. Camping. Reportedly the best surf in Michoacan.
563	Caleta de Campos. Two hotels, beach camping, restaurants.
	Hotel Yuritzi, on the bluff above the beach—double 15,000p. Spotless, very firm beds, private bath.
570	**Paraiso Escondido** restaurant.
576	Mexcalluacan. Better of the two cafes is on bridge's far side.
587	Chuquiapan. Stores, cafes.
598	Village with well-stocked grocery, restaurants.
616	Signed turn for Playa Azul. Right turn. Low key beach resort, full range of facilities.

DETOUR TO PLAYA AZUL (5k)

Full-service, low-key beach resort. Great waves, no plaza life. Why doesn't someone put in a movie theater? **Hotel del Pacifico,** at corner of Zapata and Villa—Double 13,000p. Passably clean, good mattresses, private bath. Exterior looks like it was hit by an earthquake—it was! Best deal in town.

628	Armira. Large, noisy town. Heavy traffic from here to Lazaro Cardenas.
632	Begin 9k of rolling hills.
641	Intersection with 4-lane for Lazaro Cardenas, a huge industrial city. To continue south follow sign for Guacamayas that leads onto overpass.
644	Guacamayas. Good produce market on highway. Lots of services.
650	Huge reservoir and hydroelectric station marks Michoacan/Guerrero state line. Military checkpoint.

WHAT'S AHEAD: The Guerrero Coast, from Lazaro Cardenas to Acapulco. Gentler riding and more frequent services make this section a lark compared to the adventure of Michoacan. However, there is a strong military presence, whether due to drug interdiction efforts, innate conservatism or because Guerrero was the base of a guerrilla movement in recent times. Road check stations along the highway are common. Tourists and nationals alike are sometimes searched, but travelling on a bike you may not be stopped at all. If you are, take it seriously. These baby-faced kids with the surplus weaponry don't play games.

681	Roadside cafes.
693	Petacalco. Cafes and stores, lots of mangos grown locally.
719	Detour for Playa Atracadero, 3k. Ramadas open in winter only. Cafes and stores on highway.
745	Lagunilla River. Swimming.
751	La Majahua detour, 3k. Beach, ramadas.
759	Buena Vista. Restaurants, stores.
766	Pantla. Cafes, stores.
770	Saltitreras. Stores.
776	Pemex station. Turn for Ixtapa, full service luxury resort. Rough surf. Climb mountain to Zihuatanejo.
	Camping Playa Linda. Trailer park, 3,000p per person.
783	Zihuatenejo. Full range of international tourist facilities. Calmer water.
	Casa de Huespedes Elvira, Paseo del Pescador #8, on the beach west of the basketball court—8,000p per person. Very clean, soft mattresses, common bathroom with bucket baths upstairs. Simple but utterly charming. A true find. Reservations, phone 4–20–61.
	To exit: follow signs for Ixtapa, then airport, finally Acapulco.
793	Village with cafes.
800	Signed detour for Playa Potosi, 9k. Excellent beach camping, ramadas and seafood. Begin 5k of moderately steep hills.
815	San Geronimo. Pleasant town, restaurants, stores.
834	Petatlan. Big town, lots of services, hotel.
845	Juluchucu. Copra plantation. Refrescos.
849	Las Salinas. Salt drying lagoons. Roadside salt sales, refrescos.
853	La Barrita, on the beach. Several restaurants, one hotel.
858	Road skirts ocean's edge. Fantastic view, restaurants.
873	Coyaquilla. Restaurants, stores and, reportedly, a hotel.

880	Papanoa. Big town. Power plant, lumberyard and tiny hotel.
	Hotel Chevo, main highway leaving town, across from lumberyard "Forestal Vicente Guerrero". Double 15,000p. Very clean, cots rather than beds, common toilets. We're talking humble now, facilities probably designed for use as chicken coops.
883	**Club Papanoa.** Luxury hotel, restaurant with pool.
898	Rancho Alegre. Shooting range, store.
905	San Luis de la Loma. Large town with full services, particularly on its Tuesday market day.
920	Detour through Nuxpa for stores and cafes, no added distance.
937	El Suchil. Large town, variety of services.
941	Tecpan. Large town. Fresh water available from spigot at plaza. Guest house adjacent plaza.
963	San Jeronimo. Restaurants, hotels, busses to the beach 6k.
	Posada San Francisco, on Calle Progresso about three blocks from the highway. Double 8,000p. Very clean, good mattresses, common toilet. Professional and inexpensive establishment; every town ought to have one like it.
978	Village. Cafes, stores.
991	El Zapote. Cafes, stores.
1,013	Coyuca. Big town, full services.
1,037	Pie de la Cuesta. Trailer park, beach, hotels. Begin the final climb to Acapulco.
1,047	Acapulco. Tadahhh!!!
	Guest houses glut Calle Quebrada near the zocalo. Many have a 2–3 person minimum though. For solo travelers we recommend:
	Hotel Asturia, Quebrada 45. Double 12,000p, single 10,000p. Very clean, good mattresses, private bathrooms. Small swimming pool is a refreshing bonus.

THE TARAHUMARA HIGHLANDS AND BARRANCA DEL COBRE

ROUTE: Creel–Batopilas.
DISTANCE: 135k.
RIDING TIME: 2 to 3 days.
DIFFICULTY: Ironperson. Unrelentingly strenuous.
TERRAIN: Mountainous, 100%—at altitude of 5,000 to 8,000 feet.
BEST TIME: October through April. Warning: May through September, the heat in the canyon is oppressive and the flash floods can be deadly.
ATTRACTIONS: Spectacular scenery, hiking, horseback riding, swimming, solitude, living anthropology, and a fantastic train ride.

Wow. Make no mistake about it, this route is a tough one. But you get what you pay for, and in this case you are rewarded with the sense of being transported back in time. The rugged ride to Batopilas offers recreational variety, magnificent scenery, wilderness solitude and a glimpse into the past that was life in Meso-America.

Creel, which is the jumping-off place for this tour, is just about mid-point between Chihuahua, in the north, and Los Mochis, to the southwest. Both cities are accessible from the U.S. by air, and the Chihuahua-Pacifico Railroad runs between them. The train from either city to Creel takes about eight hours, but Los Mochis to Creel is by far more visually stimulating.

The Train from Los Mochis

We chose the Los Mochis approach. Two trains depart daily, at 6 and 7 a.m. This is a strictly tourist service and your bicycle must be shipped by cargo train the previous day. The cost for shipping a 17 kg. bike is 3,500p.

With considerable justification, the Mexican government champions this rail link as one of the world's great civil engineering

Tour No. 15

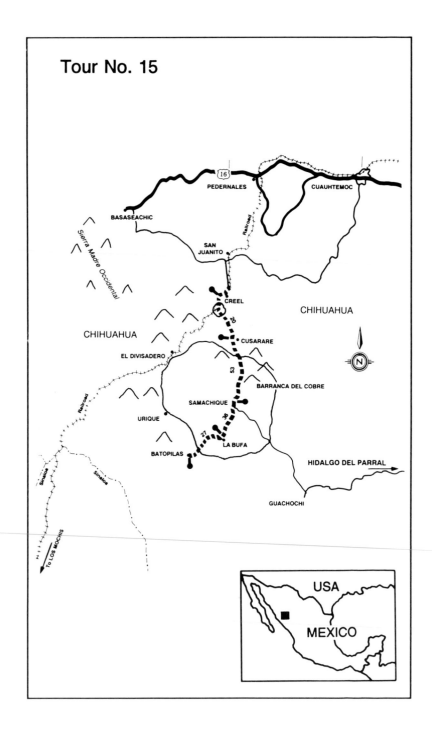

triumphs. For nine wonderful hours one enjoys the comfort of luxury rail service, ensconced in a swivel chair, observing the increasingly dramatic scenery through specially wide windows. The view changes with the twists of countless switchbacks and the approach of yet another bridge, light flickers stroboscopically with the entry and exit of the route's 87 tunnels. The cost is a mere 9,000p.

At El Divisadero the train makes a 15-minute stop at the canyon edge and passengers disembark to peer through telescopes, snap a flurry of photographs and hurriedly bargain with the laconic Tarahumara basket-weavers. This is the high point of the trip for many Barranca del Cobre visitors. Going deeper into the canyon and meeting its people requires effort and time and does not con-

Los Mochis Train Through Barranca Del Cobre

form to a busy itinerary. What is climatic viewing for most is only a preview of coming attractions for cyclists.

The Tarahumara Indians

Most of this tour is within the boundary of the recently designated Parque Nacional Barranca del Cobre. The area is the ancestral home of 50,000 Tarahumara Indians, a tribe who vigorously adhere to tradition. Some scholars believe them to be Mexico's most culturally intact people. Scattered throughout the canyon, their tiny *ranchos* are testimony to the adaptation of life in one of the world's most rugged and remote regions. This is the tribe that sends barefoot competitors to the Olympics. Don't be surprised when an old man, leg muscles rippling, overtakes you on the trail as he carries a compact-car-sized bundle of corn husks to town. Their striking physical presence is intensified by their silence. They are a serious people and brushing shoulders with them is a profound experience.

Creel

From the train platform in Creel, one looks across a valley rimmed by sandstone bluffs and crammed full of clapboard cedar shacks. Smoke curls lazily from tin chimney stacks into the chill mountain air. The only traffic is pedestrian. Riders on horseback, grim-faced as commuters anywhere, sport leather chaps, red bandanas, and cowboy hats. The scene is more befitting a movie western than modern-day Mexico. Most of Creel's 10,000 inhabitants are mestizo and its bustling railhead is the center for the Tarahumara timber harvest. Creel is the 20th-century face of mountain life.

The town is compact and finding the hotel district and overnight lodging is easily accomplished. Adjacent to the plaza are several inexpensive hotels as well as the luxurious **Parador,** one of a chain of Paradors in Mexico. If spending $40 a night does not fit your budget, perhaps the snug but humbler **Koriachi** will. It costs about $5 a night.

Across from the Koriachi is **Marguerite's,** an unpretentious guest house. Marguerite and her husband Daniel have watched

Tarahumara Dancer

this house, where he was born, transformed from a *casa de huespedes* to a small hotel. It has become a popular stop on the "gringo trail."

Inside, 30 or so travellers are accommodated in private rooms, a dormitory, and the livingroom floor. On our visit the make-up was two parts rucksack-toting Europeans to one part Canadian retirees, with a sprinkling of Norteamericanos. The house is a crossroad of global travel information. Dinner was served over a polyglot discussion about nuclear disarmament. Second helpings were on the house.

Included in Marguerite's heavily annotated guest book is an entry by Carl Franz, author of *The People's Guide to Mexico*. Carl has never mentioned a single facility by name in his book, but even his code of objectivity was broken by Marguerite, and he gave her his only six-star rating.

There's lots to do near Creel and you may decide to stay for several days. Near Marguerite's kitchen door hangs an area reference map, and a list of suggested activities which include hiking, horseback riding, and the Recohuata hot springs. Though easily reached by bike, all of Creel's points of interest are most fittingly visited by horseback. Daniel, who is very knowledgeable about the surrounding back country, is available for hire as a guide to locations as distant as Basaseachic Falls. Basaseachic, the second-highest single-drop waterfall in the world, is a day's journey by car from Creel.

It should be noted that further afield than Creel, traveler's checks become barely negotiable, groceries are scarce, and luxuries such as liquor virtually disappear. All of the money you think you will need for this tour should be converted into small denominations. Anything larger than 2,000 pesos (approx. US$1.00) is troublesome to use in the backwoods *bodegas* you will frequent. In Batopilas, traveller's checks can be cashed with some difficulty, at an exchange rate that is shockingly awful.

Cheese from Chihuahua's large Mennonite community is available for the last time in Creel, as is the opportunity to visit a *panaderia*, or bakery. It will be your last chance to purchase bottled water and, following its consumption, you are advised to start using water treatment pills. Buy a gallon here for your last unsullied enjoyment.

This is a demanding three-day trip and completing it in two is extremely strenuous. Opting for the slower pace permits you, with careful planning, to lodge in the most conveniently located communities. Armed with instructions from Daniel and a topographic map bought at the Mision Tarahumara Artesanias in Creel, we pedalled off for Batopilas. (The map costs 4,000p and is available, it turns out, from the International Map Company, University of Texas, Box 400, El Paso, TX 79968–0400, U.S.A.)

The governor of Chihuahua is "road happy" and has begun the lengthy project of paving the entire mountainous distance between Creel and Hidalgo del Parral, about 300k. Current progress extends just beyond Cusirare and the first 24 kilometers of your tour will be on a really nice tree-lined two-lane road. Stone fences and cordoned pastures pass by, kivas and rural homes dot the landscape. An intelligent reforestation program coincides with the landclearing for highway construction. Surrounded by thick forests and rolling hills, one is seduced into feeling "elsewhere."

All daydreams that you have actually been riding on Virginia's Blue Ridge Parkway end as you overtake the highway construction crew. "Andale! Andale!," they urge, "Way to go! Do it!" The road makes a sudden and crude transition from velveteen blacktop to diamond-hard gravel. Most of the traffic you now see are trucks ferrying lumber to the mill in Guachochic. The percussion of their passing shakes loose a stream of cobbles and the road is covered with a layer of lithic debris. For the sake of traction and to prevent permanent nerve damage, your bicycle tires should resemble those of the trucks. The trip can be done on 1.5's but 1.95's are the minimum we recommend and 2.25's are even better.

The first of many major climbs begins 12k south of Cusirare and brings you to the town of Naneruchachi. Surrounded by a magnificent panorama, the town consists of one cedar shack that sells candy and soft drinks through an open window. Eight kilometers further, largely downhill, is the considerably more amenable Basihuara. A small restaurant offers sitdown service, and lodging (sans bed) is available in the adjacent building. The canyon floor is wide here, the towering cliffs are stunning and, at this low elevation, the nights are warm. Consider making this your first night's destination.

Morning dawns with the cruel realization that the glinting scar on the canyon wall is the road ahead. Just beyond Basihuara begins a bumpy climb up to the start of a harrowing 5k descent to Umira, a village nestled on the shore of the Urique River. The Urique is the river primarily responsible for excavating Barranca del Cobre.

From Umira the road goes up. In the next 10k you gain a demanding 2,200 feet in altitude before reaching Mesa Napuchis. Here, a private home sells groceries and provides icy water from a nearby spring. Another 3k of rocky, rolling plateau brings you to **La Casita,** the only restaurant on this 135k route permanent enough to bear a name. It is a popular truck stop and marks the junction for Batopilas. Lodging is available in private homes in nearby Samachique and the surrounding forest offers unlimited camping. It is a good goal for your second night. Or, if it is still early enough in the day and you feel sufficiently motivated, continue another 20k to Quirare.

At the "La Casita" junction, the road narrows abruptly to a single lane and, miraculously, its surface improves. After two days of navigating over the grapefruit-sized rubble of the logging road, you can at last relax and enjoy the view. Hardwoods and pine trees embrace little cornfield clearings. Birch trees stand like sentinels against an evergreen backdrop. In the distance a brilliantly adorned Tarahumara woman chases her goats home. The road tilts gently up, the road tilts gently down, and quiet as a whisper you coast into Quirare.

Quirare is the largest Indian town on this route. It is famous locally for its small yellow apples and orchards line the road. It is home to a school for children from the outlying ranchos. Strangers are noted with wariness. The bicyclist is met with astonished silence. The children flock from the playground to stare curiously at you and admiringly at your bike, but even that is not enough to draw them out from their customary reticence.

The road from Quirare begins a downhill descent in earnest, and for the next 15k you will squeeze the brakes tightly. But the unrelenting incline is just one factor. Cattle and goats have an annoying habit of appearing on the narrow ledge with no warning. Dust, fine as talc and as effective a lubricant, is another. Besides cutting your coefficient of friction to just about zero, it is piled inches deep and hides the most jarring obstacles. Your attention is diverted from the scenery to the challenge of staying astride your bike. For an hour Eric followed the sandal prints of a Tarahumara, the serrated ridges of his automobile-tire soles delicately preserved in the dust as if in newly fallen snow. Peering over his handlebars he obliterated them, one after another, sending them skyward in a tail of dust that slowly settled on the canyon floor.

The View from Below

At the riverbed, after two days of gazing across valleys and into the canyon depths, you now look up at the wedding-cake tiers of monstrous sandstone walls. The road crosses the Batopilas River and begins a rugged one-kilometer climb to La Bufa.

La Bufa, an ochre-stained sulfate dump, seems to have been carried upward like a fishing dory on the back of a surfacing whale. The town, a collection of tiny shacks, perches precariously on the only flat surface for 20 miles around. Barricaded entrances to deep mine shafts are interspersed with the houses. There is a cafe and a place to buy groceries. Camping involves a considerable hike down to the river and, while lodging can be found, you are advised to push on to Batopilas.

It is tempting, however, to underestimate the effort required to complete this final 32k lap. The overall descent from La Bufa is 1,600 feet. Local topographic maps, straining to take in two degrees of longitude, depict the route as neatly paralleling the gently descending river. They reduce all features to a wholly unreliable scale. Don't fall for it. The burro trail you are travelling is depicted as being one-eighth of a kilometer wide!

Within the tight confines of the canyon a horizontal deviation of 100 feet can mean covering two hundred feet. This section of road does precisely that often enough to render the 1,600-foot drop meaningless. Grinding up and down the talus-strewn track of the eastern canyon wall requires three to four hours. You labor in solitude and the marvelous views are your private joy. Jagged arroyos worry their way across the trail. Tributary streams dump their slurry load of sediment like a burst sack of groceries on the kitchen counter. Deep green pools cry out for weary bikers to part their waters.

Five kilometers from Batopilas a series of freshets burst out of the canon wall. Closer study reveals them to be high-pressure leaks from an ancient stone aqueduct. Each opening is obscured by a profusion of vegetation that grows high in the mouth of the artificial spring.

The grueling ride from La Bufa and the monotonous battery of harsh trails, dull your reflexes. Three days of wilderness in which the only human occasion is the observation of indigenous poverty, tends to minimize one's expectations. All you ask of Batopilas is a chance to quit your bike.

Batopilas

The town catches you off guard. Skeletal remains of its mission rise unexpectedly over your shoulder. Cobbled streets and whitewashed walls, so typical elsewhere in Mexico, seem to have fallen out of the sky. Traffic is nonexistent. Electricity is by caprice of a kerosene generator. The streets go dark after sunset. Over 200 years ago Batopilas was a boom-town city of riches. Until 12 years ago, when the trail was widened enough to permit the passage of trucks, the town was supplied by foot and mule. Its tranquility has survived. It is a window back in time.

There are three hotels in town. The **Hotel Batopilas** is the best value at 2,000 pesos a night (US$1). The local **Artesania** shop has similar quarters at double the price, and yet one more **Parador** offers the most luxurious accommodations, with rates to match.

The town's culinary capital is up a short flight of stairs on Michaela's front porch. There's a refrigerator next to the dinner table and if you've managed to find the one store in town that sells beer, Michaela will keep it chilled.

When you are ready to explore there's the even more recondite town of Satevo, with its great mouldering cathedral, 6k and one cable footbridge downriver. High-country exploration is best done with the services of an experienced guide, and Santiago Felix and Elloy Hernandez, Sr. are two we recommend. For the remarkably low price of 15,000 pesos a day (US$8), which includes the use of their burros to carry the gear, they will take you on a walking tour of distant Tarahumara villages. Tourists are unusual but welcome guests. In the expectation that you will buy some baskets and leave any unused food, a guest room is made available for your use.

Even with burros to carry the weight, canyon hiking is strenuous. After the rigors of your journey it's more likely you'll spend days wandering the shady streets, swimming in the river, and wondering how they got the ship of Batopilas into the bottle of Barranca del Cobre.

A Few Last Words

Wilderness areas in the Third World tend to be underpopulated rather than unpopulated. Even what appear to be vacant slopes

Locals Hanging Out In Batopilas

are often the grazing land for a herd belonging to a local family. Though renowned for their shyness, the Tarahumara are tolerant of and, indeed, receptive to visitors. Consider that one more good reason to invest in the services of a guide. Despite the grinding poverty, the Tarahumara possess a tranquility and harmony with their environment that is so palpable you feel you can reach out and touch it.

There are only four cafes and four bodegas at which to buy a few meager groceries along this 135k route. With the exception of Creel and Batopilas, there are no hotels. Camping, while not essential, is a simple option. Lodging for the night can usually be found with inquiry. If you do spend the night at a Tarahumara *rancho,* a simple gift such as sewing needles and thread or some extra food is in order, in addition to the few pesos you will be asked to pay. Do not bring large bills and expect to be able to use them. Anything larger than the equivalent of US$1 will be virtually useless.

Because of the heat, the dust, and the physical exertion, you will need to drink about one gallon of water a day. Most wells are contaminated, and you should assume that they all are! *In addition* to chemical treatment or filter, it is recommended that water be boiled 30 to 45 minutes.

The Tarahumara object strongly to having their photographs taken. Respect their rights. Good quality color slides are available for sale at the Tarahumara artisan shops in Creel and Batopilas.

There is bus service between Creel and Batopilas. Busses depart from Creel at 6 a.m. three days a week and return the following day, departing Batopilas at 4 a.m. It is an eight-hour ride, and cyclists less than thrilled by the prospect of pedalling up a vertical mile of dirt road will be pleased to know that bikes can be carried on the bus for no extra charge.

ROADNOTES

WHAT'S AHEAD: Nearly all manner of civilized convenience ends in Creel. Beyond town, a few backwoods *tiendas* exist and there may even be an opportunity to spend the night on someone's dirt floor but plan to be totally self-reliant for the 2–3 days it will take to ride to Batopilas.

Kilometer 0	Creel. Stores, restaurants, maps available at the "Artesanias" shop on the plaza.
	Marguerite's Guest House, next to the plaza. A cheap and popular stop on the Gringo Trail.
3.5	Bridge. Continue straight for Batopilas, or . . .

DETOUR TO VALLE DE LAS GIGANTES (1.3k)
Cattle gate marks the turn to the whitewashed Tarahumara village of Ejido San Ignacio de Arreco. Cemetary and church. 7k further to the 80-foot-high wind-sculpted sandstone spires.

6	Lake Arareco. Clean enough for swimming but oh so cold.
19	Raramuchi. A few scattered homes, no services.
20	Road forks. Continue straight, or . . .

DETOUR TO CUSIRARE (1.8k)
Food and lodging. **Hotel Parador** marks the turn to Cusirare Falls, another 3k. Involves three crossings of shallow water where a carpet of algae makes footing extremely precarious. The falls, 90 feet high and surrounded by a deep gorge, are worth the effort.

21	Bridge over River Cusirare. Begin steep climb to 7,200-foot elevation. Parallel river.
24	Tucheachi Aserrado. A dozen homes, no services.
29	Pavement ends.
30	El Manzano. A house, a store, a view of the valley and the lumbermill.
31	Elevation 7,500 feet. From 26k to 31k takes a strenuous one and a half hours.
43	Basihuara. Town is about 2k from the river. Drop in elevation takes about one hour. Food and lodging. Recommended to spend the first night here, rent a room in a house, or camp.
46	Elevation 6,200 feet. Begin 800-foot descent.

54	Umira, elevation 5,500 feet. There is supposed to be a restaurant in town. One hour to reach Rio Urique bridge, four hours to "La Casita."
59	Rio Urique bridge. No services.
71	Mesa Napuchis junction. Groceries, good spring water.
73	**La Casita** restaurant. Good food, groceries. Junction to Batopilas, begin 10k of rolling hills on a narrow, slightly improved road.
76	Basigochito. Scattered homes, no services.
81	Arroyo Borachique. No services.
83	Elevation 7,400 feet. From 73k to 83k takes about one hour. From here to 107k begins an overall 4,000-foot drop in elevation, about three hours riding time.
85	Basogochi. Scattered homes, no services.
94	Quirare. Largest Indian town on the route. There's a mission and a school. One can probably find food and lodging with inquiry, or camp.
97	Begin last leg of the descent to La Bufa.
107	Rio Batopilas, bridge, elevation 3,200 feet.
109	La Bufa. Cafe. Rooms are available with inquiry.
130	Junction. Arroyo Cerro Colorado and the huge red mountain Cerro Colorado are on the opposite side of the river. Quimova mountaintop is used by the Tarahumara for summer grazing.
134	Bridge.
136	Batopilas. The road ends. Hotels, restaurants, groceries. Swimming and relaxation.
	Hotel Batopilas, on the left as you enter town. Simple rooms, kerosene lanterns, 2300p ($US 1).

INTRODUCTION TO BAJA CALIFORNIA

Baja is Mexico's gift to lovers of outdoor leisure. Sea-kayakers, dirtbikers, wilderness hikers and "Air-Stream" commandos seek their respective visions of heaven throughout the length of the peninsula's 1,700 kilometers. Two coastlines shelter uncounted coves and sandy hideaways and meet at one of Mexico's most glamorous resorts, Cabo San Lucas. Warm, clear blue waters, both east and west, are a wellspring for sports fishing. Sailing, surfing, swimming and sunning can't be beat.

Bicyclists are no longer in the rear guard of this recreational army. We met a greater concentration of independent bikers here, overall, than on the mainland. Several tour companies combine cycling and camping holidays in Baja.

Thrust between the Pacific Ocean and the Gulf of California, Baja is botanically unique. Dozens of plants found nowhere else populate this arid land, including huge *cardon* cacti and raggedy-topped *yucca valida*. *Cirio* trees truly prosper only here. Their peculiar tentacle-like forms have earned them the nickname "boojum" for a character created by Lewis Carroll.

Central Baja's west coast is the wintering grounds for the California grey whale. Females give birth in tepid, shallow lagoons before the herds return to the Bering Sea. Once hunted unmercifully, an estimated 100 whales survived the turn of the century. But, since gaining protective status, they have made a significant comeback. From December through March the greys can be observed from the shore near Guerrero Negro. See Tour #17 for more info.

Baja California is comprised of two states, B.C. Norte and B.C. Sur. The territory was settled by Jesuit missionaries in 1697. Like Johnny Appleseeds, the padres established missions and planted a trail of date orchards which flourished wherever water allowed. Some became the nuclei of communities which thrived, from Loreto, far south, to San Francisco in the United States.

Even so, nearly three centuries later, Baja remains largely untamed. Modern industry has spread roots along the northern border and developers scour the peninsula for potential resort sites, but these are anomalies. Baja is symbolized best by the tattered villages and abandoned missions strung across the desert. Fiercely beautiful and spartan as hell, the peninsula is a fascinating, challenging land, the perfect place for veteran cyclists to meet Mexico.

Near the United States border, English is the *lingua franca.* Prices throughout the peninsula are often quoted in U.S. dollars. Yet, there is no question that this is a "foreign" country. Crossing into Tijuana you are smacked in the face by the cultural and economic differences. The crowded streets surge with buyers and sellers, young and old, rich and poor, the familiar and the new.

Salt Flats On The Sea Of Cortes

It is only a matter of a few hours and some kilometers before the clash and refuse of civilization are outdistanced. Air pollution is minimal. Mexico's National Observatory is located here for good reason; the night sky is spectacularly clear. Sleeping beneath the diamond firmament is one of Baja's most compelling allures. Camping is safe and the vast desert offers infinite places to spend the night.

Between each shimmering oasis, virgin shore and tranquil campsite is one big heap of sunblasted desert. Biking Baja calls for self-sufficiency. Shade is rare. Water is frequently not available. Plan to carry four liter bottles and fill them at every opportunity. Unlike the mainland, towns are few and far between. Lodging is erratic, camping sometimes unavoidable. Marshall supplies and plan ahead.

Generally, provisions are available every 20k to 25k. In the most desolate areas, ranches and cafes average twice that distance apart. The long, hot, contemplative intervals make every pitstop a providential joy. Baja is a mind-blowing wasteland surrounded by water and abundant with the most astonishing variety of plant and animal life. Making its acquaintance from a bicycle seat is an unforgettable adventure.

THE BAJA DAY RIDES

No doubt about it, easy access from the U.S. is one of the great charms of the Baja Day Rides. Cross the border and more than just the cultural surroundings are different. With each pedalled kilometer the topography changes dramatically. These border rides offer a satisfying taste, but less than a full meal, of the many treats to be found in Baja.

The Tecate-to-Ensenada ride begins inland, winds through dusty, difficult, nearly uninhabited mountains, and descends into populous Ensenada. Many cyclists turn out for this tough ride, an annual spring event sponsored by Monday International. If interested in joining a cast of thousands, contact them for info at 4275 Mission Blvd., San Diego, CA 92109.

While we're on marathons, the Rosarito-to-Ensenada ride, a route covered in Tour #17, occurs twice yearly. In 1988, 16,000 bikers participated in the autumn ride, sponsored by Bicycling West, Inc., P.O. Box 15128, San Diego, CA 92115-0128.

Mex 3 bisects the peninsula from the Pacific Ocean to the Gulf of Mexico. It's a lovely ride, of moderate difficulty. But best of all, this route provides access to many of northern Baja's infamous back roads.

Of the three rides included in Tour #17, we found the Mexicali-to-San Felipe ride to be the most challenging, not for its effort but its monotony. Yet each year hundreds of cyclists show up, en masse, to bike the furnace-baked salt flats which lie between the United States and the Gulf of Mexico. Write Monday International if interested in elbowing with the crowd.

Day Ride 1

A MOUNTAINOUS
PLEASURE RIDE

ROUTE: Tecate—Ensenada.
DISTANCE: 116k.
RIDING TIME: 1 day.
DIFFICULTY: Moderately difficult.
TERRAIN: Sinuous road through dry, deserted mountains.
BEST TIME: Year-round.
ATTRACTIONS: A challenging ride, great scenery and little traffic.

There are two approaches to Ensenada from the California border. Most cyclists choose Mex 1, the coastal route from Tijuana (see Tour #18), but our own preference is Mex 3. It is a mountainous pleasure ride that originates in Tecate.

Tecate's economy is dependant on agriculture and industry rather than tourism and, as border towns go, it is uncommonly pleasant. Tourists are not constantly assailed to buy, buy, buy. There is no strip of gaudy bars, and prostitution—nearly synonomous with border life—is absent. The tranquility of this typical Mexican town lives on in Tecate's tree-shaded plaza.

Mex 3 begins as Calle Ortiz Rubio, the street which borders the plaza's eastern edge. Follow it south, cross the meager Tecate River, shift into low gear and climb through rock-studded, chapparal covered hills. The steepest grades are encountered early.

Valle de las Palmas, k 28, is a small farming community whose cafes and stores are reliably stocked. It's a good place to fill water bottles. On the far side of town a hefty climb commences. Refreshments are next available at Testerazo, k 50. From here, Mex 3 maintains elevation. The region becomes more intensively cultivated. A long downhill run begins at Ejido Zaragoza, k 64, at the large olive grove and processing plant. Sordo Mudo ("Deaf and Dumb"), another 6k, is noted as the home of Domecq Vineyards.

The village of Guadalupe, k 77, provides refrescos and a chance to stretch your legs. The terrain flattens until Santa Cruz, k 91. Then it's mostly downhill to El Sauzal and the junction with Mex

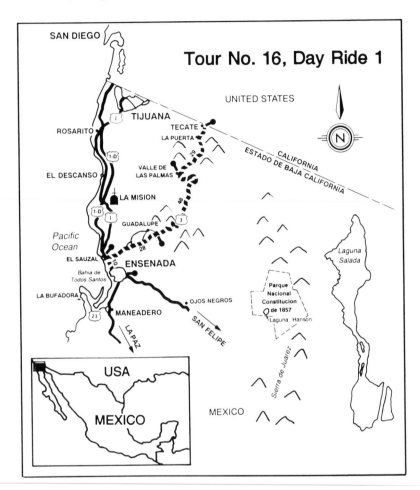

1D. As gravity relents, the wind kicks in and prevailing wester-
lies supply a great cross-tail. On a good day gusts usher you the
final 10k to Ensenada.

After the austerity of this ride, Ensenada exerts an irresistable
pull. A choice of restaurants and great revelry at such revered
institutions as **Hussong's Cantina** and **Papas and Beer**
beckon. To loosen up prior to getting loose check out the lodging
suggestions in the Tour #18 Roadnotes.

ROADNOTES

WHAT'S AHEAD: a long, rewarding day's ride over the route that paved the way for south-of-the-border riding. Tecate, neither a hectic state capital like Mexicali, nor a Jezebel like Tijuana, is a nice border-town that just happens to be home to a wonderful brewery. A veritable Milwaukee of the desert. Refill water bottles often. Refreshment stops come at infrequent intervals. Wonderful scenery and a dearth of traffic make this 112k a joy to ride.

Kilometer 0	Tecate. Full service. Leave town on Calle Ortiz Rubio, eastern edge of plaza. Begin climb.
14	Top of climb. Canada el Yaqui. No services.
28	Valle de las Palmas. Stores, cafes, Pemex. Begin climb.
37	Top. Rancho Viejo. No services.
50	Testerazo. Country town, wood carvings for sale. The store is sometimes open. Terrain levels.
75	Sordo Mudo. Store. Home of Domecq Vineyards.
77	Guadalupe. Rural community settled by Russian immigrants. Stores.
91	Rancho Sta. Cruz, no services. Fast descent begins.
106	El Sauzal. Marks the outskirts of Ensenada.
115	Ensenada.

SAN FELIPE, THE LONG WAY

ROUTE: Ensenada—San Felipe.
DISTANCE: 236k.
RIDING TIME: 2 or 3 days.
DIFFICULTY: Moderately difficult.
TERRAIN: Low mountains and desert plains.
BEST TIME: Year-round.
ATTRACTIONS: A gorgeous ride between the northern peninsula's east and west coasts.

Mex 3, the most scenic paved road in northern Baja, turns inland from Ensenada. Kilometer for kilometer, it's the least trafficked northern highway and, for all around pleasure, it can't be beat.

This route offers multiple opportunities for off-road adventure. We crossed paths with one couple who were making a holiday of cycling dirt roads from Laguna Hanson, high in the Sierra de Juarez, to Picacho del Diablo in the Sierra San Pedro Martir.

The ride out of Ensenada is a sobering series of climbs which rise from sea level to 2,600 feet. The first and longest of these is 9k. The road is very sinuous and at times turns to gravel. Watch for cars and flying debris.

There is a sign for Agua Caliente at k 28. The thermal resort has a reputation for friendly service and good food. Camping is permitted. You'll need a mountain bike to visit, though. The unpaved 8k detour is rough.

Continuing south, the interminable climbs terminate at k 36, shortly before the enormous, fertile valley of Ojos Negros.

Ojos Negros

Each November the peninsula's fabled auto race, the Baja 1000, briefly drowns Ojos Negros in high-decibel activity. The other 360 days of the year, this is one quiet burg. The town has no clearly defined center, unusual in Mexico, and a web of dusty roads connect its scattered homes. It may take some searching to find a cafe that serves dinner. At one end of town the **Albercas**

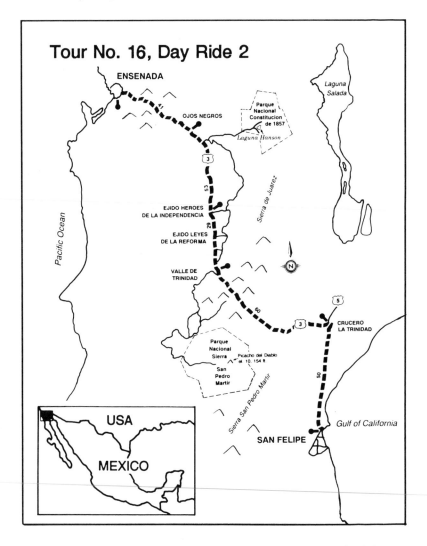

Los Casian balneario, closed for winter, made a wonderful over-night campsite where no one bothered us. When it's open, it seems likely camping would be permissable.

A gravel detour in Ojos Negros provides the best access to La-guna Hanson, located in the Parque Nacional Constitucion de

1857, one of Baja's two federally created parks. The lake is stocked with various fresh water fish—largemouth bass, bluegills and catfish. The map depicts a forest service station there, but whenever roaming off Baja's beaten trail, expect no assistance. Take lots of food and be prepared to treat drinking water. Laguna Hanson is about 40k from Ojos Negros. Reputedly, the road is driveable by passenger car and sounds worthy of mountain bike investigations.

Back on Mex 3, road quality improves. The terrain remains gentle. Rounded hills tumble to the horizon, mountains rise up in the distance. Between highway kilometer markers 59 and 60 there's a lovely little spring, a good place to picnic in the shade of cottonwoods. An abandoned ranch appears at k 67 and the cafe **Esperanza** at k 69. Chapparal gives way to grass and the road crosses a plain known as Llano Colorado. Refreshments and supplies are available at Ejido Heroes de la Independencia, k 95, and the **Vallejo** is likely the best of its restaurants.

At Ejido Leyes de la Reforma the road drops in elevation. While still swooping valleyward you pass the turn for Valle de Trinidad, k 123, the largest town in this neck of the ... uh ... desert. Somehow the turn is easy to miss. There are stores, cafes and restaurants.

A Pemex station marks the undramatic summit of San Matias Pass, a low saddle that separates the Sierra de Juarez from the towering Sierra San Pedro Martir. Nearby is the turn for **Mike's Sky Ranch,** a rustic retreat up a 35k dirt road. From there, a four-wheel drive trail continues on to **Meling Ranch,** another tourist facility. It's 48k from Meling Ranch to the crags of Picacho del Diablo, Baja's tallest peak (10,154 feet) and home of Mexico's National Observatory. We've never attempted this assault but casual observation suggests it is an appalling climb.

After coasting down the backside of San Matias Pass the party ends. The San Felipe valley floor is about as exciting as riding an exercise bike. Crucero La Trinidad, k 199, is located at the intersection of Mex 3 and Mex 5. **Three Poles** restaurant is a decent place to soak up some drinks before getting back on the treadmill.

The final 51k to San Felipe are hot, flat, and heavily trafficked. Shucks. Just when you thought you had a few minutes to practice conjugating irregular Spanish verbs, the RV's and Chevy Blazers warrant caution.

San Felipe's many tourist facilities make it a comfortable place to regenerate from the taxing ride.

ROADNOTES

WHAT'S AHEAD: Mex 3 is a scenic route through the low mountains and sparsely settled farm country of northern Baja. It is a far more interesting ride to San Felipe than Route 5.

Kilometer 0	Ensenada. Intersection of Av. Juarez and Av. Ruiz. Follow Juarez east to Calz. Cortez.
2	Monument to Benito Juarez. Turn left onto Calz. Cortez, which becomes Mex 3.
4	Start 9k climb. Briefer climbs follow.
28	Junction with dirt road to Agua Caliente, thermal resort. Begin 3k drop.
36	Climbs end. Enormous, fertile valley of Ojos Negros comes into view.
42	Ojos Negros. Campground, groceries, cafes, all sometimes open. If detouring to Laguna Hanson, ask directions for which gravel road to take.
	Albercas Los Casian balneario, closed in winter but possible to camp.
50	Junction for alternate route to Laguna Hanson.
52	Spring. Nice place to picnic and possibly camp.
67	Abandoned ranch.
69	Cafe **Esperanza,** k marker 80.
72	Peak elevation, 3,600 feet. Llano Colorado, no services.
95	Ejido Heroes de la Independencia, k marker 90. Restaurant **Vallejo,** cafes, Pemex.
106	Ejido Leyes de la Reforma, k marker 103. One store.
123	Begin 6k descent, pass entrance to Valle de Trinidad. Groceries, restaurants, Pemex.
140	Signed detour for **Mike's Sky Ranch,** 35k south via dirt roads. Rustic retreat, horseback riding, trout fishing.
143	San Matias Pass. Begin long descent into San Felipe valley.
144	Pemex.
199	Junction with Mex 5. Pemex, **Three Poles** restaurant.
250	San Felipe.

Day Ride 3

SOME LIKE IT HOT

ROUTE: Mexicali—San Felipe.
DISTANCE: 186k.
RIDING TIME: 1 day.
DIFFICULTY: Easy pedalling but way too much of it.
TERRAIN: Flat, flat, flat.
BEST TIME: Spring and fall.

Shielded from the moderating effects of the Sea of Cortes and low in elevation, Mexicali has the most hellish climate in all of Mexico. With the possible exception of Hermosillo, no place else comes close. And in winter it can be damn cold. In short, this run is a favorite of those who think that fun should hurt, and their numbers appear to be growing. In 1989, over 1,000 cyclists turned out for Monday International's annual Mexicali-to-San Felipe race. Some really do like it hot.

To establish a proper frame of mind, snuggle up close to your toaster oven while reviewing these tour highlights:

Eight kilometers from the border, Calz. Lopez Mateos crosses Mex 5. Turn right and go on auto-pilot.

Choose your personal rehydration serum from cafes and stores between La Puerta (k 40) and Campo Sonora (k 58). At k 71 the road begins to cross the Laguna Salada. The briny flats represent the desert at its least hospitable. For 48k the salt flats splay out. There are no services. The void mercifully terminates in La Ventana, k 114. Eat, drink and be merry.

Further south the highway develops fleeting relief, then quickly retreats to an overwhelming levelness. Other than a restaurant and gas station at the junction with Mex 3, the flatlands stay flat all the way to San Felipe.

Sounds like too much fun to us.

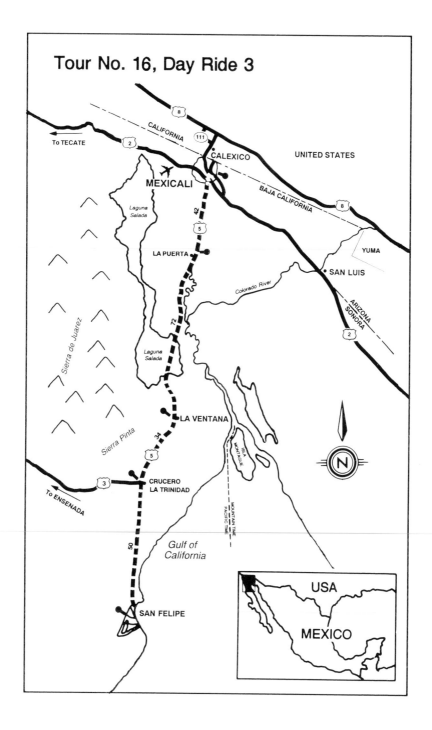

Tour No. 16, Day Ride 3

To TECATE

CALIFORNIA

8

111

2

CALEXICO

UNITED STATES

MEXICALI

BAJA CALIFORNIA

8

Laguna
Salada

42

5

YUMA

LA PUERTA

SAN LUIS

Colorado River

ARIZONA
SONORA

72

2

Sierra de Juarez

Laguna
Salada

N

Sierra Pinta

34

LA VENTANA

5

ISLA
MONTAGUE

3

CRUCERO
LA TRINIDAD

To ENSENADA

MOUNTAIN TIME
PACIFIC TIME

50

Gulf of
California

USA

SAN FELIPE

MEXICO

ROADNOTES

Kilometer 0	Mexicali, modern capital of Baja California North. From border crossing, take Calz. Lopez Mateos southeast. It becomes Mex 2.
8	Junction with Calz. Benito Juarez, which becomes Mex 5. Turn right onto Mex 5.
40	La Puerta. Cafe, store and two Pemex stations.
41	**El Topolobampo** restaurant.
43	Roadside tiendas, *marisco* stand.
44	Pemex station.
45	**Nayarit** restaurant.
48	**La Aurora** restaurant.
58	Campo Sonora. Store.
71	Road begins across the Laguna Salada.
114	La Ventana. Cafe, Pemex.
149	Junction with Mex 5. Pemex station, restaurant.
180	**Campo Don Abel** trailer park, first of many.
198	San Felipe. Full service.

TOUR 17

TIJUANA TO LA PAZ

ROUTE: Tijuana–Santa Rosalia–La Paz.
DISTANCE: 1,489k.
RIDING TIME: Two weeks.
TERRAIN: Mostly flat, maybe 15% mountainous.
DIFFICULTY: Hard. Physically and mentally taxing.
BEST TIME: Spring or fall. In winter, northern Baja may be cold and rainy.

The ride from Tijuana to La Paz is a bona fide marathon, a 1,500-kilometer endurance test. The landscape is dry and desolate, largely forsaken but for a kingdom of appalling vegetation. For fans of wide open spaces, however, this is the strength as well as the challenge of riding Baja. The dues are high but rewards are ample: unblemished natural beauty and solitude. To tackle the peninsula on a bicycle, expect privation. Carry a minimum of four liters of water and fill them at every opportunity. Camping sometimes is obligatory.

Approached in stages, the idea of riding Baja becomes a manageable concept. Plan it as you would a military campaign. A scraggly string of Pacific coast communities is the scene of opening exercises. The terrain starts out level. But the days are long and boredom emerges as the chief enemy. After endless hours to El Rosario the road turns inland and the real battle begins. A lightning thrust across the Vizcaino Plain—a single grievous day—and the lush oasis of San Ignacio appears, providing much needed succor. R & R continues at the Sea of Cortes but the job is unfinished. The final week is a mopping-up exercise, tedious but required to reach La Paz, gem of the south.

But, back to reality—and the starting line.

Tijuana is the quintessential border town, queen of the buffer zone that is the U.S./Mexican demarcation. Exciting and garish, loud, full of genuine bargains and shoddy replicas, the city unabashedly hustles the zillions of *Norteamericanos* who stream across the border daily. Tijuana, now Mexico's fourth largest city, is expanding rapidly. Its dramatic progress in many ways em-

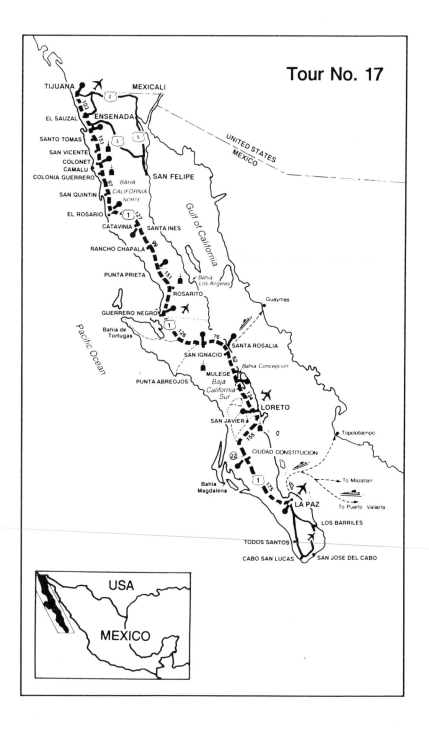

Tour No. 17

TIJUANA
MEXICALI
103
2
EL SAUZAL
ENSENADA
SANTO TOMAS
151
3
5
SAN VICENTE
COLONET
CAMALU
COLONIA GUERRERO
BAHA
CALIFORNIA
NORTE
SAN FELIPE
SAN QUINTIN
97
EL ROSARIO
1
CATAVINIA
127
SANTA INES
RANCHO CHAPALA
98
Gulf of California
PUNTA PRIETA
151
Bahia
Los Angeles
ROSARITO
GUERRERO NEGRO
Guaymas
1
Bahia de
Tortugas
128
76
SANTA ROSALIA
SAN IGNACIO
63
Bahia Concepcion
PUNTA ABREOJOS
MULEGE
Baja
California
Sur
134
LORETO
SAN JAVIER
Topolobampo
155
CIUDAD CONSTITUCION
22
To Mazatlan
1
To Puerto Vallarta
Bahia
Magdalena
175
LA PAZ
LOS BARRILES
TODOS SANTOS
CABO SAN LUCAS
SAN JOSE DEL CABO

Pacific Ocean

UNITED STATES
MEXICO

USA

MEXICO

bodies the country's emergent dreams. On a bicycle, however, it's a nightmare.

Tourist Permits

If you don't already have a tourist card, it can be gotten at the *Servicios Migratorios* office at the border crossing. As of this writing, the building is undergoing renovation. Permits are issued at an improbably tiny shack adjacent the walkway just beyond the *Bienvenidos a Mexico* sign. Remember, if travelling south of Maneadero, you *must* have a tourist permit. Although U.S. citizens do not need a passport to enter Mexico, having one will expedite the paperwork. Tourist card safely tucked away, struggle past the insistent taxi drivers and *serapé* dealers. Follow the signs for *Centro* to downtown Tijuana, four and one-half high-speed, traffic-plagued kilometers away. Things improve, trust us.

Escape from Tijuana

From central Tijuana, signs for Ensenada direct traffic to Highway 1-D, a toll road which is closed to bicycles. Our route is via Mexico Highway 1, the Transpeninsular. To reach it, follow the main drag, Av. Revolucion to the park "18 de Marzo." Make a left onto the unsigned Boulevard Agua Caliente. One kilometer further, turn right onto Calle Cuauhtehmoc. This becomes Benito Juarez, a four-lane road that climbs through a slummy river valley. You're on Mex 1 now, for the next 1,500 kilometers. Couldn't be easier.

Mex 1 to Ensenada

Mex 1 is either narrow or very narrow throughout Baja and in this northernmost portion of the state traffic is consistently heavy. Even so, the industrial stench soon gives way to more wholesome agricultural aromas. At k 23 Mex 1 crosses beneath Mex 1-D to reach Rosarito and the sea. Little more than a dusty strip of hotels, restaurants and craft shops, Rosarito may be the plaster of Paris pop and religious icon center of the world. Three-foot statues of Jesus, Mary, and Kermit the Frog stand in the thousands on both sides of the road.

Continuing south, the road creates a sandy corridor that is filling quickly with vacation homes. Billboards extoll their low prices and mar the view. It's not until Pto. Nuevo that construction abates, sand dunes rise, and the beach becomes appealing. At k 56 the road again ducks under Mex 1-D, climbs a steep hillside and drops into the valley of La Mision. Any lingering doubts about Baja's astounding majesty evaporate.

A tough 8k climb, atypical of northern Baja, begins on La Mision's far side. Traffic abates and what lies in store for the next umpteen hundred kilometers abounds: fantastic scenery and scant services. A lone soda pop stand appears at k 77, halfway between La Mision and El Sauzal, a community on the outskirts of Ensenada.

Ensenada, the most logical place to call it a day, is a genuinely amenable city. Camping is possible but the beaches are inconveniently distant. To properly enjoy Ensenada seek out a hotel. The budget choices are on Calle Gastelum, where humble rooms with common toilet and shower rent for approximately 7,000p ($3) a night. Bike and panniers safe, go out and enjoy Ensenada's nightlife. Similar opportunities won't occur until La Paz, weeks away. Of the local bars, **Hussong's** is the loudest and liveliest. They bottle their own beer, a bitter pilsner, and blend a deliciously volatile tequila.

Before leaving Ensenada, do a last-minute bicycle check. Spare parts can be purchased at **Pedal Y Fibre,** a bike shop in Calle Miramar #426.

Pacific Coast Communities

South of Ensenada Mex 1 runs parallel to, but rarely in sight of, the Pacific. Occasionally the road meanders inland, crossing low mountain passes. The terrain is otherwise gentle. Towns appear on average every 50k to 80k. Cafes, provisions, and water are abundant, but lodging is spotty at best and camping is often preferable. Unless in dire need of a shower you'll do as well to sleep under the saltbush.

The San Pedro Martir mountains are Baja's loftiest, snow-covered in winter, and site of the National Observatory. They come into view around k 280, on the approach to San Quintin, the last tourist destination of consequence in northern Baja. Numerous hotels suit a range of budgets. Leading out from the town's center, sandy roads plumb the edges of an unusual double embayment. Relics from a 19th-century English farming community are scattered among the dunes. Rotten wharf pilings and a wind-swept cemetery write its epitaph.

Leaving San Quintin, the pedalling is again easy until k 345, where a long climb commences. Then a screaming descent culminates with an alarming 90-degree turn and runway-style landing in El Rosario's main street. **Mama Espinoza's Lobster Burrito** shack is here, but don't expect the prices to be so folksy. There's a decent hotel in town and a well-stocked grocery.

El Rosario marks the start of Baja's central desert, the peninsula's most desolate and demanding territory. Try to buy supplies the night before—don't forget the bottled water—and shoot for a dawn departure. And carry lots of film; the upcoming scenery is some of the most outlandishly beautiful on the planet.

The Central Desert

The push into Baja's dessicated heart begins innocently enough. The road parallels the usually dry Rio del Rosario past fields of gloriously bright red and green chili peppers. After crossing the wide valley it begins climbing. The land puckers from erosion and becomes increasingly laden with cacti. The highway roller coasts through a spiny botanical garden of ever more peculiar specimens. They thrive in such improbable spots, the steepest ravines, the least nourishing substrates, emerging from jumbles of towering boulders.

San Agustin could only get a writeup in a place as vacuous as this. The AAA guidebook describes San Agustin as "an abandoned Pemex station, an abandoned . . . trailer park and a highway maintenance camp." Don't get your hopes up, the maintenance camp is abandoned too. Granted, it's not the most scenic spot to lounge, but those shattered gas pumps provide a tasty bit of shade. **Tres Enriques** cafe, 3k further, is a more commodious facility.

By now, *cirio* trees, unique to this part of the world, introduce a new dimension of weirdness. The plants grow to thirty feet and are vaguely reminiscent of Zippy's pinhead. The tree's dried skeleton is a woody lace more delicate in appearance than the living plant, but it's strong and is used locally for construction. Look for the distinctive hollow timbers in roadside cafes.

Offroad Anyone? Near Catavina

In the vicinity of Cataviña the land bursts forth with new varieties of desert flora. Tall fan palms fringe the edge of a dry streambed. Elephant trees, *cholla, ocotillo, cardon,* and *yucca* dot the splendorous terrain. But man's attention span is short. Graffiti splashes the rocks in Spanish and English. There are many dips along this stretch, caused by arroyos intersecting the highway. Be cautious of loose sand and even water.

At Cataviña's **La Pinta Hotel** rooms rent for 115,000p ($50) a night. Bar, restaurant and—here it's a bit iffy—swimming pool, are open to the public. Order a drink before asking about the pool. Drinking water is available from the staff and camping, near an arroyo 200 yards away, is excellent. Lying on the sandy flats, gazing through palms silhouetted against the star-emblazoned sky is one of Baja's finest attractions.

Not in the mood for simple pleasures? **Rancho Santa Ines,** 2k further, offers dormitory-style rooms and good food at travellers' prices.

After Cataviña the road climbs to a 2,700-foot-high summit, mellows out and, at k 577, reaches the junction for Bahia Los Angeles. A gas station, grocery store and the **Parador Punta Prieta** mark the turn.

Bahia Los Angeles is a tempting 68k detour to a starkly beautiful bay hemmed in by barren mountains. Headquarters for a no-nonsense crowd of sports fishermen, trailer hookups and mechanic shops outnumber the nightspots. There is no shade. Either pack a tent or plan to spend a lot of time in the bar.

On the Trail of Sebastian Vizcaino, Charles Scammon and the California Grey Whale

It is a long, *long* way from the junction for Bahia Los Angeles to Guerrero Negro, in which the road transects the vast, windswept, bleak Vizcaino Desert. The **Cafe Mauricio** in Rosarito, k 629, has the best cooking en route. Frequented by truckers, the front lot is studded with tractor-trailers. Inside, the walls are plastered with snapshots of confident stetson-bedecked drivers with their rigs. On the counter a pickle jar holds the restaurant's mascot, a yellowish scorpion the size of a small rock lobster. The waitress says only the small ones are lethal but this baby no doubt packs a wallop. It's an effective reminder to check your shoes each morning.

After Rosarito the terrain flattens. Let's be candid—it's a challenge to stay awake. By Nueva Esperanza, the road assumes the attitude of a light ray, passing unrefracted through Villa Jesus Maria. Thirty kilometers later it reaches the border of Baja California North where an extraordinary monument, 140 feet of rusting girders meant to look like an eagle, welcomes you to Baja California South.

Guerrero Negro, the first major town in B.C.S., is the world's largest producer of salt. Behind a drab exterior lies a surprisingly homey town. Out of season, competition keeps hotel prices reasonable and good fish tacos can be found on the main strip. You were expecting sushi maybe?

But it is nearby Scammon's Lagoon that put Guerrero Negro on the map. Between late December and early March the lagoon is the winter calving grounds of the California grey whale. Slaughtered to near extinction, these giant mammals are now protected.

One of the best places to see them is the Parque Natural de las Ballenas Grises, located on the Laguna Ojo de Liebre, 30k west from Guerrero Negro. An observation tower facilitates viewing. Scammon's Lagoon is reached by continuing south on Mex 1 about 9k, and turning right onto a dirt road signed "Refugio Ballena Gris/Grey Whale Refuge."

There's little besides whale watching to hold you here, except the thought of the desert ahead. The Vizcaino spreads south for yet another 140k. This saltbush wasteland is best crossed in one long day and one short one. The land is virtually featureless until the busy Vizcaino junction, where the terrain finally begins to roll. Now the Tres Virgenes volcanos come into view. Thorny forests of *cardon* cactus and *yucca valida* reappear.

San Ignacio

The first sight of San Ignacio is arresting. After the mind-numbing, interminable Vizcaino Desert the town seems a mirage, a rent in the desert floor brimming with verdant,

Lagoon, San Ignacio

wind-rustled palms. The tall, overarching trees shield a splendid lagoon—a wonderful place to stop for a swim. In the background the spire of an 18th-century Dominican church breaches the wall of green. San Ignacio is delightfully untrammeled. Unofficial camping is possible at the lagoon or on the grounds of a large date orchard, both on the way into town. The rich yellow and red sprays of these fruit abound, spicing your visit with freely scattered treats. In the hills nearby are caves protecting hundreds of ancient paintings. To hire a guide and transportation inquire with Oscar Fischer at the general store adjacent the plaza.

Inspect your brakes before leaving San Ignacio. At k 895 the steepest grade in all of Baja begins, an elevator shaft plunging to the Sea of Cortes. That people manage it in mobile homes is a marvel.

The East Coast Communities: Sta. Rosalia to Loreto

Santa Rosalia, like Guerrero Negro, is a company town and it bears the indelible stamp of industry. Slag heaps, abandoned machinery and rail cars, remnants from its copper smelting history, surround the outlying district. But the center of town, overlooked by most tourists, is quite pleasant. On the plaza, the pre-fab metal church of Santa Barbara was designed by A. G. Eiffel, of "Tower" fame. In addition to inexpensive lodging in Santa Rosalia, there are long-distance telephones and major banks. Count your pesos, it's still a way to La Paz.

Santa Rosalia is Baja's northernmost ferry port. Some people, sated with desert touring, may opt to transfer to the mainland from here. As of this writing departures for Guaymas are on Tuesday, Thursday and Sunday. Guaymas is a delightful city with excellent beaches but, when continuing on from there, consider taking the train. Reports from cyclists travelling Mex 15 through Sonora and, especially, Sinaloa, have been overwhelmingly negative: too much traffic, too little beach and too many thugs.

Sixty-two kilometers south is another remarkable Baja oasis, Mulege, abundant with hotels, stores and even a laundromat. But, unless desperate for such civilized amenities, get groceries and water, and keep moving. You're about to strike it rich.

Beautiful Bahia Concepcion

Only twelve miles further, the astounding Bahia Concepcion comes into sight, a tuck in the coastline of the Sea of Cortes. A fresh breeze ruffles your hair. Sunlight glints across the water, clear, blue, swarming with marine life. Beds of shellfish offer a smorgasbord on the halfshell. At night, phosphorescent plankton illuminate the water and draw schools of leaping mullet who comport themselves with the racket of a paddlewheel steamer. These tasty fish can be taken with hook and line, nets, or even stampeded ashore.

Maps show a slew of *playas publicas,* beaches open to the public, along the western shore of Bahia Conception. It's an ambiguous designation. Some are free, some charge to camp, and some are private. Santispac, the first of them, has a restaurant, grocery and good anchorage, making it the most popular. Palappa-style campsites fetch 11,500p ($5) a night.

Posada Concepcion, El Coyote, and Requeson, smaller beaches and more primitive options, cost as little as nothing. El Coyote has a small restaurant and Requeson offers the best clamming. *Catarina* and *chocolati* clams can be gathered in knee-deep water with astonishing ease, and scallops are found a little further out. The same was undoubtedly true of the other beaches not long ago. Be thoughtful to collect only as much as you will eat.

Departing Bahia Concepcion is not easy. Recondite coves beckon. Between Santispac and Requeson, ride with caution. The road twists sharply through rocky headlands. Traffic is moderately heavy and prone to appear in the middle of the road on blind curves. The miles to Loreto are long and beaches of Concepcion's ilk won't soon be seen again.

Loreto, Baja's oldest city, was capital of the peninsula until a hurricane levelled it in 1829. It then fell on hard times, until recently. The government is trying to develop the area for the tourist trade, but construction lags for lack of funds. Prices in Loreto are generally high and there's no reason to stay here unless in need of a laundromat.

There are some fine beaches south of Loreto, where new resorts are planned; construction is already underway in Nopolo. Swimming at Playa Notri is good, but the beach is uncomfortably close to the highway. Juncalito, though buggy, is a better bet and is the last chance for oceanfront camping before the road turns inland. There is a restaurant that caters to Americans at Pto. Escondido and a cafe at the village of Ligui. Don't forget to fill your water bottles.

Mountains and the Magdalena Plain

The Sierra de la Giganta are aptly named and no piece of cake. On a hot day—not uncommon hereabouts—-they are a brutal challenge. With legs toughened from weeks of riding, you may even find the vista worthy of the climb. At the end of a second climb, less extreme in grade and length, the highway marker corresponds to a rest stop called **Cafe K 54.** It is the first food and water break since Ligui, 31k behind. The mountains end, the Magdalena Plain begins. The region is topographically similar to, but far more fertile than the Vizcaino Desert.

At Cd. Insurgentes, k 1,254, the road bears left. If your bike is equipped with a gyroscope and sail, take a bearing and stretch

Sierra De La Giganta

out for a nap. The road follows an arrow straight trajectory for 72 b-o-r-i-n-g kilometers, barely acknowledging Cd. Constitucion as it passes into the desert beyond.

Cd. Constitucion, a full blown city, is 214k short of La Paz, still a two-day ride. It is a good place to find a hotel room. The next night will of necessity be spent outside. In the upcoming desolate country cafes continue to identify themselves by kilometer markers. There are good ones at k 154 and k 129.

At El Cien—k 100, get it?—the road enters severely eroded hills. One treacherous gulley, marked by a large roadside memorial, is resting place for several wrecked and (it's difficult to imagine otherwise) bloodstained chasis. Had the unfortunate drivers navigated the turn they'd have arrived at a high overlook, k 1428, and a fresh glimpse of the beauteous Sea of Cortes.

The sight triggers a surge of adrenaline. After weeks in pursuit of a phantom finish line, La Paz seems much closer than the 32k indicated on the map. The proximity tempts you to sprint. Legs turn to jelly.

La Paz, Gem of the South

The city of La Paz, population 150,000, is situated along a narrow channel in the huge Bahia de La Paz. The harbor is not well flushed by the tide, and for this reason, ceremonial end-of-tour dousings are cautionary. Sunbathe here; more swimmable waters are only a short bike ride away.

La Paz is one of the least touristy resort towns in Mexico. Its duty free shops are stocked with imported goods seldom seen in much of the country. The city is clean and, except for the thriving commercial district, has the feel of a much smaller place. You'll have to look around to find some nightlife. Try the hotels and restaurants along the *malecon,* the lovely palm-lined waterfront.

Surprisingly, La Paz does not have a stellar reputation for food, but there is the quite good **Restaurante Vegetariano** in Calle El Quinto Sol. The best fish tacos in all of Baja, perhaps in all the world, can be found at a tiny street stall called **Taqueria Los Amigos.** It's located on Calle Degollado near the Pension California.

Travelling by Ferry

Ferries to the mainland are as pleasurable as purchasing a ticket can be infuriating. Schedules suffer frequent disruption, the ticketing system is less than efficient. Boats to Los Mochis and Mazatlan are the most reliable in that they consistently depart from La Paz. The trip to Pto. Vallarta sometimes begins from Cabo, sometimes from La Paz, and sometimes not at all.

Visit the ferry office on arrival in La Paz. It's located at Calles Ejido and Ramirez. If there are *cabina* or *turista* vacancies, grab one. *Salon* class seats, located in the huge chamber amidships, are usually available the day prior to departure. The 24-hour voyage to Pto. Vallarta is a particular favorite of ours, a real poor man's cruise. For 12,000p ($6) you get a semi-private cabin with fresh linen, and a shower down the hall. Bikes ride free. Bring food—restaurant service is not reliable. Picnic on the open deck and watch for porpoises. Note: Lax officials sometimes allow cyclists to wheel bikes up the narrow gangplank. Not advisable. Insist on locking it below with the automobiles.

Pichilingue, site of the ferry terminal, is 17k north of La Paz. Across from the dock a row of open air restaurants serve the hundreds of truckers heading to and from the mainland. Excellent food, generous portions, good prices, and often there's live music.

The Local Beaches: Baja's Finest

But for swimming and camping, not much can surpass the pristine, isolated coves just north of Pichilingue. Both Balandra and Tecolote can be cycled to on dusty, well manicured dirt roads. Bring food and lots of water; there's none to be had beyond the terminal area. Given the seclusion, women should not go alone.

Pull out a cold "Pacifico," kick back, and let the sound of the waves wash over you.

ROADNOTES

WHAT'S AHEAD: Tijuana. Mayhem. Tijuana's pedestrian and vehicular traffic is legendary. From the border crossing follow signs which say "Centro" to downtown. Traffic is fast, heavy and unaccustomed to bicycles. Watch out for those taxis.

Kilometer 0	San Ysidro border crossing.
2	Turn left from Calle Carrillo Puerto onto Avenida Revolución.
2.5	Jai alai stadium.
3	Road splits at municipal park, "18th of March." Take a left onto unsigned Boulevard Agua Caliente.
4.5	Right turn onto Avenida Cuauhtemoc. Sign for Rosarito. Begin long uphill, four-lane road through an ugly poverty-stricken valley.
5	Sign for Ensenada Libre. Avenida Cuauhtemoc becomes Benito Juarez.
11	Top of climb. Road shrinks to two lanes. Surroundings become agricultural.

WHAT'S AHEAD: Rosarito to Ensenada. The road is narrow and there is no shoulder but the urban clutter of Tijuana disappears and traffic relents. La Mision signals the start of fantastic Baja scenery and the first of two major climbs before rejoining the coast at El Sauzal.

23	Rosarito.
32	Ocean comes in view.
61	La Mision. Cafe.
64	Begin climb.
70	Top.
77	Store. Only one between La Mision and El Sauzal.
83	Start down.
86	Orphanage.
94	El Sauzal. Full service. Road joins four-lane.
103	Ensenada. Full service.
	Budget Hotels are located on Calle Gastelum and Calle Mateos. To exit town; follow Av. Lopez Mateos to Mex 1, turn right at Gigante supermarket.

WHAT'S AHEAD: Ensenada to El Rosario. Perhaps the easiest leg of the tour. Communities appear at regular 30k-40k intervals and significant climbs are infrequent.

117	City limits of Ensenada, scenery becomes rural.
119	Turn for "La Bufadora" blowhole.

DETOUR TO LA BUFADORA (22k)

12	La Jolla. Hot springs reportedly on beach, trailer parks, private homes. 5k climb begins.
22	La Bufa. Parking lot, bikes free. Camping 4,500p ($2). Frankly, it's not worth the effort to get here by bike.

120	Maneadero. *Aduana* station. Last place to secure tourist card.
129	Begin mountainous terrain. Road turns inland towards Santo Tomas, famous for vineyards.
146	Road flattens, grapes everywhere.
149	Santo Tomas. Beautiful valley home of Mexico's largest winery, "Bodegas de Santo Tomas," winery tours are in Ensenada however. Motel, nice restaurant and trailer park. Camping 4,000p ($1.85).
157	Start tough 4k climb, 8% grade.
161	Climb ends. Begin a steep descent.
175	Start another 4k climb.
187	San Vicente. Pemex, bus station, restaurants.
206	Cross Rio San Antonio. Begin steep 3k climb.
224	Colonet. Pemex, groceries, various services. Terrain mellows out.
243	Colonia Jaramillo. Groceries. Gravel road along the San Telmo River leads to **Meling Ranch, Mike's Sky Ranch,** and the National Observatory atop Picacho Del Diablo, Baja's tallest mountain (el. 10,154 feet).
254	Camalu. Pemex, groceries, cafes, short detour to beach.
270	Colonia Guerrero. Banamex, Pemex, bike shop, restaurants.
286	San Quintín. Hotel, restaurants, bike shop.
330	Ocean comes into view, terrain grows increasingly rugged.
351	El Rosario. Hotel, restaurants, grocery. **Hotel Rosario.** Last good budget motel before Guerrero Negro, 22,000p/dbl ($9.50). **Mama Espinoza's.** 12,000p lobster burritos!

WHAT'S AHEAD: El Rosario to Santa Rosalia. Classic Baja i.e., desert and lots of it. El Rosario to Cataviña is marked by steep twisting hills that require caution. Mobile homes are liable to overtake you while you're distracted by the breathtaking desert scenery. After Cataviña the terrain becomes increasingly bland and between Guerrero Negro and San Ignacio it reaches its hot featureless worst, the Vizcaino Desert. The oasis of San Ignacio offers relief, as does the Sea of Cortes one brief day later.

361	Begin Baja's central desert. Short steep hills, many blind turns, spectacular scenery.
414	Cafe.
439	San Augustin. No services.
442	**Tres Enriques Cafe.**
470	**Cafe Tarajumara.** Nice cafe, beans cooking on a stove in the middle of the floor, tables and chairs made from dried cirio.
472	Cataviña. **La Pinta Hotel,** Supermarket, good cafe across from La Pinta.
474	Arroyo, good campsite, perennial stream.
475	Turn for **Rancho Santa Inez.** Restaurant and dormitory-style motel. Rooms 11,500p ($5), camping 2,000p ($.85).
504	El Pedregoso, a huge mountain of boulders. No services. Flat terrain.
529	Rancho Chapala. Restaurant on dusty shore of Laguna Chapala, a huge, dry lakebed. Mountainous terrain begins 4.5k later.
577	**Parador Punta Prieta Restaurant.** Pemex, Bahia Los Angeles turnoff.

DETOUR FOR BAHIA LOS ANGELES (68k)
Turn left, go straight, no services en route.
68   Bahia Los Angeles. Motels, restaurants and a trailer park which cater to sport fishermen.

588	Punta Prieta. Tiny grocery.
629	Rosarito.
	Cafe Mauricio, an excellent truckstop cafe.
671	Villa Jesus Maria. Pemex, cafe, groceries.
703	Border between Baja Californias North and South. Trailer park, camping 11,500p ($5).
728	Junction for Guerrero Negro.

DETOUR FOR GUERRERO NEGRO (5k)
Turn right, go straight.
5   Guerrero Negro. Full services, whale watching.

Smith-Sanchez Hotel; in town's center. Managed by a terrific lady. 20,000p/dbl ($8.70).

757   El Arco turnoff. Road quality, previously awful, improves.
784   Busy Vizcaino junction, turn for Bahia Tortugas. Pemex, restaurant.
810   Turnoff for San Francisco de la Sierra.

DETOUR FOR S.F. DE LA SIERRA (36k)
Gravel road leads to the town.
36   San Francisco de la Sierra. Nearby caves house hundreds of life-sized paintings.

854   San Ignacio. Exquisite oasis town. Camping, swimming and most of the amenities.
895   Big downhill after first of the Tres Virgenes.
912   First sight of Sea of Cortes. Begin extraordinary descent.
922   Sea of Cortes.

WHAT'S AHEAD: Santa Rosalia to Pto. Escondido. Easy riding, beautiful desert, magnificent beaches. Live it up.

930   Santa Rosalia. Hotels, restaurants, ferry service to Guaymas.
Hotel Blanco y Negro, inexplicably painted yellow. 6,000p/dbl ($2.60).
992   Mulege, riverine oasis with various facilities and awful cobbled streets.
1013   Playa Santispac. Popular beach with restaurant, groceries. Palappas rent for 11,500p ($5).
1015   Posada Concepcion. Private residences, grocery.
1019   Playa Coyote. Camping, restaurant, good clamming.
1035   Playa Requeson. Camping, no services.
1050   Restaurant and cafe.
1059   Sierra de la Giganta comes into view atop tough 4k climb.
1067   Nondescript, no-name cafe that forever lives in our memory—huge fish fillets and quarts of beer for a buck.
1075   Rancho Bombador. Small oasis, cafe.
1104   Cafe.
1118   Cafe.
1126   Loreto. Full service.
1129   Signed detour for San Javier, a largely abandoned community with a magnificent Jesuit mission.
1134   Nopolo turnoff. Upscale resort in the works.

1138	Playa Notri. More construction.
1158	Juncalito. Good beach camping.
1162	Puerto Escondido. Mobile home community, restaurant, good place to top off your water bottles.

WHAT'S AHEAD: Ligui to La Paz. Tough stuff. The ride from Ligui to Cd. Insurgentes is intimidating. Beginning at sea level it climbs through the Sierra de la Giganta to reach the Magdalena Plain. Thereafter the terrain is utterly flat but distances remain long. Services, thankfully, are regular. Cafes are frequently named for a corresponding highway kilometer marker.

1170	Ligui. Last opportunity to buy groceries for a while.
1173	Begin 5.5k climb. View of the original unpaved "Highway One" and Sea of Cortes.
1201	**Cafe K 254.** First since Ligui.
1254	Cd. Insurgentes. Several stores. Cotton and alfalfa fields.
1281	Cd. Constitucion. Full service.
1334	Santa Rita. Pemex, **Cafe K 154.**
1367	**Cafe K 122.**
1375	**Cafe Rosie.**
1428	Sea of Cortes comes into view.
1456	La Paz comes into view.
1489	La Paz, capital of Baja California Sur. Full services. The ferry office is at end of Calle Ignacio Ramirez.
	Posada San Miguel, Calle Belizario Dominguez #1510. Charming bougainvillea-shaded courtyard, spacious rooms, firm beds, private baths, 15,000p/dbl ($6.50). A steal.
	Hotel California, Calle Santos Degollado #209. Funky but fascinating. Shared baths, so-so beds, great courtyard, 15,000p/dbl ($6.50).
	Taqueria Los Amigos. A fish taco stand on wheels in front of the Pension California. Abundant and unimaginably good!
1493	El Coromuel. Good beach, restaurants.
1506	Pichilingue. Ferry terminal, restaurants, great beaches nearby.

LOS CABOS

ROUTE: La Paz—Todos Santos—Cabo San Lucas—San Jose del Cabo—
La Paz.
DISTANCE: 395k.
RIDING TIME: 4 to 5 days.
DIFFICULTY: Moderate to hard.
TERRAIN: Desert. Sometimes mountainous, always arid.
BEST TIME: Fall through spring.

Cyclists who have toughed the marathon ride from the border
may find La Paz a fitting place to conclude their epic journey. But
for others, riding Baja is incomplete without a circumnavigation
of the Cabos. The highway dangles like a noose from the peninsula's narrowest point to its most southerly, wide enough to touch
the shores of east and west. The 378k loop includes dazzling scenery, seaside fun, and Baja's glitziest resort, Cabo San Lucas.

Prevailing northwesterlies favor a counter-clockwise approach.
Mex 19 through Todos Santos capitalizes on the zephyrs scudding
in from the Pacific. The return leg, inland from San Jose del
Cabo, is in the lee of the Sierra de la Laguna. Going clockwise,
taking Mex 1 south dispenses with the most difficult terrain up
front, but you're gambling with the wind.

Whichever approach, the departure from La Paz begins the same.
Follow Calle Cinco de Febrero 1.5k southeast to Mex 1 and bear
right. Traffic is heavy but the road is amply wide and well
marked. The topography is utterly level, a thorny plain chock full
of cardon and cholla cactus. The village of San Pedro, k 28, is a
good place for a breather and a beer. Things heat up fast in south
Baja (!) so top off your water bottles before pushing on. The turn
for Mex 19 is just ahead and the next decent food and beverage
stop is another 29k.

Todos Santos

Restock supplies and plan to bivouac for the night at Todos
Santos, a pleasant, mid-sized town. Lodging is available but we
headed directly for the beach. An unsigned dirt road beyond town
near highway marker k 54 leads to the ocean.

Natural Arch, Cabo San Lucas

Waves pound against the sharply inclined shore. Bathers are few. At dusk the Punta Lobos Fishing Cooperative returns from sea. Beyond the breakers, mere yards away, their dories bob quietly, waiting for a tidal surge. Perfectly timed, helmsmen gun the engines, men leap over the gunwales to push the last few feet. The cooperative's ice truck drives onto the sand and loads the day's catch.

Red snapper, corvina, a young hammerhead shark. We try to buy a fish and are given, instead, a gift. A fisherman sharpens his knife on an outcrop of stone, fillets the fish and washes the blade in the sea. We camp nearby while a sentry watches over the boats.

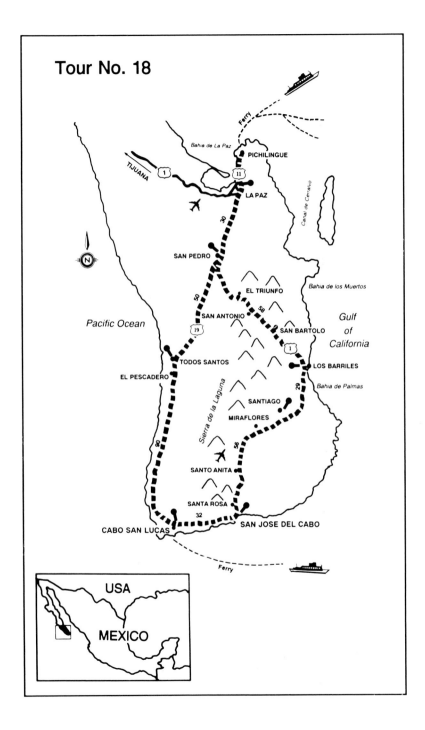

Tour No. 18

In the morning—though it seems later the same night—the fishermen come back. Helping each other, they pivot the dories to face the sea. Timed with the outrushing water, they run to meet the waves. In minutes they are gone. Voices fade, a trace of diesel exhaust lingers. The stars begin to dim. Feeling like sluggards, we lay back and wait for sunrise.

South of Todos Santos, wild Pacific beaches draw close to the road. The surroundings are visually magnificent but utterly bereft of services. Purchase food and water at El Pescadero, about 12k beyond Todos Santos. It is yet a day's ride to where east meets west.

Los Cabos

Cabo means tip, or end, and along this southern perimeter two towns claim the moniker. Cabo San Lucas is the better known, a settlement grown fat on tourism, a cornucopia of ritzy hotels, sailfish tournaments and cruise liners. The lowest priced accomodations will set you back. Even at happy hour, margaritas at places like **The Giggling Marlin** won't make you happy. Groceries, as well, cost more than elsewhere.

Mexico's shoreline is nationalized, open to anyone, even though hotel managers in places like Cabo San Lucas are loathe to acknowledge it. Camping on the pristine sands of Cabo is possible, but security people will insure you don't sleep late. For more hospitable arrangements pedal east. Beaches for the next 55k are often accessible, seldom secluded.

On leaving Cabo, Land's End comes into sight. These rocky promontories, Baja's southernmost point, jut through turbulent, azure waters, dividing the Pacific Ocean from the Gulf of California (aka Sea of Cortes). Cycling becomes effortful again, brief climbs along bluffs which dash to the sea. In the distance surfers ride the waves.

If camping, a good place to spend the night is near the **Trailer Park Brisa del Mar.** Or, for a few dollars, stay at the trailer park; showers, you know, and a food stall too.

Only 4k from Brisa del Mar is San Jose del Cabo, the largest town south of La Paz. The surf is gentler here, much better for swimming, and prices are lower than in Cabo. Despite considerable tourist development the town retains a relaxed, Mexican "feel." Camp unmolested on the beach, eat at inexpensive seaside ramadas. And rest up well, the return to La Paz is arduous.

The Return to La Paz

The international airport near Santa Anita is built at the edge of a plain. The road drops into the San Jose river drainage and the serious riding begins. There's a cafe and beer stand at the turnoff for Miraflores, but no worthwhile detours for another 17k.

Road signs for gas, a washout, and an elephant, mark the turn for Santiago, k 53. Separated from the highway by a steep hill and streambed, Santiago calls itself *el paraiso del sur.* Expansive orchards of tropical fruit thriving amidst this desolate land account for such exuberance. There's a good restaurant and hotel in town, called the **Palomar.**

Oh, yes . . . the elephant. No one seems to know what the government had in mind when they chose to put a zoo in Santiago. As it happens, there are no pachyderms. But a number of Mexico's

San Jose Del Cabo

native wildlife are housed here, including jungle cats and birds of prey. Admission is free.

The road hugs the coast one last time at Las Barriles. A number of hotels, restaurants and one trailer park serve the community of Canadian and American fisherfolk who vacation here. The beach is nothing to write home about but the camping facilities at **Martin Verdugo's** trailer park are immaculate. Cyclists pay 4,500p ($2) for a campsite and hot showers. The **Playa Hermosa** restaurant, next door, has an international library culled from the foreign encampment. Don't miss such cold war classics as *Communism, Can It Happen Here?* Our guess is, not likely.

Luckily, between the slamming of RV doors and revving of outboard engines, there is little risk of oversleeping in Los Barriles. An early start behooves you, the going gets tough. The first climb into the Sierra de la Laguna, just 2k, is enough to register a climatic change. Coastal humidity disappears. The arid desert still holds the night's chill. Eleven kilometers into the morning you reach the **Pame** restaurant, a better breakfast bet than anything in Los Barriles.

Palmy, picturesque surroundings and a wide selection of food are available in San Bartolo, k 293.

Rolling hills wind through a typically Bajamian backdrop for the next few hours. Roughhewn mountains, abandoned mines, vultures circling lazily against the sky, horizons of pastel rock and bluish-green cacti. Difficult ascents guard the approaches to San Antonio and El Triunfo, defunct mining towns now dependent on tourism. After El Triunfo the terrain settles. The final 51k (26mi) is a satisfying, swift beeline for La Paz.

ROADNOTES

WHAT'S AHEAD: La Paz to Cabo San Lucas (via Todos Santos) 226k of mostly level cruising. Deep arroyos in vicinity of Todos Santos create the only wrinkles. Services are infrequent, access to the Pacific, unlimited.

Kilometer 0	La Paz. Intersection of Calles Abasolo and 5 de Febrero. Follow signs for Cabo San Lucas and Mex 1.
25.5	San Pedro. Cafe, groceries.
30.5	Junction with Mex 19.
73.5	Turnoff for dam and reservoir, Presa de Santa Inez.
81	Todos Santos. Farming and fishing village with hotels. Last good place for groceries before Cabo San Lucas. Beach camping 2k out of town. **El Molino Trailer Park,** south end of town, camping 20,400p ($8).
93	El Pescadero.
117	Col. Plutarco Elias Calles. Big name, small town. Last supplies for a while.
171	Cabo San Lucas. Full range of services and the highest prices in Baja. **El Faro Viejo Trailer Park,** one mile northwest of Mex 1 on Calle Matamoros. 13,800p/2 people. ($6)
177	View of Land's End.
205	**Brisa del Mar** trailer park. Camping 11,500p ($5).

WHAT'S AHEAD: San Jose del Cabo to La Paz. San Jose is a wonderfully unpretentious town. Palappa-style restaurants and primitive camping on excellent beach at Pueblo La Playa. Beyond San Jose the road turns inland. Numerous climbs of 2k between Sta. Anita and Los Barriles. Slightly longer climbs between Los Barriles and El Triunfo.

209	San José del Cabo. Full service.
213	Santa Rosa.
220	Airport entrance. Terrain becomes mountainous.
222	Sta. Anita.
247	Miraflores turnoff, 2k to town. Parador restaurant at junction.
258	Tropic of Cancer. Named for the Henry Miller novel.
261	Junction for Santiago, largest town between La Paz and the Cabos. 3k detour. **Restaurant/Hotel Palomar,** excellent on all accounts. 25,000p/dbl. ($11) and worth it.

290	Los Barriles, small village overwhelmed by gringo fisherfolk.
	Trailer park. Next to Playa Hermosa restaurant. Camping 4,500p ($2).
302	**Pame Restaurant,** a good breakfast stop.
310	San Bartolo, set in a pretty ravine. Restaurant, groceries.
337	San Antonio, former mining town. Restaurants, groceries.
344	El Triunfo, former mining town. Want to buy a cheap Victorian home? Short climb beyond town is the final one.
352	Out of the mountains, road flattens to the horizon.
365	Junction with Mex 19.
395	La Paz.
	Accommodations. See Tour #18 Roadnotes.

CALENDAR OF
NATIONAL HOLIDAYS

Jan. 1	New Year's Day.
Jan. 6	Santos Reyes, day of the Three Wise Men.
Jan. 17	St. Anthony's Day. Animals are blessed.
Feb. 2–8	Virgin de la Candelaria. Bullfights, parades, dancing.
Feb. 5	Constitution Day, legal holiday.
Feb. 24	Flag Day, legal holiday.
Mar. 21	Birthday of President Benito Juarez.
May 1	Labor Day.
May 3	Feast of the Holy Cross, honors construction workers. Endless fireworks and drinking.
May 5	Commemoration of Mexican victory over the French in Puebla, 1862.
May 15	Day of San Isidro, patron of rain and agriculture. Village priests bless livestock. Flowers galore.
June 1	Navy Day. Heroes are honored.
June 24	Feast of St. John the Baptist. Much prankishness. Especially big in Guanajuato and Puebla.
July 18	Commemorates death of President Benito Juarez.
Aug. 15	Assumption Day. Flowers galore.
Sept. 1	President gives annual State of the Nation Address. Legal holiday.
Sept. 15–16	Independence Day. Very big in Mexico City and San Miguel de Allende.
Oct. 12	Dia de la Raza. Commemorates the discovery of America by Columbus, uniting Hispanic and Indian peoples. Legal holiday.
Nov. 1–2	Day of the Dead. Big in Patzcuaro.
Nov. 20	Anniversary of the Revolution of 1910.
Dec. 8	Feast of the Immaculate Conception. Big in Patzcuaro.
Dec. 12	Feast of the Virgen de Guadalupe. Much merriment, especially at her shrine in Mexico City.
Dec. 16–24	Nine days of religious celebrations.
Dec. 25	Christmas Day.

Three days preceding Ash Wednesday: Carnaval. Big merriment, especially in Acapulco, Mazatlan, Guaymas, Guadalajara, Mexico City, Monterrey, Tepoztlan, Tampico and Merida.

Easter Week, from Palm Sunday to Easter Sunday.

Holy Saturday, around this time of year, no specified date. Papiermache representations of Judas are burned.

Corpus Christi: An unspecified Thursday in late May or early June. Opening day of a week-long, very colorful fair in Papantla, Ver.

Hundreds of other specialized travel guides and maps are available from Hunter Publishing. Among those that may interest you:

MEXICO TRAVEL MAP
1:3,000,000 scale. Full color map shows all roads, with practical travel information on the reverse. Map measures 2' x 3'/$6.95

BACKPACKING & TREKKING IN PERU & BOLIVIA
by Hilary Bradt
Walks in the Andes, including Cuzco & Macchu Picchu. "All a backpacker needs to see as much as possible with minimum hassle" (*South American Explorer*).
5 x 8 paperback/150 pp./$13.95

BACKPACKING IN CHILE & ARGENTINA
by Hilary Bradt
The best book on the subject, now revised and updated.
5 x 8 paperback/204 pp./$13.95

CLIMBING & HIKING IN ECUADOR
by Rob Rachowieki
A complete guide to the mountains and trails. Ascents of all the major peaks, walks along the Inca Trail, the Pacific Coast.
5 x 8 paperback/160 pp./$11.95

THE ADVENTURE GUIDE TO BAJA CALIFORNIA
by W. H. Morrison
History, best driving routes and excursions, hotels, all practical details. Maps & color photos throughout.
5 x 8 paperback/320 pp./$15.95

BEST DIVES OF THE WESTERN HEMISPHERE
by Jon & Joyce Huber, C. Lofting
Scuba & snorkelling guide to 200+ best sites in Caribbean, South & Central America, Hawaii, Florida, California. Full color, with maps.
5 x 8 paperback/320 pp./$16.95

THE ADVENTURE GUIDE TO THE PACIFIC NORTHWEST
by Tom Arnold
Hiking, cycling, mountaineering in the most beautiful parts of Idaho, Washington, Oregon, & Northern California.
5 x 8 paperback/224 pp./$12.95

CALIFORNIA POCKET GUIDES
FARM TOURS OF NORTHERN CALIFORNIA
THE COMPLETE GOLD COUNTRY GUIDEBOOK
THE COMPLETE LAKE TAHOE GUIDEBOOK
THE COMPLETE MONTEREY PENINSULA & SANTA CRUZ GUIDEBOOK
THE COMPLETE SAN DIEGO GUIDEBOOK
THE COMPLETE SAN FRANCISCO GUIDEBOOK

THE COMPLETE SANTA BARBARA GUIDEBOOK
THE COMPLETE WINE COUNTRY GUIDEBOOK
Each guide is 4¼" x 8½", illustrated with maps and photos. Packed with practical details on attractions in each region, the books also contain hundreds of annotated hotel and restaurant listings.
150 pp./$7.95 each

CARIBBEAN GUIDES
ANTIGUA & BARBUDA 160 pp./$11.95
THE BAHAMAS 208 pp./$13.95
CUBA 288 pp./$17.95
CURACAO 72 pp./$6.95
GRANADA 136 pp./$11.95
BERMUDA 170 pp./$12.95
These are a few of the many Caribbean guides we offer. All are full color throughout. *5½ x 8 paperbacks.*

MICHAEL'S GUIDES
Included in this series are volumes on:
ARGENTINA & CHILE
ECUADOR, COLUMBIA, & VENEZUELA
BRAZIL
BOLIVIA & PERU
Each is packed with practical detail and many maps. These pocket-sized paperbacks tell you where to stay, where to go, what to buy.
4¼" x 8¼" paperbacks/200 pp./$7.95 each

ALIVE GUIDES
BUENOS AIRES ALIVE
GUATEMALA ALIVE
RIO ALIVE
VENEZUELA ALIVE
VIRGIN ISLANDS ALIVE
Researched and written by Arnold & Harriet Greenberg, owners of the celebrated Complete Traveller bookstore in New York. These guides are the ultimate source for hotel, restaurant, and shopping information, with individual reviews for thousands of places—which to seek out and which to avoid. Sightseeing information as well.
5" x 7¼" paperbacks/296 pp./$10.95

HILDEBRAND TRAVEL GUIDES
Among the titles in this series are:
MEXICO 368 pp./$10.95
JAMAICA 128 pp./$8.95
HISPANIOLA 143 pp./$9.95
The New York Times describes the series: "Striking color photographs, concise fact-packed writing, valuable practical information and outstanding cartography, including a fold-out map inside the rear cover."
4½" x 6¾" paperbacks

Plus

HUGO'S SPANISH PHRASEBOOK 128 pp. $3.25
Words and phrases are arranged by categories such as Hotels, Restaurant, Shopping, and Health. A special *menu guide* lists 600 dishes or methods of food preparation. An 1800-item *mini-dictionary* also included.

HUGO'S SPANISH IN 3 MONTHS $29.95
HUGO'S EL INGLÈS SIMPLIFICADO/ENGLISH FOR SPANISH SPEAKERS $29.95
These are intensive cassette-based courses in conversational speech. Each course comes in a vinyl album containing a 160-page book and four 1-hour cassette tapes designed to speed learning and to teach pronunciation. Together, the tapes and books take the absolute beginner to a good working knowledge of the language. The books are also available without the tapes at $5.95 each.

The above books, maps, and tape courses can be found at the best bookstores or you can order directly. Send your check (add $2.50 to cover postage and handling) to:

HUNTER PUBLISHING, INC.
300 RARITAN CENTER PARKWAY
EDISON NJ 08818

Write or call (201) 225 1900 for our free color catalog describing these and many other travel guides and maps to virtually every destination on earth.